PREPARING
LEADERS
FOR DEEPER
LEARNING

PREPARING LEADERS FOR DEEPER LEARNING

Marjorie E. Wechsler
Steven K. Wojcikiewicz

with

Julie Adams
Desiree Carver-Thomas
Channa M. Cook
Daniel Espinoza
Madelyn Gardner
Maria E. Hyler
Anne Podolsky

HARVARD EDUCATION PRESS
CAMBRIDGE, MASSACHUSETTS

Paperback ISBN 978-1-68253-840-1

Library of Congress Cataloging-in-Publication Data is on file.

Published by Harvard Education Press,
an imprint of the Harvard Education Publishing Group

Harvard Education Press
8 Story Street
Cambridge, MA 02138

Cover Design: Ciano Design
Cover Image: kali9/E+ via GettyImages
The typefaces in this book are ITC Stone Serif, ITC Stone Sans, and Museo Sans.

CONTENTS

CHAPTER 1

PREPARING SCHOOL LEADERS FOR DEEPER LEARNING

In the evolving and interconnected world of the twenty-first century, conceptions of schooling are changing. The demands of life, work, and citizenship in an information-rich and technology-driven society are raising expectations for education systems. Advances in the science of learning and development are doing the same. Meeting these new expectations will require a transformation of school structures and classroom practices to provide engaging and comprehensive learning experiences—deeper learning—to all students.

Such a transformation will depend heavily on school leaders, who play an essential role in shaping teachers' instruction and students' learning. Leadership development, too, will have to evolve for school leaders to acquire the knowledge, skills, and dispositions to enable, encourage, and sustain deeper learning. That is the focus of this book: understanding what deeper learning leadership looks like and how leadership preparation and professional development programs can best prepare principals for this new type of leadership.

A CALL TO DEVELOP SCHOOL LEADERSHIP FOR DEEPER LEARNING

Rethinking schooling for the twenty-first century begins with research on the science of learning and development. In recent years, researchers, building on decades of previous work, have made rapid progress in expanding our knowledge of how people learn.[1] In this emerging picture, learners constantly construct knowledge and build novel understandings through experience, proceeding along individual developmental trajectories embedded within, and intertwined with, social relationships, physical environments, and cultural contexts. Learning is as much social and emotional as it is cognitive and academic, shaped by students' mind-sets, enabled by their knowledge of themselves and their metacognitive processes, and hindered by trauma, adversity, and chronic stress.

By itself, this new understanding of learning and development points to the need for an overhaul of our educational system, in which too many schools still follow long-familiar industrial-era models of standardized rote learning.[2] Yet the goal of aligning schools toward deeper learning experiences is also driven by new demands on learners. Emergent technologies and expanding access to information require learners to develop enhanced capacities for critical reasoning, cross-contextual knowledge acquisition and application, and nonroutine problem-solving.[3] In this dynamic environment, preparing students for college, careers, and citizenship requires an increasing focus on developing the analytical and communication skills needed for lifelong learning.[4]

Organizing for the future also means confronting the inequities of the past and present. Our industrial-era educational system was never designed to provide a high-quality, challenging, and empowering education for *all* students. Indeed, school structures and practices have perpetuated inequities. Tracking systems have denied students of color, English language learners, and students from low-income families access to meaningful learning opportunities; schools serving these students have been more likely to adopt narrow, one-size-fits-all curricula focused exclusively on basic skills, often in response to policy trends and accountability-related initiatives.[5] The scale of these systemic and historical issues makes "access to deeper learning . . . a primary equity challenge," though this challenge has not been addressed by policy makers at the state or federal level.[6] Bringing all schools up to twenty-first-century standards will require deliberate dedication of resources and effort toward ensuring that all students, especially populations that have been underserved by our educational systems, have such access. In other words, *a commitment to aligning schooling to deeper learning brings with it a concurrent commitment to educational equity.*

Changing conceptions of learning and development, emerging societal needs, and the moral imperative of addressing inequitable educational opportunities all point toward a realignment of our educational system for deeper learning. Questions remain, however, about how this might be accomplished. One answer, which has received increasing attention in recent years, is to prepare teachers so that they are able to teach for deeper learning.[7] A related answer is to have school leaders play a central role in systemic transformation toward increased access to deeper learning opportunities. School leaders strongly influence teacher working conditions, classroom instruction, school environments, and student learning by establishing direction and vision for their schools, guiding professional development, and driving priorities and practices through the allocation of resources and the design of school structures.[8]

Growing recognition of the importance of school leaders' influence on schools has already led to an expansion of how school leadership is conceptualized. Today's leaders are expected to provide instructional leadership, engage in systemic thinking regarding school effectiveness, and support teachers' collaboration in developing and executing sophisticated pedagogy.[9] Professional standards for leaders emphasize managing school improvement, employing culturally responsive practices, creating professional communities and learning opportunities for educators, and engaging families and local stakeholders, all while maintaining a focus on student learning.[10]

As expectations for leaders continue to evolve, leadership preparation and professional development must do the same. But what does school leadership for deeper learning look like? What are the features and practices that define programs preparing leaders to create schools in which deeper learning thrives? This book provides answers to those questions.

WHAT IS DEEPER LEARNING?

Deeper learning stands on a strong foundation of educational research, developed over a century of exploration of the cognitive and social nature of learning and its interactions with development.[11] Deeper learning is not knowledge acquisition through memorizing facts and practicing problems. Rather, it is the development of conceptual frameworks that allow learners to transfer knowledge to the application of novel problems.[12] It also recognizes the connections between cognition and emotion and their embeddedness in social, physical, and cultural contexts. Deeper learning, then, is a complex and comprehensive concept, referring to a variety of experiences, through which learners

- cultivate, practice, and master deep content knowledge, including key principles in a discipline and complex conceptual frameworks, allowing transfer and application to new situations, contexts, and problems;[13]
- develop problem-solving and inquiry skills by applying critical thinking skills in cycles of research and inquiry, enabling the identification of novel solutions to a wide range of problems, including complex challenges;

- acquire multimodal communication and collaboration skills through authentic learning experiences, including well-structured collaborative opportunities to reason critically and solve real-world problems with peers and expert teachers;[14]
- develop metacognitive skills and strategies, including active regulation and evaluation of learning though engagement in meaningful tasks in which they set goals, create plans, and monitor progress aided by feedback from continuous assessment;[15]
- attain social emotional awareness and academic mind-sets necessary to succeed in college and career, cultivating individual beliefs and attitudes, motivation, and self-efficacy to persist through the learning process, including in challenging tasks or subjects.[16]

This complex conception of learning brings a host of implications for the design of school environments.[17] Deeper learning is enabled by inquiry-based, student-centered teaching that builds on students' assets and prior experiences and engages their full range of social and emotional needs and identities. To create such experiences, educators provide students with relevant learning activities, supported by scaffolded activities and shaped by formative feedback, aimed at challenging goals that foster motivation and engagement. Incorporating deeper learning also means a focus on creating safe and positive school climates, environments that foster strong relationships and support the whole child.[18]

A STUDY OF LEADERSHIP PREPARATION FOR DEEPER LEARNING

School leaders need to understand this conception of deeper learning and have the capacity to build systems and learning environments that enable teachers and students to instantiate it in practice. However, leadership for deeper learning is a new concept. The practices and structures that enable deeper learning, though backed by substantial research, are for the most part aspirational rather than actualized in the majority of today's schools. Guidance for leadership preparation and professional development programs focused on deeper learning is thus hard to find as the knowledge, skills, and dispositions of deeper learning leadership are still emerging.

Therefore, rather than deriving the features of development for deeper learning leadership by working backward from practice, we started with leadership development programs already focused on instilling deeper learning–aligned practices. This approach was modeled on a previous study, *Preparing Teachers for Deeper Learning*, which examined how seven pioneering teacher preparation programs equipped future teachers with the skills and mind-sets needed for twenty-first-century student learning.[19] That study found that the features of deeper learning are as applicable to teacher education as they are to children's learning. Effective programs teach and support their candidates in the same ways they want the candidates to teach and support children. In setting out to study leadership preparation for deeper learning, we began with the assumption that the through line from preK–12 student learning to teacher learning would continue through school leader learning. School leaders would need to understand deeper learning by experience in order to implement it.

Study Focus

To understand deeper learning leadership and the program features that prepare administrators for this role, we purposely focused on the entire continuum of leadership learning, from initial preparation through in-service professional development (see figure 1.1). Multiple factors contributed to this choice. One of these was the policy context around school leadership. While programs determine what and how principals learn, state standards, accreditation, and licensure requirements also play important roles, and these affect both initial preparation and professional development. Another factor was the characteristics of school leaders. Approximately one-third of principals nationally are in their first three years in school administration; for two-thirds of principals, their learning about new leadership concepts will necessarily come through in-service professional development.[20] Given the importance of deeper learning leadership for creating more equitable

FIGURE 1.1   **Principal learning opportunities**

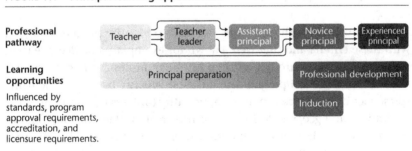

learning opportunities and outcomes, programs through which principals can develop the necessary skills must be available at all levels.

While both the policies and the population of school leaders make it important to understand preparation and in-service development for leaders, another reason to look across both is that the job of school leader has a natural career ladder. Preparation begins before entry into a licensure program through program recruitment and selection. Once it begins, the preparation experience encompasses the structures and content of coursework, clinical placements, and assessment. After program completion, administrators may work as assistant principals, then start again as novice principals, with some participating in induction programs. Leaders continue to learn through in-service programs, possibly taking on mentor roles themselves as experienced principals or moving to larger and more challenging schools or even into district leadership roles. Whatever their path, school leaders' work offers evolving challenges and ample opportunities to step into ever-growing roles, with continued learning along the way.

Methodological Overview

The first step in our study was to develop criteria for identifying programs focused on preparing deeper learning leaders. These criteria included

- coursework that explicitly models project-based learning and authentic performance-based assessments;
- coursework that is deeply integrated with field experiences;
- an explicit focus on educational equity;
- clinical placements that are highly collaborative, focus on personalization, and provide authentic curriculum and assessments;
- coursework and clinical experiences that emphasize developing relationships with students and their families and understanding their communities and contexts.

We consulted with experts in the field to identify programs aligned with these criteria and that were known for exemplary practice. We then narrowed the field through research on program designs and outcomes. We selected five focal programs to ensure diversity—by size, participants (preservice or in-service), administrative entity (university, nonprofit, state, or district), and geographical scope (district, region, state, nation)—and to broaden the applicability of findings. Even with this diversity, the programs stood out in the degree to which their features were aligned with the principles of deeper learning, even in cases where the program did not use the term *deeper learning*.

We then constructed case studies of each program. Our examination of key program design features included program goals, curricular content, practices, and contexts. We also explored barriers to implementing high-quality leadership development programs and how programs are addressing them. We drew data from interviews with program faculty, mentors, participants and graduates, district leaders, and community organizations; surveys of program participants and alumni; observations of participants in their schools and program courses; and document review (see appendix for methodological details and full survey results). We collected all data between spring 2017 and spring 2018. Program descriptions and study participants' names and job titles reflect information at the time of data collection.

After completing the case studies, we looked across programs to identify the dimensions of deeper learning leadership along with the program features aligned to those dimensions. We explicate these dimensions and aligned program features in chapter 7. However, we include them here in brief as they provide important framing for the following case studies (see table 1.1).

TABLE 1.1   **Dimensions of deeper learning leadership and aligned program features**

Dimensions of leadership for deeper learning	Aligned dimensions of leadership preparation for deeper learning
Leaders follow and share a vision for deeper learning	Programs follow a vision centered on deeper learning
Leaders prioritize equity	Programs align leadership priorities with equity and social justice
Leaders build collaborative communities of practice	Programs create communities of learning and practice and emphasize collaboration and distributed leadership
Leaders provide deeper learning opportunities by creating developmentally appropriate and improvement-focused staff supports	Programs use and model instructional strategies for leaders to experience deeper learning
Leaders adopt a contextualized approach for systemic alignment for deeper learning	Programs prepare leaders to think strategically about, and create supportive systems for, deeper learning

Programs Studied

The programs highlighted in this book represent five distinct approaches to school leadership preparation and development for deeper learning. Some serve aspiring school leaders, while others engage current principals or are a combination of the two. Two of the programs are led by institutions of higher education; the others are run by a nonprofit organization, a state-wide partnership, and a school district. Collectively, they serve leaders in both urban and rural schools located in a variety of states and cities. They confer a range of credentials or designations and operate at varying scales, providing a broad view of what is possible in the field of school leadership development.

The University of Illinois Chicago (UIC) Urban Education Leadership Program is an intensive, clinically based, and academically challenging multiyear doctoral program. The program's first phase integrates thoughtfully structured coursework with a fully funded, full-time residency in Chicago Public Schools supported by a mentor principal and university coach. Completing this stage qualifies participants for the Illinois P-12 Principal Endorsement. In the second stage, participants work as school administrators while receiving coaching and completing additional university coursework en route to a doctoral degree.

The Principal Leadership Institute (PLI) at the University of California, Berkeley, is a master's degree program that develops school leaders who are capable of improving education opportunities for historically underserved students in California's public schools. Candidates in the PLI program complete four semesters of intensive coursework and engage in identity-, equity-, and inquiry-based learning activities as part of a structured cohort. Those who complete the program receive initial administrative licensure.

The Long Beach Unified School District (LBUSD) district-operated leadership pipeline develops leaders at all levels, from assistant principals to cabinet-level roles. The leadership pipeline encompasses a number of initiatives, including the Future Administrators Program, which supports district staff in becoming school administrators, and the Aspiring Principals Program, designed to prepare candidates for principal positions. Both of these one-year programs provide a series of learning opportunities and supports, including workshops, site observations, and mentoring.

The Arkansas Leadership Academy's Master Principal Program is an in-service professional learning program that supports school leaders in creating equitable deeper learning environments and catalyzing system improvement. The selective, three-phase program engages public school principals in developing leadership skills and knowledge through intensive residential sessions bridged by relevant research and activities. Principals who complete all three phases are eligible to apply for recognition as a Master School Principal in Arkansas, a selective designation that recognizes a track record of enacting meaningful school improvement and that carries financial incentives.

The National Institute for School Leadership (NISL) serves school administrators in all stages of development. It is implemented by the National Center on Education and the Economy, a nonprofit organization, in close partnership with states and districts, and is delivered through a series of in-person workshops facilitated by specially trained instructors. The program is driven by a research-based curriculum that emphasizes school leaders as drivers of equitable and transformative change that culminates in deeper learning and enhanced achievement among all students.

In the subsequent chapters, we share rich descriptions of the visions, structures, and practices that enable these programs to prepare leaders who are capable of promoting deeper learning and equity in schools. We also describe the leadership practices of program graduates, making explicit what deeper learning leadership looks like in practice. We then focus on the common aspects and outcomes of leadership preparation for deeper learning, delving into both the dimensions of deeper learning leadership and the program features through which these dimensions are developed. We close the book with a focus on policy recommendations to enable wider adoption of the features and practices highlighted here. In doing so, we aim to enhance efforts to equip school leaders with the knowledge and skills to support deeper learning experiences for all students.

CHAPTER 2

THE POWER OF INNOVATION AND PARTNERSHIP

University of Illinois Chicago Urban Education Leadership Program

The Urban Education Leadership Program at the University of Illinois Chicago (UIC), a multiyear doctoral level program, aims to equip school leaders with the knowledge and skills to drive improvement in Chicago Public Schools (CPS). UIC serves as a model of a residency-based principal preparation and in-service program that is building a district-wide network of leaders whose practice is aligned to deeper learning.

PROGRAM HIGHLIGHTS AND HISTORY

UIC's Urban Education Leadership Program prepares principals who are capable of transforming urban schools. It is an intensive, clinically based, two-stage doctoral program (see table 2.1). The first stage, spanning eighteen months, consists of coursework integrated with a funded, full-time residency in CPS, with support from a mentor principal and a university coach. Completion of this stage qualifies participants for the Illinois P-12 Principal Endorsement. The second stage, lasting three or more additional years, is completed while participants work as school administrators and includes advanced coursework and in-service coaching. The program culminates in a doctoral capstone project in which participants document efforts to build their school's organizational capacity to improve student learning.

Before 2002, UIC offered a typical master's degree–level principal preparation program. In 2000, motivated by its central vision and goal—to consistently prepare a new generation of school principals able to transform urban schools—the university began a two-year process to reimagine the preparation experience. UIC administrators set their sights on a multiyear preparation program that was highly selective, cohort-based, clinically focused, and dedicated to improving educational achievement in Chicago's schools.[1]

TABLE 2.1 **Overview of UIC Urban Education Leadership Program**

Program type	Preservice and in-service
Mission	To prepare and develop principals who lead significant improvement in the culture, climate, and student learning outcomes of high-need urban schools
Targeted places	CPS
Program duration	1.5 years to earn principal certification; approximately 3 additional years to earn EdD
Degree or designation conferred	Illinois P–12 Principal Endorsement after first 18 months EdD for completion of full program Certificate of Advanced Study for those who complete all requirements but the EdD capstone thesis
Program highlights	Partnership with CPS; coursework in instructional leadership, organizational leadership, and practitioner inquiry; paid, full-time, full-year residency with support from a UIC coach and mentor principal; performance-based projects using cycles of inquiry; postresidency leadership coaching; capstone project that demonstrates participants' abilities to build a school's organizational capacity
Key staff	University faculty; university leadership coaches; mentor principals
Costs and funding supports	Participants pay UIC tuition (just under $60,000 for the entire program); many participants have residencies paid by CPS; others have full-time, paid jobs in which they fulfill residency requirements

Around the same time that UIC began transforming its program, the Illinois legislature established a task force, chaired by Steve Tozer, director of UIC's Urban Education Leadership Program, to craft policy recommendations for improving principal licensure statewide. The task force's recommendations were influenced by the success of the revamped UIC model and included requiring more rigorous participant selection, establishing formal partnerships between preparation programs and school districts, and mandating supervised internships. These recommendations were given force in 2010 when the legislature enacted changes to principal preparation program accreditation.[2] The board of education gave all principal preparation programs two years to redesign their offerings and reapply for accreditation under the new, more rigorous program standards.

Chicago took the statewide emphasis on improving school leadership a step further. In 2011, CPS created the Chicago Leadership Collaborative, a partnership between the district and four leading principal preparation programs, including UIC's. The collaborative was designed to create a principal pipeline to provide every public school with a highly effective leader capable of driving change, improving student achievement, and graduating every student college and career ready.[3] With initial funding of $10 million, the collaborative tripled the number of funded residency seats in the district from thirty-two to one hundred. Half a decade later, the collaborative includes partnerships with eight preparation programs and continues to be a critical component of Chicago's commitment to effective and equitable principal preparation.[4] For UIC's part, participation in the collaborative has created ongoing opportunities for participants to receive hands-on preparation that supports their readiness for leading deeper learning–oriented schools from day one.

PROGRAM PHILOSOPHY

UIC's principal preparation program stands apart from many traditional one-year programs in its length and philosophical approach to principal development.

Building Transformational Leaders over Time

Realizing that it takes years to develop leadership expertise, program faculty embedded leadership development in a doctoral program taking at least 4.5 years to complete. Program developers believe that this extended learning time, far exceeding the former one-year timeline, was necessary to "scaffold the developmental process over time through cycles of preparation, practice, assessment, and reflection."[5] They believe this process is essential for principals to develop the knowledge and skills to be transformational school leaders.

Learning by Leading

The UIC program is also rooted in the belief that the best way to develop leadership skills is through real practice. This foundation is evident in the partnership between the university and clinical site schools, the strategic integration of coursework and practice-based learning experiences, and the collaboration of academic and site-based faculty in supporting participants' learning. UIC program director Tozer likened the program's approach to that of medical schools:

> We are trying to demonstrate the importance and the difficulties of making a shift in . . . school leader preparation that parallels the shift

made in US medical schools almost exactly a century ago: a shift from nonselective to selective admissions; from non-site-based to site-based intensive preparation; from nonscientific instruction to the strategic combination of academic and practitioner faculty to ensure optimal integration of research and practice; and from no formal partnerships with institutional sites of practice such as clinics and hospitals to formal partnerships.

For UIC, the ability to focus on student learning is predicated on adult learning driven by collaborative, sustained inquiry at the building level. This is why the first program stage is built around the eighteen-month, full-time residency in which program participants serve as school leaders under the guidance of mentor principals. Learning in practice continues in the second program stage as participants lead their own schools as principals or assistant principals, developing their capacities, with support from UIC, "in the heat and challenge of high-stakes leadership after licensure."[6]

Focusing on Critical Content

The UIC coursework is organized into three strands that are critical for school leadership: instructional leadership, organizational leadership, and practitioner inquiry. Through courses such as Leading Improvement of Mathematics Learning, Leading Improvement of Literacy Learning, and Leading Classroom Diagnostics and Interventions, participants learn to promote and support instruction that gives students the opportunity to engage in deeper learning practices. UIC faculty understand that creating deeper learning classrooms is a new concept to many teachers and leaders. As described by Tozer, "I want them to understand the culture of teaching in American schools, which is largely privatized practice and not set up for teaching for deep meaning. And the challenge for teaching for deep meaning is fundamentally an organizational and adult learning challenge."

The organizational leadership strand includes courses such as Improving Education Organizations, Developing Organizational and Leadership Capacity, and Organizational Theory in Education. These courses focus on organizational effectiveness and improvement. They provide the historical understandings of schools as organizations, theories of organizational change, and the practical aspects of developing human resources, engendering parent and community support, and creating supportive learning environments.

At the heart of the program is a focus on leading schoolwide cycles of inquiry, a "central disciplinary way of thinking and acting for school leaders."[7] Cycles of inquiry encompass designing data collection plans to identify problems, collecting and analyzing data, reporting findings, selecting improvement strategies and establishing goals, implementing the plan, and using data systems to track progress and make adjustments. Linking schoolwide improvement to systematic organizational learning, the faculty have embedded cycles of inquiry in course projects in both program phases. As Tozer said, "The practitioner inquiry strand is really all about how principals can lead professional communities that use data as the source of their learning. It's not simply about principals who can use data. It's about leading."

Recruiting Promising, Diverse, Equity-Minded Participants

The UIC program's commitment to advancing equity guides program recruiting. Alfred Tatum, dean of the UIC College of Education, explained that student diversity in CPS requires that UIC "recruit and support a diverse group of leaders," a goal that the program is meeting: approximately 50 percent of UIC participants identify as people of color, a higher proportion than most US programs.[8] UIC also seeks applicants with strong leadership potential and a commitment to transform inequities and improve learning opportunities in urban schools. Tozer summarized the ideal characteristics: "One, demonstration of instructional expertise. We don't want someone who knows the literature on good teaching but has not been able to demonstrate that. We want to see evidence that someone knows how to teach. . . . Two, fire in the belly. We need to see people who are absolutely committed to doing this work because it's really hard work. . . . We want to see someone who feels like 'If I don't do it, nobody is going to do it.' . . . And thirdly, there needs to be some track record of leading adults."

To ensure participants meet these qualifications, UIC boasts a rigorous, highly structured recruitment and selection process. Program applicants must have a master's degree, four years of successful teaching, and experience in a teacher leadership role. Their applications are comprehensive, including descriptions of past leadership roles and accomplishments, letters of recommendation, an analytic essay on urban school performance, a professional portfolio, a written analysis of a teaching video, and a two-hour interview. Each applicant is reviewed by a panel composed of faculty members, leadership coaches, and EdD graduates. The panel is seeking participants who have been effective in supporting student learning, leading change processes, collaborating with adults, and working with families, *and* who are amenable to coaching and capable of completing challenging practical and academic work.

PREPARING DEEPER LEARNING LEADERS

UIC's aim is to develop transformational leaders who are capable of creating systems to support teaching that is experiential and collaborative, builds on students' assets, addresses their social and emotional needs, and innovatively assesses their development. As principals, they must be able to create positive school climates, foster strong relationships, and support the whole child. UIC's structures and practices—the residency, coaching, assessment practices, coursework, and cohort design—are specifically designed to develop principals' knowledge and skills in these deeper learning competencies.

Providing Deeper Learning Leadership Practice Through Residencies

One hallmark of UIC's program is the full-year residency. After taking pre-residency courses in the spring and summer, participants begin their hands-on engagement with school leadership in the fall, working five days a week in a "resident principal" administrative position.[9] Residents are mentored by onsite principals, receive coaching from UIC clinical faculty, and participate in developmental leadership activities. Residencies give participants the opportunity to experience deeper learning in practice and to hone their skills as deeper learning leaders.

CPS PLACES PROGRAM PARTICIPANTS IN SCHOOLS THAT MODEL DEEPER LEARNING INSTRUCTION AND ASSESSMENT. Whenever possible, CPS, with UIC input, places residents in schools that value and model the principles of deeper learning. In these schools, participants see firsthand the structures and supports that principals must establish to enable deeper learning environments. During residencies, participants take an active role in day-to-day operations, review and write lesson plans with teachers, and analyze formative assessment results, among other activities. These authentic tasks help the UIC participants practice leadership moves that enable teachers to adopt deeper learning–aligned approaches. Indeed, 86 percent of the residency completers surveyed said they felt well or very well prepared to lead instruction that focuses on developing students' higher-order thinking skills.

Many placement schools emphasize inquiry-based instructional practices, a key element of deeper learning. For example, one UIC resident was placed in an elementary school in which students often work on projects that they define. The resident shared how she benefited from this hands-on engagement with inquiry-based curricula and instruction: "There was a lot of becoming familiar with the curriculum through reading it and talking with people and understanding how things are done here. And learning as you go. By the second quarter I was much more familiar with how units are written here, what best practice was for those units by understanding the practices that were happening in some really strong classrooms. So, [with] that, I could have a little more critical eye when those practices weren't happening." Seeing how project-based units of study were designed and how her mentor principal supported the process helped the resident identify how she might lead similar work when she became a principal.

Many residency placements also focus on performance-based assessments—a natural outgrowth of inquiry-based instruction—which measure mastery of higher-order thinking and critical skills through application to real-world scenarios. One resident described the advantages of being placed in a school emphasizing mastery learning: "A lot of those structures that a lot of schools don't have in place to really focus on deeper student understanding have been built here . . . so it is great for me to study." Another resident described how teachers in her residency site used formative assessments to understand students' existing knowledge, learning needs, and areas of interest, then used this information to design future learning opportunities. She had the opportunity to assist with analyzing formative assessment data, contributing to her learning about inquiry-based approaches to school leadership.

CPS PLACES PROGRAM PARTICIPANTS IN SCHOOLS THAT ADVANCE EQUITABLE AND SOCIALLY JUST LEARNING. Reflecting another deeper learning principle, CPS, with UIC input, also strives to place participants in schools working to advance equitable and socially just learning. In these schools, UIC participants are immersed in the challenges of addressing educational inequities. One CPS administrator described the types of activities in which UIC residents engage:

> They are looking at the data and determining where is the school missing its mark and delving deep into the disaggregated data. So looking at: Is it a type of student? Is it a certain population in the school that is just not moving? And starting to ask those questions of why. And working with the teachers to determine how to isolate what is actually needed for that grade level or what is needed for that subgroup of students. And building a plan of action around that. . . . Are we teaching to the level of rigor for the standards? Are we dumbing down the standards for students who have not met the mark? Or are we building capacity within the teachers to be able to scaffold and keep students at grade level in grade-level content?

Residencies enable UIC participants to experience social justice theories in practice as they grapple with the challenges they will face as school leaders. One participant explained how his placement helped him understand the ideas covered in his coursework: "We talked about . . . how you run schools that have economically, culturally, linguistically diverse learners. Truthfully, being in a school is the best way to really understand how to use that."

RESIDENCIES PROVIDE OPPORTUNITIES FOR PARTICIPANTS TO PRACTICE DEEPER LEARNING LEADING. Once they are placed in schools that enact deeper learning principles, residents are provided opportunities to practice leading critical thinking and inquiry-based learning. For example, in his residency, one UIC participant was coaching first-year teachers to move from teacher-centric to student-centered instruction, getting feedback from his own coach on his use of instructional leadership practices. One teacher reported that the coaching helped him understand the need to create more active, student-centered lessons: "One thing we talked about a lot was me doing the heavy lifting. . . . I was really carrying a lot of the load." He reported that after the coaching "it got much better."

Residents also have opportunities to support teachers in addressing students' social and emotional needs. One resident, with support from her mentor principal and coach, developed a program for eighth-grade boys who had social-emotional learning challenges. Another resident worked with a cohort of teachers to develop more personalized learning practices. Yet another developed a social-emotional assessment tool for incoming freshmen that helped teachers understand students holistically and address their needs more effectively.

Residencies also help participants learn to support productive communities of practice among teachers. Mentor principals typically use collaborative, distributed leadership models that prioritize the development of teachers' instructional leadership abilities and create a collective commitment to instructional improvement. Residents, then, learn to support these models. For example, one mentor principal asked her resident to lead the school's efforts to develop a multitiered system of supports. The resident had to interact with teachers, social workers, guidance counselors, and various service providers to develop a functional system, garner support for the system, and implement it with fidelity. With guidance from her mentor principal and leadership coach, she learned to manage the various teams, personalities, dynamics, systems, and structures of this complex assignment, developing her own capacities in the process.

Providing Individualized Support Through Leadership Coaching

Another central aspect of the UIC model is intensive, long-term, individualized coaching. Residents receive on-the-job support from their mentor principals and from a university coach. At any given time, UIC has four to six coaches on staff, all former CPS administrators who previously improved student outcomes in schools with high percentages of students of color and students from high-poverty families.

INDIVIDUALIZED COACHING HELPS PARTICIPANTS IMPROVE TEACHING AND LEARNING FOR ALL STUDENTS. UIC coaches conduct weekly site visits, communicate frequently about issues or questions that arise, and tailor feedback to participant needs. Coaches work with residents to create professional development plans, help them prepare for CPS principal eligibility assessments, and provide advice on their capstone projects. They also help participants learn how to address racial and socioeconomic inequities. UIC charges its coaches with "help[ing] make explicit the social context knowledge necessary for school leaders" to raise "standards and academic achievement for all students and teachers."[10]

Consider, for example, a resident who wanted to ensure his work bringing deeper learning practices to the school would be sustained, even though both the resident and the mentor principal were leaving the school. The resident planned to empower a teacher leader to pick up the mantle of instructional improvement, but he did not know how to execute this plan. His coach, knowledgeable about the school, encouraged the resident to lay out next steps and work with the teacher leader to plan how she might have the conversation with the new principal around influencing the professional learning plan. The coach encouraged the resident to use his own professional development plan to lay out and document next steps.

Even as they individualize their support, coaches coordinate closely with one another to ensure consistency and quality, meeting biweekly to engage in professional development and determine ways to improve their support of participants. As Program Director Tozer explained: "The potential downside of coaching is it's . . . not programmatic. It's so individualized that your success in the program depends on who you get. And you don't want that. . . . We have a community of professional practice of coaches that meets a minimum of two hours every two weeks around problems of coaching practice. . . . How do you coach? What are our most important aims? What are our procedures? What are our protocols?"

COHERENT, COORDINATED COACHING TURBOCHARGES LEARNING TO LEAD. Critical to the UIC model is the tight coordination of support provided by the mentor principal and the UIC coach. UIC has developed a monthly triad meeting in which the resident, the mentor principal, and the UIC coach come together to examine the resident's competency development. At these meetings, which are facilitated by the resident, the three participants discuss issues related to the resident's leadership work, review data to monitor progress, and plan appropriate next steps. Following each meeting, residents complete a written reflection, prompting them to adopt a metacognitive perspective toward their development.

The triad meetings are designed to accelerate the resident's leadership development through coordinated, collaborative dialogue and support. They provide a critical triangulation of perspectives on the participant's residency experience, leadership development, and short- and long-term developmental goals.

The Power of Coordinated Coaching

It was ten o'clock on a June morning when UIC participant Didi Swartz called her triad meeting to order. She was joined by her mentor principal, Nicole (Nikki) Milberg, and her leadership coach and UIC instructor Paul Zavitkovsky. Swartz was completing her residency at the school where she had worked since the previous summer as a resident principal. Together, these three individuals form what UIC calls a triad, and Swartz was leading one of their routine check-ins to discuss her performance at the school. With everyone seated, Swartz passed out paper copies of the agenda she had prepared. It read, "Strengths, opportunities, reflections: Multi-tiered Systems of Support structures and processes, social-emotional supports, parent engagement, and coaching." Swartz started the discussion about the multitiered systems of support, a comprehensive instruction and intervention framework to help ensure every student, regardless of need, has the support to be successful. Swartz had been leading the overhaul of the school's support system over the course of the year, gaining valuable experience in the process.

Reflecting on her work, Swartz shared, "The takeaway product is a handbook—that still needs some refinement—but it outlines new processes for next year. I feel proud that that is something we developed as a team." "Do you think there are ways you could have done it that were more inclusive, so you are not doing so much of the lifting?" Milberg probed Swartz. The conversation then shifted to unpacking the development of the handbook and the leadership practices Swartz incorporated: Did teachers feel engaged with the process? Did Swartz do enough to actively cultivate teacher buy-in up front? What are the pros and cons of possibly having slowed the process down to ensure greater levels of collaboration? What are the adequate levels

(continues)

of support and facilitation that Swartz needed to provide to ensure the process was teacher-driven yet focused on the priority of the assignment? Each topic was considered in turn as Swartz, with the help of the others, engaged in this guided self-reflection exercise.

At another point in the hour-and-a-half meeting, Swartz dove into her reflections on a partnership program she designed with a local high school to offer mentoring and positive behavioral examples for a group of eighth-grade boys struggling with academics and social-emotional issues. She asserted, "I think we need to find better ways for [the middle grades teachers] to plan with them so that they can take better leadership within the sessions with the students." Swartz also pondered the frequency of interaction as Zavitkovsky, seeking to affirm and push Swartz's thinking, inquired about evidence of effectiveness: "Is there one kid that comes to mind? What [does] that one kid's story sound like?" Swartz brightened as she related the positive changes she's seen one eighth-grade boy make over the course of the semester; Milberg contributed additional background details about the student.

The ensuing dialogue prompted timely consideration for Swartz's future. Her residency was nearing its end, but she had not yet secured an administrative placement for the following year. The triad considered the range of possibilities where Swartz may find herself next year and what she can do to have a positive impact for her future students' social-emotional development. Zavitkovsky began by posing a question about social-emotional supports: "What are your thoughts about some kind of scalability? If next year, the kinds of behaviors that are relatively more isolated here became more normative . . . what would you do?" Swartz paused, then proposed a few possibilities. Zavitkovsky and Milberg each offered feedback on the possibilities while Swartz hurriedly captured their feedback in the margins of her agenda.

The meeting concluded with a frank discussion of Swartz's next career steps. "I'm still torn about whether it would be beneficial to be in an assistant principal role where I can develop understanding," Swartz admitted. Unlike many of her peers, Swartz was working at the district office before enrolling at UIC and was several years removed from the classroom. Hearing Swartz's hesitancies, the others offered no uncertain advice. "Assistant principal can be great as long as the principal is great. . . . Everything ties to that kind of professional marriage." Nodding in agreement, Milberg encouragingly added, "You should be at a school where you have a co-leadership position, otherwise you will not be happy." Swartz smiled in agreement.

Building Knowledge Through Authentic Assessments

UIC has embraced formative and performance-based assessments that provide rich information about participant learning throughout the program. These assessments reflect the deeper learning principles UIC is preparing leaders to enact in their own schools.

ASSESSMENTS REFLECT DEEPER LEARNING AND DEEPEN PARTICIPANT LEARNING. UIC enacts deeper learning principles by using formative and performance-based assessments to provide ongoing information about participants' progress and needs. Faculty and coaches use this information to create multiple opportunities for participants to revise their leadership practices and demonstrate competence. It also helps faculty identify participants who consistently fail to meet UIC's standards and may need to be counseled out of the program.

One such formative assessment is the Leadership Development Plan. This living document, collaboratively developed at the beginning of the school year among a resident, a mentor principal, and a UIC coach, details the participant's goals, progress, and edges of growth. Residents use these plans to document evolving leadership challenges and development throughout the residency. They revise these plans as cycles of inquiry unfold, new data are gathered, and new obstacles emerge. The plans also serve as anchor points for triad meetings. For example, one participant's goal was to coach new and struggling teachers by leading them in cycles of inquiry. The resident recorded her progress and struggles in her plan and routinely strategized with her mentor principal and her coach on how to more effectively support the teachers.

One performance-based assessment used by UIC is the juried review, which takes place after completion of the residency. Professor Shelby Cosner described the challenging nature of this assessment, which requires participants to compile artifacts and complete a written reflection: "It's not an essay about 'Here is what I've learned.' It's . . . artifacts from the work that they've been doing over the course of the year. And it might be a thirty-page write-up, but it might have links to forty documents that are artifacts that show things that they have been working on in their school. . . . When we assemble all the work, what are the patterns of problems that we see?"

As with the formative assessments, UIC faculty and coaches use data from the juried review to understand participants' progress and the refinements needed to support their growth.

PARTICIPANTS PRACTICE DEEPER LEARNING LEADERSHIP THROUGH THE CAPSTONE THESIS. After participants finish their residencies and complete two years as a principal or vice principal, they move to the capstone thesis. This final step before participants earn their EdD focuses on their ability to demonstrate and analyze strategies for improving schools. It is not a traditional doctoral dissertation; rather, it takes the form of a written case study detailing participants' cycles of inquiry, improvement efforts, and organizational capacity-building at their schools. Participants use data collected from their schools, ground this information in relevant research literature, and analyze their case from leadership practice, practice development, and organizational development perspectives. They provide evidence of how their school has changed over time and how they have developed the requisite interpersonal, cognitive, and intrapersonal skills to become school leaders. Each capstone is defended before a faculty committee, first as a proposal and later as a final case study.

One graduate's capstone project illustrates the tight connection between the assessment and the real problems of practice faced in her school. Her thesis focused on understanding how to create more avenues for teacher leaders to emerge. For her, this meant moving away from "handpicking" leaders to "helping people emerge in their strengths." Working on the project helped her grow as a leader and benefited the school as she expanded and strengthened distributed leadership, contributing to deep engagement by teachers.

Tying Coursework to Fieldwork

The UIC program provides in-depth coursework with immediate application to schools. The curriculum is organized into three themes: organizational leadership, instructional leadership, and practitioner inquiry. UIC's courses are sequenced to build on each other, are focused on participants' work transforming historically underserved schools, and reflect the continuous collaboration between academic and clinical faculty.

UIC EMPHASIZES ACTIVE AND PROBLEM-BASED LEARNING BY MELDING COURSE-WORK AND FIELDWORK. UIC's coursework provides frequent intersections between theory and practice. Topics, assignments, and discussions are deliberately linked to the work participants are doing in their schools, either as residents or, later, as licensed administrators. This blending often takes the form of course-embedded, clinically enacted tasks. For example, in the Leading Improvement of Mathematics Learning course, participants assess the rigor of mathematics instruction in their schools by analyzing student work and observing lessons. They discuss findings during class, implement improvements in practice, and create a feedback loop connecting both. Faculty want program participants to both understand the theory behind leadership and have opportunities to practice it. Professor Cosner explained, "We take really seriously the difference between understanding and practice development. When you're thinking about leadership preparation and you look at standards . . . they are performative in nature. . . . For us that translates for our courses to be about not only developing new understandings but developing new practices."

Another course-embedded, clinically enacted project is the Grading and Assessment Inventory. For this assignment, residents collect instructional materials and assessments from teachers in their schools, analyze them, and code them using a framework designed to identify the rigor and complexity of a task or assessment. They then report their findings to the school's faculty. This assignment engages residents in the technical work of their schools and opens opportunities for connecting with teachers about instruction.

COURSEWORK PUSHES PARTICIPANTS TO CONSIDER THE INFLUENCE OF RACE AND CLASS IN THEIR SCHOOLS. UIC's coursework pushes participants to consider the influence of race and class in their schools and how they can address educational inequities. UIC has structured its curriculum so that all courses address how disability, race, ethnicity, language, gender, and social class influence teaching, learning, and leadership in schools. UIC expects program graduates to "demonstrate a professional-level, research-informed response" to questions about the social construction of intelligence, the relationship between race and ethnicity and building social trust, gender, and class and how they relate to student achievement, and professional standards and how they relate to leadership for social justice.[11]

In the first course of the program, Organizational Leadership, participants read *Racism Without Racists: Color-Blind Racism and the Persistence of Racial Inequality in the United States*, by Eduardo Bonilla-Silva.[12] Program Director Tozer explained the significance of having students begin with this book and topic. "You can talk about justice all you want, but if you don't have a theory for changing institutions, you're not serious about social justice." UIC teaches that advancing social justice requires an awareness of how schools and communities have been structured to the detriment of many people of color. Grappling with issues of race and social justice in their coursework equips participants to lead such conversations in their schools. As one participant said, "When you have those courageous conversations in your courses, then you see it modeled how to have those courageous conversations around race with the adults that you're leading." Focusing on race and class helps participants appreciate the historical roots of the challenges occurring in their schools and develop strategies that support students.

Developing an Understanding of Race and Justice

Most UIC courses build participants' understanding of race and justice. Consider Paul Zavitkovsky's course, Introduction to Practitioner Inquiry. At the beginning of one class, Zavitkovsky—also a full-time coach—shared with his students that the goal of the class was to "[move] from the unconscious to conscious and making the invisible visible." One focus of the class is for participants to learn how to address the racial achievement gap that persists in CPS. A key aspect of this development is for participants to learn how to make the teachers and staff in their schools aware of the root causes of the gap. Zavitkovsky reminded the participants about the issues they encountered while reading *Racism Without Racists*. He connected the challenges of racial inequality to participants' experiences in the schools where they have taught: "When it comes to the discipline, punishment, and the exclusion side, I ask you to think about schools where discipline is a problem, and think about the discipline rates and exclusion rates that go on and how those things break out by race and class. There is no mystery about how those things break out by race and class."

After that, Zavitkovsky charged the participants with reflecting on conventional approaches to educating students from lower-income families and students of color. "I ask you to think about race and class from the point of view: What it is that we think kids can actually do, particularly poor kids of color? What it is that we think they are capable of doing? To what extent is our curriculum for those particular youngsters guided by our implicit sense that we really have to deal mostly with basic skills and the most fundamental things before we think they can deal with the most interesting things? I ask you to think about that."

Participants then broke into small groups to, as Zavitkovsky described, "[generate] some starting points for leading conversations that help [them] and others stop being unwitting parties to institutional racism and classism." A student in one group raised the challenges she has faced when trying to push her school to move from conventional supports to transformational supports for teaching and learning:

> I've seen multiple times that schools, leadership, someone will say, "Just give me the silver bullet. We are drowning and we're not doing good work by our kids. We need something to fix this problem now." And I always argue that while I understand your motivation, over the long term, there's no system in your school. You're just giving someone a scripted curriculum and assessments that go with it and saying "Use this and you'll be fine." You might have the appearance of fixing the problem. But you don't. You just perpetuate the same thing. Because no one has an investment in the work and actually developing as an instructor as part of this long, drawn-out, difficult, messy, complex process.

The student's comment reflected an awareness for how instruction for students from low-income families and students of color has traditionally been more focused on developing basic skills—in part because of the pressures that have accompanied

(continues)

test-based accountability policies.[13] The student recognized that making shifts in organizational culture and practice takes time and requires collaboration among teachers, staff, and leaders. These shifts also require leaders to make the negative effects of short-term solutions visible to staff so that they will invest in sustainable deeper learning instructional strategies with that promise to improve the learning of all students.

PARTICIPANTS PRACTICE LEVERAGING DATA THROUGH CYCLES OF INQUIRY. Central to UIC's curriculum are cycles of inquiry, a "signature pedagogy" used in courses both during and after the residency, applied to participants' real-world experiences in CPS. Through cycles of inquiry, UIC urges participants to use data to identify patterns of underperformance by different student groups, investigate root causes as critical steps in addressing educational disparities, and empower teachers to improve their practice. A UIC graduate described the value of learning to conduct cycles of inquiry:

> We spend two and a half years where most of our coursework is about how to collect data relevant to instruction, how to analyze the data. Not data in terms of this multiple-choice test and how many people got number seven wrong, but rather, "Here's a framework for understanding the rigor of math instruction. So let's see what that looks like in our schools. Let's do a diagnostic around that." . . . So you do that diagnostic work and at the end of that you come up with a vision of where your school has to go based on your context.

Indeed, after the residency year, 93 percent of surveyed participants said they felt well or very well prepared to use student and school data to inform continuous school improvement. That percentage increases to 97 percent among EdD completers.

Fostering Learning Communities Through a Cohort Model
UIC utilizes a cohort structure to offer supportive and collaborative learning experiences. Program participants—typically fifteen to twenty per cohort—take courses, complete residencies, and develop their leadership abilities together. This structure allows participants to foster deep, trusting personal and professional relationships with one another that increase participant persistence and highlight the importance of collaboration in leading schools. Further, this peer network endures beyond the program;

peers, even those across cohorts, rely on one another for support and professional advice well into their careers.

A COHORT EXPANDS LEARNING OPPORTUNITIES. UIC recruits and admits participants with shared values and skills, including a commitment to advance social justice and to work collaboratively. This shared commitment creates a strong foundation for mutual respect and trust upon which productive communities of practice are formed. The collaborative nature of the cohort enables participants to push each other's thinking and provide alternative perspectives.

The coursework takes advantage of cohort collaboration to prepare participants for a variety of schools, not just the ones in which they have experience. Consider the course Leading Improvement of Mathematics Learning, in which participants conduct classroom observations and collect artifacts such as lesson plans, instructional materials, and student work in math classes in their schools. They then return to the UIC campus and collaboratively make meaning of those data, looking at data from their own schools and from their cohort members' schools as well. Professor Cosner explained the importance of the cohort in broadening participants' perspectives:

> If they were just doing this in the clinical setting, they would only have one set of data to look at to make meaning of. But when they collect the data in a clinical setting and bring it back into the course, I can now get them in a long-standing group with two or three other students and now they get to see these mathematics program data and instructional data from . . . other settings. . . . And part of what they are doing is discussing with their peers, "As we start to look across these three or four assortments of data that we are collecting, what do we notice?"

ACCOMPLISHMENTS AND DEEPER LEARNING LEADERSHIP IN PRACTICE

UIC's focus on connecting theory and practice has brought tangible benefits to the school leaders it has prepared, the schools they lead, and the students they serve. In the first fifteen years of the program, 207 UIC participants completed their residency year, achieved state licensure, and went on to work in leadership positions. Over this time, UIC maintained a

95 percent placement rate in administrative positions, with 70 percent serving as principals. Of this group, 146 became urban school principals, 108 of them in Chicago, nearly all working in historically underserved urban schools. The remaining 48 became assistant principals or system-level leaders.[14] It speaks to the quality of the UIC program that system leaders who are program graduates included a CPS network chief (principal supervisor), the heads of the CPS Office of Language and Culture and Early Childhood Education, and the CPS chief executive officer (Chicago's equivalent of a superintendent).

UIC has been recognized for the quality of its program.[15] In 2012, the Council of Great City Schools awarded UIC, in partnership with CPS, the Urban Impact Award, recognizing the positive and significant impact their partnership has had on student learning. That same year, the George W. Bush Institute's Alliance to Reform Education Leadership named UIC to Exemplary Status, the first higher education program to obtain this status. In 2013, the program received the first Exemplary Educational Leadership Preparation Program Award from the University Council for Educational Administration for its strong outcome evidence of program effectiveness.

Research also has demonstrated that high schools led by UIC principals improve attendance, freshman on-track rates, and graduation rates at significantly higher levels than comparable CPS high schools. Compared with all other CPS schools, schools led by UIC principals were more likely to increase a full level in CPS school quality rankings and less than half as likely to decline in rankings.[16] Over an eleven-year period, 72 percent of UIC-led elementary schools and 60 percent of UIC-led secondary schools exceeded the state's average student growth gains by the end of the principals' first year.[17] And, nearly all (90 percent) UIC students passed the CPS principal eligibility process in their first attempt, in contrast to less than 40 percent for all non-UIC prepared eligibility seekers.[18]

In a survey, most residency completers (87 percent) and nearly all EdD completers (97 percent) reported that the UIC program prepared them well or very well to be a principal. Reflecting the program's emphasis on deeper learning, both residency completers and EdD completers reported that they were very well or well prepared to lead curriculum and instruction that focuses on students' higher-order thinking skills (86 percent and 80 percent, respectively). Nearly all residency completers and EdD completers felt especially prepared to use data to inform continuous school improvement (93 percent and 97 percent, respectively) and engage in their own continuous learning (93 percent and 97 percent, respectively).

Considering UIC's focus on developing leaders capable of improving the organizational capacity of schools, it is notable that residency completers and EdD completers felt well or very well prepared to redesign the school's organization and structure to support deeper learning for teachers and students (93 percent and 82 percent, respectively).

Not only do UIC alumni feel prepared to lead for deeper learning, but their work inside schools also shows that they are, in fact, enacting deeper learning leadership.

Encouraging Teachers to Use Active Learning Pedagogies

In deeper learning classrooms, children engage in active, hands-on learning, from manipulating objects, to engaging in discourse, to running experiments. As school leaders, UIC participants and alumni work to ensure that teachers enact these types of active learning pedagogies. One UIC-prepared principal, for example, used deeper learning practices in the professional development she led for teachers so that the teachers could understand the practices she expected them to use in their classrooms. This principal found that the teachers were able to implement these practices in their classrooms after engaging in the practices themselves. UIC participants learn through experience that to get others to champion active learning pedagogies, they must show them firsthand, through experience, their benefits.

Leading Schools Where Inquiry Projects Are Ubiquitous

Deeper learning calls on students to use critical thinking to investigate open-ended questions rather than relying on teachers' expertise. In schools led by UIC participants and alumni, students engage in complex inquiry. In one such school, led by a UIC-prepared principal, inquiry projects were the norm in all grades. In first grade, learners experimented in small teams to create the stickiest glue, starting with a collection of ingredients, noting their properties, and making predictions about which would work best. Older students engaged in more elaborate inquiry assignments. One required learners to develop a method for determining whether each of three tanks was full of oxygen, half full, or empty and then use that method to run experiments and document and share their findings. Sixth-grade students chose an early twentieth-century American history topic, investigated it, and wrote reports that they shared schoolwide, creating hallway posters with QR codes linked to more information. The focus on applied learning was reinforced by the language and culture of the school. In hallways and classrooms, posters encouraged students to see themselves as "inquirers," "thinkers," and "*investigadores*"—the latter critical given the school's large

English language learner population. Classroom walls covered with student work refer to students as "scientists" and "engineers."

Enacting Equitable and Socially Just Learning

UIC-prepared principals advance more equitable and socially just learning in the schools they lead, demonstrating a critical aspect of deeper learning. In one school, for example, a core value is "International Mindedness," which the school describes as "we embrace diversity." Kindergartners through eighth graders study different cultures and gain an appreciation for the diversity of different groups of people. Kindergarten students studied the culture and traditions of people from China. Another class studied Native American tribes and learned about their clothing, food, and shelter. These lessons help students develop an appreciation for cultural differences, contributing to a classroom environment where students' differences are celebrated. The school also communicates its expectations of transforming inequities through democracy and civic engagement with quotes from civil rights leaders lining the halls.

Developing Productive Teacher Communities of Practice

During and after their residencies, UIC participants focus on developing collaborative teacher teams capable of directing their own learning. One resident, for example, led a grade-level meeting focused on creating the year's professional development plan. She took a back seat at the meeting, coaching the teachers to identify the agenda and formulate the issues they should discuss to move forward productively. Under the resident's guidance, the team leveraged the collective expertise and experience of each member. In another example, a UIC graduate took steps to restructure her school's instructional leadership team as a collaborative unit. The prior principal had used the team to disseminate information and instructions to the teachers. She, in contrast, envisioned the group leading teacher teams to deeper understanding through active learning techniques. She attributed her understanding of professional learning communities to her UIC preparation. She operated on the assumption that authentic collaboration entailed meaningful engagement around tasks, not just simultaneous task completion.

Focusing on the Social and Emotional Needs of Students

UIC-prepared principals also push for more attention to the social and emotional needs of students. One resident, for example, developed an assessment tool for incoming freshmen to measure their social-emotional readiness. The purpose of the tool was for teachers to understand, and subsequently address, students' needs beyond their academic skills. Another resident established a mentoring program for eighth-grade students specifically to address their social and emotional learning. Program graduates used grant funding—in one case to bring in a clinical program that supported students through meditation to reduce anxiety and stress, and in another to purchase a curriculum focused on children's social and emotional development.

UIC-prepared principals also support a whole-child approach, setting goals to revamp disciplinary policies and practices to be more supportive and less punitive in order to foster, rather than interrupt, student growth. One UIC-prepared principal, for example, noticed that her teachers were quick to suspend students. In response, she banned the practice and implemented Saturday detentions, where she uses the time to get to know the students.

FACTORS INFLUENCING SYSTEMIC DEEPER LEARNING LEADERSHIP DEVELOPMENT

UIC has transformed principal preparation and development from a one-year course-heavy program to a multiyear, practice-based doctoral program with a strong track record of preparing principals who can design systems and support teachers to enact deeper learning. UIC faculty have a deep understanding of adult learning and the complexities of the principalship, and a vision for how to prepare principals to successfully wrestle with these complexities. However, there are factors that contribute to the success of the program while others present challenges.

Investing in Program Improvement

The strength of UIC's program can be attributed, in part, to the program's emphasis on continuous self-assessment and improvement. It has five full-time doctoral-level research staff who study program impact based on a comprehensive data system that includes information on licensure, achievement rates on the CPS principal competency assessment, and job placement and retention, as well as graduates' impact on schools. According to Tozer, "UIC is committed to collaborative, sustained research into how to develop school principals who inspire school cultures with high expectations, who engage key staff in leadership roles, and who build professional communities that improve adult and student learning through collaborative, sustained inquiry at the building level."

UIC has used the data regularly to make notable programmatic changes. For example, to enhance participants' abilities to address inequities in their schools and strengthen their engagement with communities, program designers revamped coursework to more effectively complement the on-the-ground support provided by coaches. Other program revisions included updating tools and protocols to better support participants through successive stages of leadership development, enhancing collaboration with CPS to strengthen residency experiences, calibrating enrollment to balance district needs with program capacity, and working toward more sustainable funding.[19] Cycles of program research and revision are continuous. As UIC dean Alfred Tatum said, "They are always striving to get it right. Although this program is being recognized nationally . . . they are continuing to ask the questions or push the envelope or seek expertise."

Sharing a Mission with UIC's School of Education

Most universities are not known for recognizing or rewarding faculty for practice-facing work. UIC is the exception. As Tozer described, "The tagline for this college of education, which we take really seriously, is 'Making good on the promise of public education.' . . . You really need institutional support to pull this sort of work off." University support has been manifest in many ways: the establishment and funding of the Center for Urban Education Leadership, the commitment of funding for three clinical faculty members to provide leadership coaching, the negotiation with CPS to provide residency salaries, and the steady stream of research dollars. This symbiosis between the principal development program and the university is rooted in a shared mission and shared values.

Fostering Coherence Through Faculty and Clinical Staff Collaboration

UIC academic and clinical faculty are committed to collaboration, creating program coherence. For example, Professor Cosner regularly collaborates with UIC coaches so that their support for participants is grounded in the clinically enacted classroom tasks. She regularly meets with participants and their UIC coaches to work through an assignment or a challenge the student is having in their school. Faculty construct and maintain these linkages with a great degree of intentionality and do not hesitate to rely on UIC coaches to guide coursework, leveraging their firsthand knowledge of the challenges participants face in their schools. Such collaboration is unusual in university settings, which tend to recognize individual scholarship for tenure-line faculty members while relying on adjunct faculty to fill clinical staff positions. UIC works to sustain this vital collaboration through its faculty hiring. As Cosner described, "There's been a great emphasis on building a culture of collaboration and hiring people who are disposed to collaborate. . . . We've been working on creating a culture that says there is a lot of glory when we work together. . . . We have to think about it every time that you're bringing a hire in."

Creating an Expanding Network

The bonds developed through the UIC program—among cohort members, across cohorts, and between participants and coaches—create networks of support that last years beyond the program. UIC's cohorts, past and present, form a supportive network that members lean on when faced with problems of practice at their schools. One CPS principal who did not attend UIC expressed her admiration for the ongoing collaboration: "You can always tell the UIC people. This is a district that is very decentralized and isolated. [Yet] there is so much collaboration that happens between them." This network also supports the program. As more cohorts complete the program, the number of UIC-prepared principals who can serve as mentor principals has increased. Further, there are more schools that model the program's values of deeper learning and a commitment to equity in which participants can complete their residencies.

Managing the Relationship with CPS

A strong relationship with CPS is critical to the program's success. Since the program's inception, CPS has provided financial support through the Chicago Leadership Collaborative by covering salaries and benefits for the residency. The district also fully funds one leadership coach position and contributes to program liaisons. A shared understanding of strong leadership has also been a driver of coordinated and mutually supportive action. CPS developed principal competencies explicitly focused on the needs of urban schools in collaboration with principal preparation programs, including UIC's.

While the CPS-UIC relationship is strong, it is not without challenges. CPS is spreading residency slots to an increasing number of preparation programs, leaving UIC participants without the guarantee of a funded residency and shifting the responsibility of locating residency positions to the program. Meanwhile, the district has taken a more active role in deciding where participants receiving CPS-funded residency positions will be placed, which has led to some less-than-ideal matches between participants and placements. Finally, sustaining a partnership through fiscal challenges and shifts in leadership is challenging. UIC has responded by hiring an experienced non-tenure-line employee to serve as a formal liaison to the school district.

KEY TAKEAWAYS

UIC's Urban Education Leadership Program has successfully provided CPS with skilled principals who are able to foster and sustain deeper learning in their schools. Through its unique two-stage structure, yearlong residency, intensive coaching, doctoral-level work, and deeper learning–infused pedagogies, the program develops participants' knowledge and skills to be transformational leaders. The key features and practices of UIC's program are outlined below.

UIC provides sufficient time for participants to develop leadership competencies. In this four- to five-year program, principals learn and practice leadership skills over time, enabling them to develop into expert leaders capable of transforming schools. Clinical work, coursework, and coaching are embedded in a deliberate scope and sequence that prioritizes mastery while accounting for participants' individual development trajectories.

Program components that are coherent and integrated create powerful learning experiences. All program components—residency, coaching, coursework, assessment, and cohort—are mutually reinforcing. Course-embedded, clinically enacted tasks connect research and practice. Further, each component is focused on, and aligned to, a shared vision of transformational leadership that prioritizes instruction, school organization, and the diagnosis and resolution of problems in the service of educational equity.

Strong collaboration among academic faculty, university coaches, principal mentors, and participants creates coherent, consistent learning opportunities. Structures and processes, such as triad meetings, create consistent communication among faculty, staff, and participants. This communication ensures that everyone is working toward common goals related to participants' development as deeper learning leaders while providing a model of collaboration for participants to use in their schools.

UIC's yearlong clinical residency exemplifies deeper learning instructional practices and provides opportunities for aspiring principals to learn by leading. The funded, full-time residency provides active, inquiry-based engagement with school leadership that is contextualized. Mentorship from an experienced principal and coaching from a former CPS administrator help create personalized and developmentally grounded learning opportunities for residents.

Cycles of inquiry develop participants' abilities to foster instructional and organizational changes in service of deeper learning. UIC participants leverage project-based, practice-focused learning experiences to empower teachers to improve instruction in ways consistent with deeper learning. Furthermore, the cycles reflect deeper learning by developing candidates' competencies through hands-on, real-world activities.

A cohort model supports participants' learning and develops their abilities to create collaborative school environments. The cohort structure models collaborative learning. It also persists over time as participants rely on peers for support well into their professional careers. Over time, the growing UIC alumni network has amplified the program's impact.

CHAPTER 3

PUTTING EQUITY AT THE CENTER

University of California, Berkeley, Principal Leadership Institute

The Principal Leadership Institute (PLI) at the University of California, Berkeley, prepares a diverse community of equity-focused school leaders who are able to provide educational opportunities for all children, particularly those who historically have not received them, such as dual language learners, students of color, and students from low-income families.

PROGRAM HIGHLIGHTS AND HISTORY

The PLI is a cohort-based master's degree program for school leaders committed to improving education "for vulnerable and historically underserved students in California's public schools in support of social justice."[1] The program has deep roots in the state, going back to a 1999 commitment by California governor Gray Davis "to enhance the professional quality of principals."[2] The Public Schools Accountability Act of 1999 created the PLI at the state's two flagship campuses: the University of California, Berkeley, and the University of California, Los Angeles.[3]

The PLI provides aspiring school leaders with coursework, field experiences, and coaching, leading to a California Preliminary Administrative Services Credential and a master's degree in education (see table 3.1). PLI candidates complete forty units of coursework over four semesters, or fourteen months, while maintaining full-time employment as educators. Most PLI candidates work as teacher leaders, department chairs, grade-level chairs, teachers on special assignment, or literacy or math coaches.

The PLI costs approximately $29,000 in university tuition and fees, plus books and other fees.[4] A blend of philanthropic support and funding from the University of California's Office of the President provides partial scholarships, including needs-based and diversity-focused funds. Program Director Rebecca Cheung explained that these financial supports

TABLE 3.1   Overview of UC Berkeley PLI preparation program

Program type	Preservice
Mission	To prepare a diverse community of equity-focused school leaders who will improve education for vulnerable and historically underserved students in California's public schools in support of social justice
Targeted places	San Francisco Bay Area: Berkeley, Oakland, San Francisco, and West Contra Costa Unified School Districts
Program duration	14 months
Degree or designation conferred	Master's degree in education and Preliminary Administrative Services Credential
Program highlights	Focus on social justice and equity; cohort model; connections between educational theory and practice; site-based inquiry projects; individual leadership coaching; action research capstone project
Key staff	Tenure-track faculty instructors; practitioner instructors; leadership coaches; guest lecturers including PLI alumni; graduate student writing coach
Costs and funding supports	Tuition and fees are $29,000, but all students receive need-based scholarships and approximately 75% are eligible for federal financial aid. Fellowships and awards range from $3,000 to $20,000 per student, averaging $10,000.

are essential for ensuring that the PLI enrolls a diverse group of candidates in service of the program's broader social justice mission.

The PLI has four partner school districts in the San Francisco Bay Area: Berkeley, Oakland, San Francisco, and West Contra Costa. About 50 percent of the PLI's students and alumni work in these districts. They vary in size, with Berkeley serving just over 10,000 students and San Francisco serving 60,000. All four districts are located in urban areas and serve racially, linguistically, and economically diverse student bodies: the percentage of English language learner students ranges from 9 percent in Berkeley to 32 percent in West Contra Costa, while nearly three quarters of Oakland and West Contra Costa students qualify for free or reduced lunch.[5]

PROGRAM PHILOSOPHY

The PLI embraces five core leadership values:

- engaging in reflective practice
- fostering strong relationships through collaboration

- embracing distributed leadership to effect change
- taking a systems perspective
- disrupting inequity and striving for social justice in structures, practices, and policies

These core values show up as consistent drivers of the program's design and shape how members of the PLI community engage with one another.

Engaging in Reflective Practice

The PLI views reflection as a critical practice for leaders who aim to effectuate deeper learning. The program provides regular opportunities for participants to engage in self-reflective, metacognitive exercises where they consider how their racial, ethnic, linguistic, gender, and socioeconomic identities shape their worldviews, stances about learning, and individual leadership paths. Pasquale Scuderi, associate superintendent of Berkeley Unified School District, explained: "There's an expectation that our new leaders have a baseline fluency and know how to step back and understand who they are culturally, and what role that plays in terms of the dynamic that it generates with students, with families, and those from subgroups who historically aren't super connected to our schools." This reflective stance helps participants become conscious of their positionality and how it shapes their potential to engage in deep, equity-minded leadership.

Fostering Strong Relationships Through Collaboration

The second prong of the PLI's philosophy recognizes the centrality of collaboration. PLI assistant director Soraya Sablo Sutton articulated the program's commitment this way: "We believe that school leaders must work with their staff, be collaborative in nature in order to be successful. They have to have a strong vision of social justice. And they have to have the ability to bring people along with that vision, which means not landing at a site thinking that you have all the answers."

To foster school environments in which collaborative relationships are authentically valued, the PLI teaches leaders to adopt an inquiry stance. Starting with the notion that leadership is not always about problem-solving but is sometimes about making people feel heard, an inquiry stance emphasizes listening, observing, and questioning.

Embracing Distributed Leadership to Effect Change

Another foundational idea is that of distributed leadership. Distributed leadership operates through the delegation of decision-making to teachers by administrators, and teachers must be provided with time and support to make decisions that are in the best interests of students. This notion, grounded in empirical evidence about the benefits of shared governance, drives all that the PLI encourages its principals to do.[6] As site supervisor and PLI alum Linda Kingston explained, lasting change cannot live solely with the leader, "it has to live with the people."

Taking a Systems Perspective

The PLI staff believe that strong leaders approach change through a system-wide, assets-based lens. Using this lens means looking for opportunities and resources present in schools, systems, and personnel and using those assets as a foundation for change. Sablo Sutton noted that leaders adopting this perspective "can take a step back and see the big picture." They are still able to manage the day-to-day or "attend to the fires" while they take "a long view of how they're going to help to build up their school site and their community." Such leaders see schools as communities steeped in their own cultures, norms, and beliefs, composed of people with various experiences, motivations, and skills. Judith Warren Little, former dean of UC Berkeley's Graduate School of Education, explained that when leaders learn to "read the culture of a school" they are able "to really build the capacity for deeper learning" by creating coherent organizational structures along with social supports for students and staff.

Disrupting Inequity and Striving for Social Justice

Central to the PLI philosophy is a call for social justice–oriented change and the urgency to disrupt inequities in public schools. Head Lecturer Tom Green remarked that the PLI seeks to "radically transform the K–12 public education system so that it is equitable and socially just, so that over time one hundred percent of the children in their public education system have the opportunity to fulfill their potential, meet or exceed grade-level standards, and to graduate from high school with the ability to choose what they want to do next."

In preparing emerging leaders to steer change focused on social justice and equity, the PLI teaches them to think deeply about the different resource needs of students. Sablo Sutton described how this aspect of the PLI's vision of a social justice leader is operationalized:

It's about understanding that different parts of your population are going to require different types of support, and as a leader, recognizing that you actually have the power, you have influence, and you have a responsibility to notice when certain populations need extra support, when they need intervention, when they need more than others. It's your job, actually. You're sitting at the big desk, you are required to stand up and to advocate for your students of color, for your underserved populations, for your English learners, for whatever population it is.

The PLI's Leadership Connection Rubric Enacts Program Values

The PLI's philosophy is actualized in the program's Leadership Connection Rubric, developed by program staff as a guide for coaching, supporting, and assessing participants as they move from emerging to practicing leaders.[7] The rubric contains the following elements:

- Presence and attitude—communicate a compelling presence and a steadfast belief in the power of the possible.
- Identity and relationships—demonstrate personal and professional self-awareness and nourish trusting relationships in a culturally and racially diverse learning organization.
- Equity and advocacy—advocate for equitable academic, civic, and social-emotional outcomes for students who have been historically underserved by schools and society.
- Curriculum and instruction—cultivate high expectations and ensure durable academic, civic, and social-emotional learning outcomes for students and adults.
- Organization and systems—align systems, structures, and resources that sustain a culturally consonant environment in the service of student learning.
- Change and coherence—engage all adults in change efforts that respond collectively and coherently to the assets and challenges in schools and communities.
- Assessment and accountability—exhibit a persistent focus on teachers and student learning outcomes by developing, aligning, and monitoring an equity-driven assessment system.

For each element, the rubric includes descriptions of practice broken into three levels of mastery: emerging, developing, and practicing. Used throughout the program in coursework, assessments, clinical experiences, and coaching, it helps PLI participants reflect on the concrete "knowledge, skills, and dispositions [that are necessary] to deepen [their] effectiveness."[8]

PREPARING DEEPER LEARNING LEADERS

The PLI is designed to imbue equity-focused school leaders with the knowledge and skills to improve the education of historically underserved students. PLI staff expect program graduates to be "instructional leaders who are skilled in working collegially with teachers, parents, students, and the community to improve the quality of teaching and learning." They also must "develop strong visions of equity schools," "understand the change and school reform process, [and be] capable of analyzing challenges and creating solutions."[9] The core elements of the PLI—from recruitment through the culminating performance assessment—are designed to develop these skills and prepare new leaders to lead for deeper learning.

Recruitment and Admissions Process Targets Diversity, Excellence, and an Equity Orientation

The PLI's effort to prepare deeper learning leaders starts with the individuals it selects. Program staff have cultivated an intentional process of recruiting and selecting aspiring leaders who share the program's mission of transforming public education to provide equitable educational opportunities. Through extensive outreach, robust screening, and an in-depth, performance-based selection process, the PLI strives to compile a holistic understanding of applicants and their commitments and abilities to become equity-focused school leaders.

THE PLI RECRUITS DIVERSE CANDIDATES WITH LEADERSHIP SKILLS AND A COMMITMENT TO EQUITY. The PLI employs a purposeful recruitment and admissions process to ensure that applicants meet basic requirements (e.g., five years of classroom teaching experience), demonstrate a record of successful teaching and leadership, and have a passion for advancing social justice. Program faculty and alumni conduct information sessions on campus and at schools across the Bay Area to generate interest in the program and demystify the application process, especially for nontraditional applicants unfamiliar with graduate-level education. PLI alumni figure prominently in the recruitment process: about 50 percent of applicants are referred by alumni who understand the skills, dispositions, and values that the PLI seeks.

The PLI's selection process emphasizes values and skills in three areas: commitment to equity, demonstrated leadership capacity, and cohort diversity. Along with more common requirements such as letters of recommendation, a passing score on the California Basic Educational Skills Test, and a statement of purpose, applicants submit a lesson plan and teaching video. They also must attend a full day of interviews and group discussions, the latter focused on social justice issues in education. Throughout that day, PLI staff assess applicants' ability to collaborate and willingness to dialogue about social justice. The day concludes with one-on-one interviews. Assistant Director Sablo Sutton explained the rationale behind these interactive sessions: "Because our program is so steeped in ideas of equity and social justice, we want [applicants] to have some sense and commitment of that already coming in, and if they can't talk about race in the interview that's a big red flag for us."

The PLI does not expect applicants to be expert leaders when they are admitted, but rather to show potential. As Viet Nguyen, the PLI's leadership support program coordinator, explained: "We're looking for folks who can grow, who are open, who really have potential, as well as those who have already exhibited a bunch of leadership qualities. Because we also believe, just like we would with our own students, that it's about access and opportunity; not everyone has the same access and opportunity, even when you're teachers. So how do we walk that talk?"

Another of the PLI's selection criteria is an established track record of teaching effectiveness. Specifically, the PLI is looking for future leaders who show promise in leading teachers for deeper learning. This is the rationale behind the required submission of a lesson plan and classroom video. Still, the PLI faculty recognize that being a successful teacher and being able to successfully evaluate and lead teachers require different skills. Therefore, the lesson plan and video complement, rather than replace, the evidence of leadership experience.

THE PLI PRIORITIZES COHORT DIVERSITY. Since its inception, the PLI has prioritized having diverse cohorts—by race, gender, background, and other factors—to fulfill the program's mission of preparing a diverse community of equity-focused school leaders. Cohort diversity creates rich learning opportunities for exploring issues of equity central to understanding deeper learning. Head Lecturer Green shared that the PLI recruits "students who would [not] necessarily historically either apply to or get accepted into an administrative credential program, or specifically a credential program at UC Berkeley." Sablo Sutton expressed a similar point when she distinguished between the PLI's admissions process and that of traditional graduate school professional programs on campus: "We believe that our job is to help diversify the administrative force. There aren't enough [administrators] of color, there aren't enough [administrators] with diverse backgrounds and experiences, so our program, being the gatekeeper to teachers making that leap into [administration], means that we're going to accept nontraditional [graduate] students."

PLI staff have been successful in pursuing this goal. About half of PLI alumni identify as people of color, compared with less than a quarter of principals nationally.[10]

PLI Coursework Cultivates Deeper Learning Competencies

The sequence, content, and delivery of coursework contribute to building candidates' leadership competencies around deeper learning. Heavily influenced by the program's core values of collaboration, distributed leadership, and equity, the coursework and other learning experiences provide candidates with opportunities to develop their knowledge and skills through intentional modeling, scaffolding, and application of deeper learning leadership domains.

PLI COURSEWORK EXPLICITLY TEACHES DEEPER LEARNING CONCEPTS. The PLI's curriculum covers a range of topics related to leading for deeper learning, including equity and social justice, leadership identity, teaching and learning, and working collegially with teachers, parents, students, and the community. For example, the PLI's course on using data to drive school improvement aims to broaden participants' understanding of what qualifies as data, provide tools to efficiently collect useful evidence, and develop skills for analyzing and responding to patterns. Program staff stress that leaders who aim for deeper learning seek a holistic view of data to explain student outcomes in nuanced ways. Thus, the PLI helps candidates see the value of both quantitative and qualitative data, including teacher observations, video and audio evidence, and interviews with parents, teachers, and community members.

A key part of this course is a community-mapping project in which candidates investigate an issue related to equitable and healthy learning environments (e.g., transportation, housing, health, social services) in the school's community. One candidate, for example, examined the local availability of affordable, quality fresh food. The project requires students to develop partnerships in their school communities and culminates in a report and presentation about evidence collected, actions taken, outcomes or insights, and implications for school leaders. By requiring candidates to analyze how theories on data gathering and analysis play out in practice and in partnership, the community-mapping project allows candidates to experience deeper learning themselves as they apply theoretical knowledge about data for school improvement to practical issues of equity and leaders' behavior. Another element of deeper learning that is explicitly taught through the community-mapping project is that teaching and learning should be connected to students' lives. As Program Director Cheung explained, the project presses candidates "to develop a leadership lens beyond their school, to think about their school as situated in a space, in a community, with assets and values and history and legacy."

The PLI course on school supervision and instructional leadership provides another example of how course assignments explicitly teach deeper learning leadership. PLI staff believe coaching is a critical skill for school leaders, one that provides significant opportunities to influence and improve the quality of instruction. PLI candidates learn that teacher coaching and evaluation is a collaborative practice aimed at strengthening students' learning experiences. As Assistant Director Sablo Sutton described, "They learn how to not only coach, not only evaluate teachers for the official evaluation process, but how to develop an ongoing coaching relationship with a teacher, how to figure out what your coaching stance will be, and which stance is appropriate for different situations." This view requires PLI leaders to understand teachers' needs, attend to teachers' social-emotional issues, and focus on building positive relationships with teachers—all elements of deeper learning. Candidates complete a variety of tasks throughout the supervision class that help them hone these skills; for example, they participate in role-playing, mock debriefs, and "naming" exercises in which they identify different coaching stances enacted by their peers. Candidates also complete school-based activities, often assisted by PLI coaches, such as classroom walk-throughs and teacher debriefs.

THE PLI PREPARES SOCIAL JUSTICE LEADERS THROUGH A CONSISTENT FOCUS ON EQUITY. PLI instructors cultivate equity-minded leaders by highlighting specific systemic change strategies that leaders can employ to increase equitable student outcomes. One course, for example, unpacks the ways that school discipline policies have disproportionately harmed communities of color. Another course helps candidates better understand how their racial, socioeconomic, and gender identities shape their perspectives. Assignments, readings, and discussions prepare them to be personally and professionally self-aware while nourishing trusting relationships in culturally and racially diverse contexts. Role-playing, videotaped discussions, and formative feedback are used to strengthen participants' competencies in these areas, guided by explicit norms of trust and assumptions of positive intent.

Teach-ins, where staff revise course plans to address significant current events through discussions or seminars, represent another PLI instructional strategy used to both inform and model instruction. As Green described, "When an issue comes up that . . . is clearly critical to our students' ability to address social-emotional issues or issues of identity and values, we stop and talk about it." Teach-ins enable the program to be responsive to broader social and cultural milieus and to bring timely, relevant issues of equity into candidates' preparation experiences. These sessions frequently involve alumni returning to dialogue with current students, offering their perspectives for how to lead among tragic or unexpected developments.

AILEYCAMP ADVANCES DEEPER LEARNING LEADERSHIP THROUGH THE ARTS. The PLI also leverages the arts to teach candidates the importance of deeper learning by having them step into the shoes of the learner and engage in an immersive, experiential dance education program. Through this experience, candidates learn the importance of a full curriculum, the influence of social and emotional factors on learning, and the empowerment and knowledge that students derive from deeper learning. The program does all of this by partnering with AileyCamp, a nationally acclaimed summer program founded by the Alvin Ailey American Dance Theatre. AileyCamp offers underserved youth, primarily children of color, six weeks of intensive dance instruction, even though most campers have no prior dance training. The entire camp, including attire, meals, and transportation, is free. The goal of AileyCamp is to "use the power of dance to enrich and positively impact the lives of children."[11] Director Cheung explained the motivation behind the partnership: "AileyCamp is about transformational learning in an artistic area. PLI is about transformative teaching and learning in public schools. By combining the two organizations, our students have a chance to take the transformations that AileyCamp is making with students in their program and translate those to everyday K–12 schooling."

The PLI-AileyCamp partnership expands leaders' toolboxes for developing the whole child. Rigorous dance instruction, which attends to campers' cognitive, physical, emotional, and interpersonal selves, can provide deeply evocative, expressive, and humanizing modes of learning. Through multiple engagements with the camp, including a dance lesson, open house, and interviews with campers, PLI candidates deepen their understanding of these modes.

Participating in AileyCamp also offers a model for how candidates can promote culturally responsive pedagogy and deeper learning in their schools. For social justice leaders, the camp models the empowerment of vulnerable students who have been historically disempowered by schools' curricula and instruction. As one candidate described, "AileyCamp's long-term vision for its youth, its dedication to transformation through the arts, and practices that honor community pride, family engagement, and distributed leadership, can be adapted in public school settings to nurture the whole child."

AileyCamp Builds Deeper Learning Leadership Knowledge

On one of the early days of the PLI experience, the members of the new twenty-four-person cohort meet at the massive Zellerbach Auditorium at the University of California at Berkeley. After they drop their bags, they wait. As time passes, their jokes and laughter turn to hushed, nervous whispers, then silence. David McCauley, their instructor, is a tall, lithe Black man whose graceful movements confirm his years spent in the Alvin Ailey American Dance Theatre. The purpose of AileyCamp, he stresses, is to expose historically disadvantaged middle school students to the arts, while building discipline and social-emotional learning skills. He speaks with affection for his mentor, Alvin Ailey, who was known for incorporating his dancers' moves into his choreography, because "dance comes from the people and should go back to the people." The camp, McCauley shares, features daily positive self-talk and affirmations about "the way that you treat yourself and others." Students kick off each morning with phrases such as "I am open" and "I will not let 'can't' define my possibilities."

Today, the PLI students sit where the Ailey campers normally do. They've gathered here as part of their work of preparing to become social justice–oriented leaders in schools that serve historically marginalized students. Today's experience will inform one of their assignments: a paper on theories of transformative teaching and learning.

PLI staff believe that at the root of transformation is discomfort, and these students are bathing in discomfort on the stage. The lights illuminate the barefoot participants, some of whom are giggling nervously while McCauley models each dance step. Their first is a simple body roll. He tilts his head forward and rolls toward the ground, one vertebra at a time. He narrates his moves, highlighting key details, such as position and how it should feel as they roll forward. Later, he adds music to their practice.

The group soon picks up the pace as students become more acquainted with McCauley's steps. He watches them while he models, constantly assessing their needs and progress. Then he stops the cohort; over half is struggling with a particularly challenging move. They will "just practice staying on one leg first," he states jovially. The shift elicits a chorus of relieved laughter. As they move into the multistep iteration, McCauley repeats "off, fall on it, press, and close," a shorthand for the sequence, until the group is moving fluently again. They bob up and down and sway side to side as a unit, sharing a rhythm set out for them by McCauley. Before long, he has steadily increased the rigor of the sequence until the novices are doing tendus and pirouettes across the stage.

(continues)

Eventually, they break from the warm-up. McCauley shares that, because today gives just a taste of AileyCamp, they will skip forward to work that takes place later in the summer: rehearsing for the final performance. He scaffolds this sequence with ease and expertise, counting each of his movements aloud, then pausing for a beat before asking the class to follow. Next, he chunks steps together, narrating the emotion behind each progression. He holds his hands above his head, eyes wide, and mimes pushing back against invisible forces, the ones that are "oppressing you and trying to hold you down." He pauses to contextualize their learning. The dance, he explains, comes from Ailey's "Revelations." Representing the repentance of Sunday morning, it features members of the corps in a diverse array of flesh-colored costumes. The spiritual song "I Been Buked" serves as the foundation for their movements, each pose flowing with the richness of the baritone, expressing the cascading grief that comes with each word. At this point, several cohort members stand up straight, focus more intently, and let go of the remnants of their awkward giggles. The collective demeanor shifts. They have been tasked with something meaningful, spiritual, and larger than themselves. McCauley sings the spiritual as they move, some with jaws clenched in focus, others whispering the cues under their breath.

The day concludes with two performances. In each, McCauley taps unlikely students to assume leadership roles, to stretch themselves. His humor puts them at ease and makes his unwavering high expectations more welcome. By noticing the strengths, comfort levels, and dynamics of the collective, he surfaces the leadership capabilities that individuals may have but may not be comfortable exhibiting on stage. When the students perform, they melt into a shared rhythm that guides them smoothly through each step, finishing as a collective with hands held firmly toward the sky. The audience, PLI cohort members, erupts in boisterous applause as the relief, joy, and sense of accomplishment wash over all. They have done it. They are dancers now.

THE PLI MODELS COLLABORATIVE PRACTICE THROUGH ENGINEERED WORK-GROUPS. The PLI puts a heavy emphasis on collaboration among cohort members. Doing so serves two purposes for developing deeper learning leaders. First, candidates' learning experiences mirror the types of instruction their future faculty should embrace, so candidates better understand what collaborative learning looks and feels like. Second, candidates learn about their own leadership tendencies, the value of distributed leadership, and how to create environments in which teachers and other staff members are valued and can contribute productively to the school.

Throughout their courses, candidates work in what the program calls "engineered workgroups." These groups of four to five candidates are intentionally selected so that students from different backgrounds and identities have ongoing opportunities to work with one another to develop collaboration skills. As Head Lecturer Green described: "We provide them with structured activities, with rubrics that provide guidance on graduated levels of collaborative practice, descriptors of what collaboration looks like at the lowest level, of what collaboration looks like at a functional or competent level, and what it looks like at a high-functioning, highly effective level."

Nearly all coursework is completed within workgroups. Literature analysis protocols, in-depth discussions of exemplary action research, and feedback to colleagues on their action research projects are all part of workgroup sessions, as are article jigsaws, case studies, and role-playing. "They sit in their workgroups for every course," Director Cheung noted. "Their workgroups become kind of a home base for them and become a place for them to practice a lot of their leadership skills." The workgroups help candidates learn that collaboration, not isolation, is vital to effective leadership. As one candidate described, "You're always thinking and relying on the other three or four members of your group. . . . You couldn't go through the program alone, and that was very intentional."

As candidates learn how to collaborate effectively, they become better equipped to facilitate collaborative learning among their teachers and to help teachers enact collaborative classrooms. Some of this learning comes through friction, or productive struggle, that program staff seek to generate within the groups in order to provide opportunities to practice newly acquired collaboration skills. "We do not engineer these teams for maximum smoothness. We're actually looking for diversity, or conflict, or potential for growth," said Cheung.

Over the fourteen-month program, staff assemble three rounds of workgroups. As faculty learn about individuals' growth areas and candidates gain greater collaborative competencies, faculty ratchet up the potential conflicts in groups. Individuals who need practice using their leadership voice might be placed in a group of active speakers so they can see that kind of engagement modeled and find their own voice and role in the group. They, in turn, might challenge their peers to be more inclusive, self-aware, and better listeners. The dynamic becomes mutually reinforcing as candidates help each other develop collaborative leadership skills and value diverse perspectives in leadership decision-making. As one program graduate described: "Having people who are really different than you on your team is so crucial and beneficial because if you have a team of people who just agree with everything you think, then you're not actually being innovative. Your blind spots won't get exposed until further down the line when they're at the kids' detriment."

Assessments Reflect and Teach Deeper Learning Practices

The assessments used in the PLI authentically gauge whether candidates have developed the competencies for deeper learning leadership as defined by the Leadership Connection Rubric. They also reflect deeper learning practices by prioritizing performance and application.

ASSESSMENT CENTERS FOSTER DEVELOPMENTALLY GROUNDED, APPLIED LEARNING. Twice during the program, PLI candidates attend an all-day "assessment center" where instructors and coaches observe and evaluate candidates' abilities to translate and apply their learning in simulated scenarios aligned to course and clinical work. One assessment center focuses on a debrief with a struggling, yet recalcitrant, teacher; another is a mock expulsion hearing before a judge and panel. Along with these primary tasks, assessment centers include case study projects during which workgroups develop solutions to open-ended problems of practice, such as taking on the role of a new principal in a school with an overrepresentation of students of color in special education classes. Workgroups develop their response—a data gathering tool or a professional development plan, for example—and present it to a panel of instructors and coaches. The cases are structured to simulate real-life leadership challenges in which there is no single right answer; every decision has consequences and trade-offs. The PLI strives to make candidates aware of these nuanced dynamics and to use frameworks learned in their courses to guide their decisions.

The PLI has designed the assessment centers to be free from the pressures of traditional grading, awarding full credit for participation to elevate competencies and skills over a grade. The structure, content, and climate of the assessment centers combine to create a low-stakes environment that encourages risk-taking and practice of essential skills while being personalized and focused on a candidate's individual developmental needs. One candidate described assessment centers as a "relatively low-stakes environment because we knew we weren't going to fail," but, she emphasized, "we still had to dive in and practice everything that we have been talking about and reading about." Further, candidates receive timely feedback as part of the assessment center experience. Coaches provide personalized feedback in follow-up conversations and in writing to share evidence of candidate learning and identify areas for improvement.

PLI instructors believe that the assessment centers push candidates past "explicit knowledge"—knowledge of content, theory, and concepts learned from coursework. With the authentic, open-ended problems of practice, assessment centers give candidates an opportunity to experience leadership, to think on their feet, and to quickly apply what they know, developing what instructors refer to as tacit knowledge. By requiring candidates to enact their leadership competencies in active, meaningful, collaborative, and personalized learning opportunities, for which they receive immediate feedback, assessment centers authentically measure candidate preparedness and, in multiple ways, reflect deeper learning.

ACTION RESEARCH PROJECTS DEVELOP LEADERSHIP COMPETENCIES IN REAL SETTINGS. The PLI's Leadership Action Research Project, the program's master's thesis project, embraces the PLI principle that leaders must think deeply about the intersection of school context and needs, relevant research and policy, and the design of outcomes-oriented steps. Candidates work on this project for nearly the entirety of the program, identifying an issue of equity in their school and leading multiple cycles of inquiry to analyze, strategize, implement, and adapt systemic approaches to school improvement. Through the project, candidates develop their capacity to frame problems, understand how to arrive at decisions, lead collective change, and reflect on theories of action.

The rich descriptive and analytic thinking called for by the project is grounded in candidates' actual school settings and is relevant to them. As Director Cheung described, this project demonstrates how different aspects of deeper learning—personalization and analytic thinking—are connected to one another: "Following lines of inquiry that are directly connected to one's own life and practice are an important part of a candidate's deeper learning. Similar to how students may be driven to engage in a project they feel is connected to their community or lived experience, candidates are willing to dive deeply into their projects because they can see its relevance and how it will make a difference for adult practice and student outcomes at their school."

It is important to note, however, that the PLI is moving away from this assessment strategy to an oral exam for the master's degree. This new exam requires candidates to connect theory to specific problems of practice and to engage the literature in their thinking, speaking, and leadership behaviors. A version of the Leadership Action Research Project is preserved in the form of a Change Management Project. Embedded across courses, this new project is focused on conducting multiple cycles of inquiry and applying systemic improvement strategies. The Change Management Project is coupled with a new state-mandated performance assessment for all administrative preparation programs, the California Administrative Performance Assessment (CalAPA). Because the CalAPA is practice-focused and includes significant analytic and writing requirements, program leaders believe that the combination of these assessments will provide for balanced evaluations of candidates on major aspects of the principalship.

Candidates Lead for Deeper Learning in Structured, Coached Practicums

Alongside conventional coursework, the PLI includes a structured, school-embedded practicum supported by trained coaches. The practicum includes a range of leadership experiences such as shadowing administrators, facilitating faculty meetings, coaching teachers, and communicating with parents. These activities provide real opportunities to practice deeper learning leadership as candidates facilitate staff activities, advocate for equitable student opportunities, create culturally competent learning environments, and cultivate high expectations for all teachers and students.

CLINICALLY ENACTED ASSIGNMENTS BRIDGE THEORY AND PRACTICE. In the PLI, it is almost impossible to separate emerging leaders' clinical experiences from their university-based coursework. Readings give candidates a theoretical grounding in educational research and leadership practices, and assignments are designed to push candidates to use this grounding to analyze their school or apply theory to their daily work. As Head Lecturer Green described, "Every body of knowledge that is presented in class is then tied to an assignment," and each assignment requires candidates to "go back to their current sites and look at what it looks like in practice, using rubrics or frameworks we've provided."

At the PLI, producing leaders who are grounded in educational research and understand why certain actions or strategies can lead to better, more equitable outcomes for students is of utmost importance. Faculty instructor Lanette Jimerson described several ways that this plays out: "It's intentional in how you make decisions and how you dialogue, your choice of words, your choice of data, your choice of framing. . . . It's that they can intentionally draw upon the knowledge and wisdom of people who study leadership and use that as an invisible set of tools to help make visible equity issues; to help make visible our synergies and ways we can connect and collaborate; to help make visible our parents and the value we see in them; to help make visible the needs of our students. It's that kind of frame." One candidate noted that this kind of deep learning by application helped her "to think critically about issues . . . before jumping to action."

COACHES SUPPORT THE DEVELOPMENT OF DEEPER LEARNING COMPETENCIES. To support fieldwork, the PLI employs coaches who work with candidates in their school sites. Coaching sessions occur about three times per month, during which coaches see their assigned candidates in the context of their work environment. Coaches offer critical feedback, ask probing questions, and brainstorm next steps as candidates become fluent in the daily exercises of school leadership. Green described coaching as supporting leaders "in experimenting with the implementation of their training," as coaches' probing and guidance help develop candidates into thoughtful learners and leaders.

Like the fieldwork, the content of the coaching sessions is tightly connected to the coursework. Coaches ask the candidates to think about how new theories, strategies, or concepts from their readings might be relevant to their school sites, creating opportunities for learning as they facilitate these connections. PLI coach Carole Robie explained that coaches have been trained to spot intersections between coursework and candidates' experiences in schools and to make use of them: "It's not that their daily work is separate from whatever goals they're working on; it becomes, how do those goals apply to their daily work? We take the classwork that they're doing, the rubric that they're working with, the rubric that they're writing goals towards, and help them apply that to their core beliefs or ways of being at their schools."

Coaches use progress-monitoring forms to individualize the support they provide based on the candidate's development needs. One primary coaching strategy they employ is consultations, scheduled conversations during which the candidate and the coach review goals and progress to date, engage in thought partnership, and brainstorm solutions to problems. During these conversations, coaches ask probing questions and push candidates to share their thinking. For example, they might ask candidates about the ramifications of a leadership move, the identification of potential supporters for advancing leadership priorities, or the intentions behind a specific action. Another coaching strategy is observations, which can take place in a variety of settings, including professional development sessions, meetings with teachers or parents, student activities, or while the candidate is conducting teacher observations. Through these sessions, emerging leaders receive direct feedback to hone their skills, often in a debriefing immediately following the observation.

Coaches coordinate their support of candidates with PLI Director Rebecca Cheung and Viet Nguyen, coordinator of the Leadership Support Program (i.e., the post-PLI induction program), during meetings that take place two times for each cohort. In these meetings, coaches provide updates about candidates' performance, and the trio decides whether the candidates need any interventions or supports.

COACHES ARE TRAINED USING DEEPER LEARNING MODELS. Most coaches are retired school leaders, usually former principals and district office administrators. Although they bring years of experience, they are expected to ask questions and push candidates' thinking, not "download" everything they learned as administrators. These expectations drive a rigorous hiring and development process for coaches.

Coach applications include written responses to articles, a panel interview, and a role play in which they respond to a coaching scenario. This process allows PLI staff to develop a sense of how new coaches will respond to certain dilemmas, think on their feet, and handle being observed and taking feedback. Once selected, new coaches attend a three-day intensive institute in which they are introduced to the PLI philosophy and core values and trained in how to conduct coaching sessions and use questioning techniques that support leaders' growth.

All coaches meet monthly for a four-hour seminar where they discuss topics that candidates are learning about and wrestling with in their school sites. Monthly seminars also include mock coaching sessions during which coaches work through scenarios, identify strengths and shortcomings, pose questions to one another, and give feedback. Coach Barbara Armstrong noted that these sessions enable coaches to continue growing as educators. She underscored that "because [coaches] are asked to increase our own skills, we're being pushed as well as the students are being pushed; we're really having to become better as we go along." Finally, the PLI builds coaching capacity through peer coaching sessions where coaches observe one another in the field as they work in real time. Peer coaching allows coaches to share insights and push each other's thinking in the same way that they are expected to coach school leaders.

THE PLI'S SITE SUPERVISORS EXTEND DEEPER LEARNING OPPORTUNITIES. Site supervisors (i.e., the principals of the schools where the candidates work)—frequently PLI alumni who have been principals for a number of years—also act as important on-the-ground learning facilitators for program participants. Michael Essien, principal and PLI alumnus, explained how he pushes PLI candidates working at his school: "I actually put my mentees in situations where they [informally] evaluate people. I particularly send them into challenging situations and then we debrief because I have to hear how they're thinking and reflecting about what they've seen. How they think and reflect is going to be very important as to whether they become an asset to teachers and students."

Site supervisors help their mentees understand what it is like to run a school. They conduct myriad leadership activities alongside candidates, including conducting classroom visits, engaging in discipline conversations with parents and students, or meeting with a teacher's union representative. Site supervisors employ some of the same questioning techniques that coaches use to "challenge the [candidate's] mind-set so they can actually grow," as site supervisor Essien explained. Site supervisors push candidates to reframe conceptions of school away from an individual teacher perspective, converse with candidates about enacting a social justice vision, and help candidates navigate their positionality.

ACCOMPLISHMENTS AND DEEPER LEARNING LEADERSHIP IN PRACTICE

The PLI is an effective model for developing deeper learning leaders. One measure of effectiveness is local impact, and the PLI is cultivating a critical mass of like-minded Bay Area school leaders who share norms, values, and knowledge about how to enact equity-minded leadership strategies. By 2018, the program had graduated just under 600 school leaders. As of 2015, 98 percent of graduates continued to work in education; 90 percent worked in California, almost all in the San Francisco Bay Area.[12] According to the 2017 impact report, "During the 2015–2016 school year, 100 percent of middle schools in Berkeley Unified had PLI presence, 54 percent of schools in Oakland Unified had PLI graduates on their administrative teams, 24 percent of San Francisco Unified principals were PLI graduates, and 76 percent of PLI presence in [West Contra Costa Unified] was in school administration."[13]

PLI graduates have been recognized for their outstanding achievements by such awards as California Distinguished School, California Department of Education Academic Achievement, and Blue Ribbon School.[14] Additionally, the program has helped increase the racial diversity of the principal pool in its partner districts. In 2017, 50 percent of Berkeley's principals were principals of color, of which 70 percent were PLI alumni. In West Contra Costa, 59 percent of principals identified as people of color, of which 40 percent were PLI alumni.

Program participants reported that they are prepared for various leadership responsibilities associated with deeper learning. In a survey of PLI candidates, 95 percent reported that they feel very well prepared or well prepared to be a principal. Perhaps of most interest given the program's focus on social justice and equity, all (100 percent) of the surveyed candidates said they felt very well prepared or well prepared to equitably serve all students. Likewise, principals reported they were well prepared for a variety of leadership functions that support deeper learning, such as creating collaborative work environments and redesigning the school environment to support deeper learning.

Infusing Equitable Practices in Schools

PLI graduates have enacted equity-oriented leadership practices, such as prioritizing historically underserved students in scheduling, managing the equitable distribution of financial resources, and facilitating explicit conversations about opportunity gaps. For example, one alumna, Hollie Mack, noted how she applies an equity lens to her work as a vice principal: "It means a willingness to talk about the kids that don't necessarily get the focus; those for whom the master schedule is not necessarily built around. . . . It's the kids whose parents don't come to the school. Whose parents don't speak English as a first language. Whose kids have had an IEP and that sort of thing. It's putting those kids first and starting from there and working out."

Mack attributed her ability to use this lens to her preparation: "PLI gives you the tools, the framework, and legitimacy to be on the site and actually speak with authority about the importance of those kids, their needs, and their families." PLI alumnus and principal Vernon Walton echoed this sentiment when he explained how he applies theoretical concepts to actionable decisions that translate to more equitable outcomes for students: "Where you put your resources is where your belief systems actually are. Looking at my master schedule or how I allocate funds toward developing programs to support students who have been historically marginalized—that's taking money from somewhere else, and so that really is a belief system. It is a tangible thing that a leader can do to really frame equity . . . just put your money where your mouth is."

Promoting Schoolwide Improvement Through Collegiality and Self-Reflection

The PLI effectively imparts the value of distributed leadership to effect systemic, schoolwide change. This emphasis is reflected in participants' perceptions of their preparation. All surveyed participants reported that they felt well prepared or very well prepared to lead a schoolwide change process to improve student achievement. Additionally, 95 percent indicated that they felt well prepared or very well prepared to redesign their school's organization and structures to support deeper learning for teachers and students.

Site supervisor, PLI alumna, and principal Summer Sigler shared how she worked to create a schoolwide culture that, rather than being top-down or compliance oriented, stimulates critical thinking across faculty members. To deepen her own leadership practice and, ultimately, to do what is best for students, she encourages her entire staff to challenge her thinking, modeling the role of "lead learner." Initially Sigler's assistant principal was reluctant to provide critical feedback, but Sigler told her, "No, keep pushing!" Sigler's remark underscores that continuous, schoolwide change requires continuous, individual-level change.

Another alumna, Shannon Williams-Zou, explained how her PLI preparation helped her become a strategic thinker. Rather than just jumping in, she thought about what leadership actions would support her long-term equity vision. She asked herself, "How can I be strategic in helping to move the ship?" Thus, for example, even though she wanted to implement affinity groups, she recognized that coming in new and mandating such groups would not be effective. Instead, she built the idea into her strategic planning and then successfully launched affinity groups with great faculty support for them and lasting power.

Enacting Collaborative Faculty Environments

PLI alumni create collaborative school environments, enacting what they experienced in the PLI. For example, Principal Sigler takes an inquiry stance while listening to staff concerns: "It was always modeled to be egoless and to take feedback and to be nonreactionary to feedback. And I think that has saved me a million times to say, 'Wait. I'm not going to react to this right now. I'm going to sleep on it and I'm going to really try to understand what that person said or needs and I'm going to come back to it.'"

PLI alumni also facilitate productive conversations. Some alumni attribute these skills to PLI instructors' modeling. For example, vice principal Hollie Mack recognized that her own techniques for guiding teachers engaging in group work derive from the facilitative guidance she received at PLI: "When we would be meeting in our different groups, [instructors] would be walking around and listening and they would give us feedback and say, 'You might want to think about,' or, 'Have you guys considered X, Y and Z?' . . . Absolutely I've done that with staff. . . . I just feel like that facilitation and awareness of people and of the things that are getting in the way of what they're trying to achieve, that's a leadership move that I think is very important."

Critically, PLI graduates understand how to develop collaboration in a school building where it does not yet exist. This ability is a hallmark of deeper learning leaders. Alumna Helida Silva shared her experience starting at modest beginnings: "One thing I had done last year with my sixth-grade team was we actually had them sit in a circle to just talk with each other. I didn't jump straight into an affinity group, but I figured we just need to sit and have a conversation as a first step to if we ever want to reach a [more collaborative] place, because that's a very vulnerable place."

Supporting Deeper Learning Instruction

In their schools, PLI alumni and candidates support deeper learning instruction. One way they do this is by coaching teachers to adopt more student-centered pedagogical practices. One PLI candidate coached her teachers to develop reflective practices in order to work toward student-centered instruction. Seeking to move teachers past the rigidity of a scripted curriculum, she emphasized teaching and learning cycles. She asked teachers to analyze formative student learning data, reflect on student needs and their own instructional practice, and develop shifts that would drive deeper learning. She also worked with teachers individually. In one coaching session, for example, she encouraged the teacher to reflect on whether her assignments were designed to rigorously and equitably assess students' learning, then brainstormed with her about holding students to high learning expectations while giving them supports to meet them.

Another principal and PLI alumna, Lena Van Haren, established multiple systems to drive deeper learning. Grade level and department teams had common planning time during which teachers discussed struggling students and strategized how to support them. Teachers regularly engaged in a multistep process of analyzing student data, examining lesson plans, and developing departmental visions aligned with deeper learning. They then designed professional development around identified priorities. Department leads were given an additional preparation period dedicated to instructional coaching so they could be in other teachers' classrooms, modeling lessons and offering feedback daily. Principal Van Haren's decisions to create systems for collaboration that empowered her teachers to deliver engaging lessons defined her approach to supporting deeper learning instruction.

Deeper Learning in Action

Everett Middle School sits at the corner of the historic Mission district and the Castro in San Francisco. The school enrolls about 700 students, about 61 percent of whom are Hispanic, 17 percent White, and 9 percent African American. Additionally, about four out of every ten students come from families living in poverty, and many students (61%) are emerging bilingual speakers. Not too many years ago the school bore the unpleasant distinction of being the lowest-performing middle school in the San Francisco Unified School District. Today, the school is a thriving learning community with a waitlist of students. This transformation is in no small part due to the passionate efforts of principal and PLI alumna Lena Van Haren and her dedicated colleagues.

Deeper learning is occurring throughout the school. In an eighth-grade math classroom, framed words on the wall define student expectations:

"In 8th grade math at Everett we . . .

- Work together, because none of us alone is as smart as all of us together
- Question each other to deepen everyone's understanding
- Justify our thinking in multiple ways
- Are brave enough to make mistakes"

Students in table groups busily work on calculating the volume of various shapes. The teacher is working with one group that is struggling. "This is where we got stuck. We couldn't get the radius," one student tells the teacher. She looks over their work and asks a probing question about how to calculate circumference. A "turn and talk" refresher gets the students in the group back on the right track; after, they turn back to each other to revisit the problem. In another group, the teacher inquires, "If you know the diameter, can you get the radius?" The gentle questioning is enough to turn on the lightbulbs for students in the group. They huddle and begin scribbling on their papers to solve the problem together.

This circulating and questioning continues for several minutes. Principal Van Haren joins as well. At a separate table she works with a group of students asking similar probing questions, helping students to reach answers themselves. Before moving to the next group, Van Haren smiles and shares with the students, "Notice how brilliant you all are!" The educators' interactions with students seem to embody a slogan framed on the wall: "Mistakes make our brain grow."

Van Haren continues moving through the school, visiting one classroom after another. Along the way she unobtrusively but noticeably picks up trash. The subtle message, she later related to us, is that everyone should take pride in the way their school looks, "and that starts with me." At one point a beaming seventh grader stops in front of Van Haren, strikes a runway pose, and shows off her pink jacket. "¿Que piensa?" she asks in Spanish. With a pleased grin, Van Haren answers with nicely accented Spanish.

FACTORS INFLUENCING SYSTEMIC DEEPER LEARNING LEADERSHIP DEVELOPMENT

The PLI has a track record of preparing a diverse community of school leaders who are committed to improving education for vulnerable and historically underserved students, and they are well equipped for the job. Many factors contribute to the success of the program. Some, however, present challenges, an indicator of the complexity of this work.

Partnerships Support Program Goals

The PLI has developed many partnerships, each of which contributes to fulfilling the program's goals of preparing principals who reflect the diversity of the communities they serve and who have the knowledge and skills to lead their schools with a social justice lens. Strong relationships with partner districts make it possible for program staff to run information sessions across the districts while district leaders act as informal recruiters, both of which strengthen and diversify the pool of applicants. The PLI's partnership with philanthropy has also contributed to the program's diverse applicant pools, with scholarships helping to increase program participation. The PLI's partnership with AileyCamp is likewise critical for the program to meet its goals, providing a unique deeper learning opportunity for program candidates to develop an understanding of the empowering nature of experiential learning activities along with a keen appreciation for providing a full curriculum, including the arts. These partnerships create unique opportunities for the program and for candidates that would not be available otherwise.

Reflective Practices Lead to Program Improvements

The PLI teaches candidates to be reflective and to make midcourse corrections if warranted, and program staff also embrace this tenet. The strength of the program can be attributed, in part, to its commitment to continuous self-assessment and improvement. During assessment centers, for example, candidates are not the only ones getting feedback on their performance; instructors and coaches are also gathering valuable information about their own contributions. In this way, deeper learning is occurring at all levels of the program—among candidates, coaches, and faculty. Importantly, lessons learned from assessment centers have tangible impacts on instruction, as candidates' strengths and needs drive adaptations in coursework. Coaches also collect information about the candidates' thinking and their application of their learning. When the coaches meet with

PLI instructors, they share their observations so that the faculty can adjust course instruction as needed.

A Critical Mass of Social Justice Leaders Fosters Systemwide Change

The PLI's impact on local systems has created a powerful network of leaders who serve as principal mentors, program recruiters, and advocates. The presence of this critical mass of deeper learning leaders creates multiple opportunities for mutual support. For instance, Principal Linda Kingston's leadership team consists of two vice principals who graduated from the program, and she also employs two teacher leaders who are PLI alumni. Because of their common training, she said, "we speak a common language. I don't have to explain myself. I don't have to have any ambiguity. It's like we know exactly how to move forward." PLI alumnus Vernon Walton described the dynamic this way: "Being a graduate of this program says something. It says something about mind-sets. . . . When I meet other administrators who look like me who are coming from the PLI, we automatically click." By creating this coalition of equity-oriented leaders who know and promote deeper learning, the PLI advances its mission to improve education for vulnerable and historically underserved students.

The Challenges of a Professional Program in a Research University

The PLI was specifically established at UC Berkeley by Governor Davis to "enhance the professional quality" of leaders. Yet housing a professional program in an elite research institution is not without challenges. The most frequently mentioned challenge from faculty and coaches was the need for additional resources and increased awareness of how resource constraints affect equity. As one program instructor articulated, "It feels like we are constantly fighting for funding and bringing revenue in so that way we can give it back to our students, because we know our students need scholarships. We have to go out and pursue these funding streams on our own." Staff have responded creatively to this challenge, proactively seeking planning grants and foundation donations to support candidates.

Another challenge arose early for the program. When it was first established, the Berkeley Graduate School of Education did not have any tenure-line faculty with extensive professional or research expertise in K–12 educational leadership. This mismatch required the PLI to hire several part-time lecturers who possessed the practical and intellectual knowledge required. In recent years, one to three tenure-track faculty members have taught in the program, and the PLI has hired full- and half-time clinical professors rather than leaning on intermittent adjuncts. The school also formed a Leadership Advisory Committee composed of tenure-line and clinical faculty members and has partnered with several tenure-line faculty members on grant- and foundation-funded research projects.

Yet another difficulty has been bridging the traditional academic culture with the needs of working students. The PLI runs on a nontraditional program schedule consisting of summer sessions as well as weeknight and Saturday classes during the academic school year. Furthermore, due to the cohort model, PLI classes tend to be larger than many other courses, especially PhD courses. These differences can make for sharp contrasts for tenure-line faculty accustomed to more traditional ways of doing things.

Adapting to State Mandates

Faculty and coaches have also grappled with a state mandate to shift to a statewide principal performance assessment. The PLI was involved with the shift early on, being one of several principal preparation programs that piloted the CalAPA in 2018. Even before the pilot process, Program Director Cheung served on the CalAPA planning committee, providing an opportunity for the PLI to share its work and inform the development of the statewide assessment.

And yet, while many pieces of the CalAPA align well with PLI's program, others were more challenging. For example, the CalAPA created additional work for candidates, such as when they had to duplicate write-ups to meet differing requirements from the state and the program. As a result, program staff had to create new assignments aligned with the CalAPA's requirements. Still, staff and candidates are hopeful that the most challenging implementation year is behind them. What is more, faculty were hopeful that this extra layer of external evaluation will ultimately be positive, motivating the PLI to continue innovating.

KEY TAKEAWAYS

UC Berkeley's PLI offers a fourteen-month preparation program for aspiring school leaders. Graduates earn a Preliminary Administrative Services Credential and a master's degree in education. The program focuses on improving schools, especially those serving vulnerable and historically underserved youth, through equitable learning opportunities, particularly for English language learners and low-income, Black, and Latino students.

With a focus on social justice and equity and its own deeper learning instructional approach, the PLI equips diverse school leaders with the knowledge and skills to support deeper learning among their teachers and ultimately their students. Since its founding in 2000, the PLI has been a cornerstone of California principal preparation, with nearly 600 alumni working in education, most in the San Francisco Bay Area. The key takeaways from the program are outlined below.

Preparing diverse social justice leaders begins with equitable recruitment and admissions practices. The PLI's dedication to diversifying the administrator workforce is reflected in its efforts to recruit and select a racially, ethnically, socioeconomically, and professionally diverse cohort. By eschewing traditional graduate school admission measures such as GRE scores or GPAs, and prioritizing applicants with clear commitments to equity and demonstrated leadership capacity, the PLI broadens access to school leadership while laying the foundation to address issues of social justice in the preparation of candidates.

The PLI has a clear vision of leadership for deeper learning–aligned teaching, learning, and organizational development. An inquiry stance, collaborative mind-set, and equity lens are central to the PLI's vision for leadership. Expert coaching, deliberate modeling, and project-based learning help candidates develop competencies in each area of this vision.

The PLI's development of effective, social justice–oriented school leaders requires collaboration among instructors, coaches, and other program staff. Routines for coach and instructor check-ins to discuss candidate development, frequent faculty discussions to rapidly adjust curriculum, and monthly coaching seminars for calibration and development undergird the PLI's programming. These processes and structures model the program's vision of collaborative leadership, which candidates can witness, experience, and adapt to their own contexts.

The PLI's organizational partners model how transformational, social justice–oriented leadership can be enacted inside schools. Because of its arts-based partnership with the AileyCamp, candidates have the opportunity to experience firsthand how they can implement a vision of social justice, one that helps adults and youth actively resist negative stereotypes and promote students' social-emotional development.

Candidate assessment is centered on demonstrations of practice and competency development. PLI staff use performance-based assessment and formative assessment to identify gaps in candidate understanding and skills and support effective interventions. Actionable assessment has evolved as a way of being at the PLI, with instructors, coaches, and eventually candidates recognizing and modeling each moment as a teachable one.

Individualized coaching bridges university-based learning and school site experiences. The PLI invests a host of resources to support, train, and develop its coaches. This focus prepares coaches to understand and connect classroom-based learning with candidates' leadership experiences in their schools. Regular communication between coaches and program faculty effectively targets supports to candidates' areas of need.

CHAPTER 4

COMPREHENSIVE, DISTRICTWIDE LEADERSHIP DEVELOPMENT

Long Beach Unified School District Leadership Development Pipeline

The Long Beach Unified School District (LBUSD) Leadership Development Pipeline prepares administrators at all levels to lead for deeper learning. The pipeline is an extension of the professional development system through which the district identifies excellent teachers as potential administrators. It builds on that system's practices in instructional design and continuous improvement, cultivating leaders who are skilled at supporting deep and meaningful classroom instruction. The pipeline develops and expands leaders' administrative knowledge and skills with mentoring, observation and discussion, reflection and feedback, and shared inquiry.

PROGRAM HIGHLIGHTS AND HISTORY

The LBUSD Leadership Pipeline is a preservice and in-service program that is the primary route to school and district leadership positions in LBUSD. The pipeline is comprehensive, preparing and supporting leaders at all levels, from assistant principal to assistant superintendent (see table 4.1). It consists of the following programs:

- Future Administrators Program: for district staff interested in becoming school administrators; completion is required to become an assistant principal
- Continuing Future Administrators Program: for former Future Administrators Program completers who have not been selected for a leadership position
- New Administrators Support Program: for first-year assistant principals
- Clear Administrative Credential Program: offered in partnership with the Association of California School Administrators; allows new

TABLE 4.1   **Overview of the LBUSD Leadership Pipeline**

Program type	Preservice and in-service
Mission	Supporting leaders to have a positive impact on every student, every day
Targeted places	LBUSD
Program duration	1 or 2 years, depending on program
Degree or designation conferred	Clear Administrative Credential Program offers the opportunity to earn a California permanent administrative credential
Program highlights	Context-specific mission and vision for teaching and learning; recruitment of experienced educators; workshops; field assignments; observations, feedback, and reflection aligned to goals; shadowing and mentorship
Key staff	Leadership development director; program coordinator; clerical support; LBUSD administrators
Costs and funding supports	All Leadership Pipeline programs are free for participants except for the Clear Administrative Credential Program, which costs $7,000 to cover coach stipends and the Association of California School Administrators program fees.

administrators holding their preliminary administrative credential to earn their clear credential

- Aspiring Principals Program: prepares second- or third-year assistant principals for principal positions; completion is required to become a principal
- New Principal Support Program: provides first- and second-year principals with coaching and support meetings
- Principals Coaching Program: offered in partnership with the Association of California School Administrators; certifies veteran principals to coach new administrators working to clear their initial administrative credentials
- Aspiring Director Program: prepares administrators for director-level district office positions
- New Director On-boarding Program: orients new directors to district offices and staff

While this case study describes the pipeline holistically and touches on all pipeline programs, it focuses on two: the Future Administrators Program, designed for teachers interested in becoming assistant principals, and the Aspiring Principals Program, for assistant principals looking to move into principal positions. In 2017–2018, these programs enrolled seventeen future administrators and ten aspiring principals.

LBUSD educates approximately 65,500 students from preschool to high school in its eighty-five public schools. Nearly 90 percent of LBUSD students are students of color, with 59 percent Latino/a, 12 percent African American, and 11 percent Asian American, Filipino, and Pacific Islander. Sixty-five percent of students come from families living in poverty, and 15 percent are English language learners.[1]

In the early 2000s, LBUSD launched its leadership development initiative with the aim to cultivate and support leaders who could thrive in the unique context of Long Beach, winner of the 2003 Broad Prize for Urban Education. Feedback provided to the district through the Broad Prize review process was a key driver in the district's decision to start a leadership development program. In 2005, LBUSD launched the first iteration of the leadership pipeline with support from a local foundation and a significant grant from the Broad Foundation. Since then, district leaders have continued to prioritize ongoing support for the pipeline, cultivating relationships with philanthropic foundations and allocating funds from the district's Local Control and Accountability Plan. The district also has continued to update the pipeline program, such as with the addition of the Continuing Future Administrators Program and the New Director On-boarding Program, both of which were added during the 2017–2018 school year.

PROGRAM PHILOSOPHY

The design, organization, and facilitation of pipeline programs underscore the district's core values and mirror the ways in which students experience deeper learning in their classrooms. As Dr. Kelly An, director of leadership development, described: "How [principals] model, how they teach, and how they work with their staff will demonstrate for teachers how to do the same with their students—that is the expectation." One implication of this belief is that teaching and learning, not budgeting and management, are considered leaders' primary responsibilities. Another is that pipeline programs need not replicate the district's extensive work in developing and supporting educator practice but can instead build on a common vision, common language, and districtwide structures to help rising leaders learn to lead.

Teacher Development as a Foundation for Leadership Development

Leader development in LBUSD is built on the district's instructional framework, called the Understandings Continuum, or just the Understandings. Created by LBUSD, the Understandings provide teachers and leaders with a shared picture of what high-quality, deeper learning teaching, learning, and collaboration look like. The Understandings are as follows:

- A thorough understanding of standards provides a foundation for high-quality differentiated instruction that results in all students meeting college and career readiness expectations through the Linked Learning approach.[2]
- Providing all learners with cognitively demanding tasks and complex text with the goal of making meaning is essential in order for students to build conceptual understanding of content and transfer their learning to new contexts.
- Orchestrating opportunities for technical and academic discourse, including collaborative conversations, allows students to develop a deeper understanding of content and support a point of view in varied contexts.
- The strategic planning and consistent use of formative assessment strategies allow teachers and students to collect evidence about where students are and to determine immediate next steps.
- Effective instructional leadership teams engage in collaboration, data analysis, problem solving and reflection in order to create a collective culture of efficacy leading to a focus on improving common instructional practice.
- Cultivating a classroom atmosphere, where teachers deliberately balance caring relationships with high expectations and supports for student success, provides a foundation for a safe learning environment that values diversity, trust, and respectful communication.

In articulating that student learning should be collaborative, cognitively demanding, and relevant and that instruction should build conceptual understanding, orchestrate opportunities for discourse, and create a culture of efficacy, LBUSD has offered its leaders a useful compass to follow when organizing and facilitating teacher development and a barometer by which to measure the effectiveness of instruction. That this shared vision is used throughout the system is "one of the things that makes Long Beach strong," according to a principal supervisor. She explained that even though principals have autonomy, their actions are "always aligned towards a common goal." The Understandings are featured in the leadership pipeline programs and are communicated from the beginning and through ascending levels of leadership.

The process of creating a districtwide focus on the Understandings starts with teachers in professional development and continues with leaders in pipeline programs. It comes full circle when new leaders impart it to teachers in their schools. This process is facilitated by the district's expectation that school leaders focus on teaching and learning. One future administrator, a high school teacher, shared that "a majority of the [Future Administrator Program] meetings that we had were focused on how to improve teaching and learning at our school sites."

Leadership Evaluation Domains and Dimensions Guide Leaders' Growth

While the Understandings create a common touchpoint for instruction, LBUSD also developed a set of leadership-specific expectations that guide pipeline programs and administrator evaluation. The Leadership Evaluation Domains and Dimensions provide a clearly conceptualized and comprehensive picture of what LBUSD leaders should know and be able to do. They cover seven topics: teaching and learning; environment and equity; communication and engagement; supervision, evaluation, and employee development; professionalism, disposition, and ethics; strategy and planning; and organization and development.[3]

Although the Domains and Dimensions do not explicitly use the term *deeper learning*, they show significant alignment with deeper learning tenets. For example, the environment and equity domain includes the following deeper learning–aligned dimensions:

- Leaders facilitate safe, inclusive, and respectful environments that meet the cultural, intellectual, emotional, and physical needs of each student.
- Leaders develop a culture of high expectations, appreciation, and celebration.
- Leaders develop a culture of equity toward students' academic achievement and college and career readiness.[4]

The Domains and Dimensions inform both the pipeline programs and the district's administrator evaluation system. By linking administrator development to the evaluation system, LBUSD ensures a connection between preparation and practice. Kelly An, LBUSD director of leadership development, noted, "This foundation ties it all together." This systematic approach to leadership development and evaluation also facilitates a culture of continuous administrator learning. The Domains and Dimensions provide clarity on what is expected of leaders and create opportunities for authentic evaluation linked to participants' personal knowledge and skills as well as the needs of schools and the district. An elementary school principal and Aspiring Principals Program mentor explained how the evaluation framework functions: "There's a real plumb line . . . from top to bottom . . . —[from district] office, to site administrator, to teachers—in consistency of what we're evaluating each other on. And the process is not typically top-down evaluation but seen as . . . collaborative in learning to improve practice together."

Pipeline program leaders encourage participants to use the Domains and Dimensions as a guide for setting their developmental goals. One middle school principal and pipeline alum recalled that "having to dig through those leadership domains while in the program helped me see . . . areas where I knew I had to grow and where I didn't have any experience or had no clue." He communicated his growth areas to his mentor: "This domain right here, I'm struggling. Can you provide me some experience here? Can you teach me something here?" With this information, the mentor could then tailor support.

PREPARING DEEPER LEARNING LEADERS

LBUSD's Leadership Development Pipeline equips aspiring and current administrators with the skills and mind-set that the district expects of its leaders. As Deputy Superintendent Dr. Jill Baker put it, "We like to think there's a Long Beach way of doing things." Aspiring administrators do not just learn about administration in general; they learn how to be an administrator in LBUSD. "There's a job-embedded aspect of all the programs," according to Dr. Baker, which means, "they're actually getting time in the field [to see] what it looks like and feels like in Long Beach to be a leader."

Leadership Development Is Founded in Teacher Professional Development
LBUSD's commitment to building leadership from within makes for leaders who know the district and are invested in keeping their experience and knowledge in district schools. By providing strong professional development and career advancement opportunities, the district builds the bench of prospective pipeline participants. The district draws on this bench to find candidates for administration, tapping talented educators and bringing them along while maintaining high standards aligned to district priorities.

BUILDING TEACHER CAPACITY CREATES A POOL OF FUTURE ADMINISTRATORS READY FOR DEEPER LEARNING. Teachers who have demonstrated expertise in teaching and leading for deeper learning make for promising leaders, and LBUSD works to bring them into the pipeline. As an Aspiring Principals Program mentor explained: "Long Beach is really proactive about keeping candidates within our district because we have our vision, we have our mission, we believe in it. It's the Long Beach Way."

Building the bench of leaders through years of investment in school staff means pipeline programs do not have to start from scratch in developing the skills and knowledge necessary for deeper learning leadership. Instead, they leverage the considerable reservoir of experience in the district. Pipeline participants credit their deeper learning skills to their extensive time in the classroom and the professional development they received as teachers. Many participants have upward of ten years of experience in the district before joining the pipeline. Pipeline staff are looking for prospective leaders whose teaching reflects the kind of instruction they expect leaders to support across the system, because, as Dr. Baker put it, "If you haven't done it and done it well, it's hard to lead it."

PROGRAM RECRUITMENT SUPPORTS DISTRICT AND PROGRAM VALUES AROUND DEEPER LEARNING. Because LBUSD focuses on recruiting, preparing, supporting, and retaining the *right* leaders, interest in entering the Leadership Development Pipeline does not guarantee acceptance. Teachers who are interested in applying must submit a letter of intent, complete an application, and submit their most recent evaluation. A select number of candidates are invited to complete a timed written exam in which they respond to a hypothetical leadership scenario, which is blind scored by personnel outside of the leadership pipeline office. Candidates who meet a set score then participate in a group interview during which they facilitate a discussion with teachers, similar to what they might do as a site-level principal. A subset of the district's executive leadership team scores this activity, the final hurdle for pipeline applicants.

Even before this intensive process, LBUSD makes a significant effort to locate promising applicants. The district enlists current principals to identify strong teachers who have the potential and inclination for leadership. Through a survey, principals highlight the talent at their sites, making note of any teachers who have already received their administrative credentials and may be considering an assistant principalship. Sometimes recruitment is in the form of a nudge, where a principal may see potential in a teacher who never considered leadership before. Sometimes it is more direct, where a principal provides additional guidance to a teacher who may already be on the path to leadership.

Program Components Prepare and Support Deeper Learning Leading

The first two pipeline programs—the Future Administrators Program and the Aspiring Principals Program—prepare LBUSD educators to assume the roles of assistant principal and then principal. Through workshops, field assignments, observation, feedback and reflection aligned to goals, and shadowing and mentorship, pipeline participants learn how LBUSD conceptualizes deeper learning leadership in ways that bridge theory and practical application.

LEADERS ENTER THE PIPELINE THROUGH THE FUTURE ADMINISTRATORS AND ASPIRING PRINCIPALS PROGRAMS. The Future Administrators Program is the beginning of the pipeline, intended for teachers interested in becoming school administrators. Teachers entering the program are required to have already earned a preliminary administrative services credential. In other districts, this credential typically constitutes eligibility for a leadership position, but for LBUSD the credential is a qualification for entering the pipeline. Other requirements include at least five years of teaching experience and demonstrated leadership experience. The program consists of six full-day workshops, monthly site visits by Leadership Development staff, and five full-day shadowing visits with a mentor assistant principal. Participants also complete readings and field assignments between workshops.

Aspiring administrators who complete the Future Administrators Program and who are selected for assistant principal positions enroll in the New Administrators Support Program, which provides mentoring during their first year as assistant principals. They also enroll in the Clear Administrative Credential Program, an LBUSD partnership with the Association of California School Administrators, through which they obtain clear, or permanent, administrative credentials over two years. The New Administrators Support Program includes four full days of professional development trainings and bimonthly site visits by Leadership Development staff in addition to the regular monthly meetings required of all LBUSD principals. The Clear Administrative Credential Program provides forty hours of coaching each year from LBUSD principals trained and certified for the role.

Not all candidates who complete the Future Administrators Program obtain administrative placements, but this does not preclude their being selected at a later date or cut off their access to the pipeline. Beginning in the 2017–18 school year, teachers who completed the Future Administrators Program but who were not selected for assistant principal positions enroll in the one-year Continuing Future Administrators Program. This program consists of five evening training sessions and monthly site visits by Leadership Development staff. These teachers stay in the assistant principal eligibility pool for up to three years after completing the Continuing Future Administrators Program.

After the Future Administrators Program, the next step in the pipeline is the Aspiring Principals Program, designed to recruit and prepare candidates for principal positions. Participants must be LBUSD assistant principals and graduates of the Future Administrators Program who have held leadership positions for two or three years, or outside candidates with comparable experience. The one-year Aspiring Principals Program includes six half-day workshops, three days of shadowing a mentor principal, one day of shadowing at the special education office, and monthly site visits by Leadership Development staff. Aspiring Principals Program completers are not automatically selected as principals, but those who have not been chosen for principal slots can remain in a pool of eligible candidates for up to three years.

WORKSHOPS GROUND NEW LEADERS IN THE THEORY AND PRACTICE OF DEEPER LEARNING. The Future Administrators and Aspiring Principals Programs each use workshops to ground candidates and leaders in the theoretical underpinnings and practical applications of deeper learning. Both programs include six workshops, each focused on one or more of the district's leadership domains. The workshops share several common features: participants read and respond to texts, district leaders present on topics related to the domain, and participants reflect on, share, and discuss connections to the context of LBUSD schools. Since program participants spend considerable time shadowing a mentor who is a current LBUSD administrator (a practice described below), these reflections and discussions can draw from experiences in their own or in their mentor's schools.

Workshops are designed to focus on high-leverage readings and experiences that participants can immediately apply as emergent leaders. For example, an elementary teacher in the Aspiring Principals Program recalled reading *Crucial Conversations* in preparation for a workshop focused on supervision, evaluation, and employee development.[5] The book offers skills for facilitating difficult conversations in productive ways that help maintain a collegial work environment. Participants applied these skills by brainstorming how they would provide feedback to teachers who were not meeting their instructional expectations, then role-played conversations to refine their approach. Another participant described the applicability of the guest speakers: "They're bringing in principals for the Aspiring

Principals . . . if you're a future administrator, they're bringing assistant principals. . . . They're bringing in people that you want to hear from." Through relevant readings and speakers, workshops facilitate learning experiences and contribute to leaders' ability to support improvement in teacher practice and student learning.

In addition to covering relevant content, pipeline workshops model strategies that leaders can use as they craft professional development experiences for teachers, and that teachers can use in their classrooms. Participants think together around anchor texts to build understanding of key leadership concepts, reflect on their roles as leaders, and consider how to adjust their leadership practice in ways attuned to their own contexts and experience as leaders.

Workshops Model Deeper Learning Practices

The Aspiring Principals Program kicked off in the fall of 2017 with a workshop that modeled strategies that rising leaders can use as they craft professional development experiences for teachers, who, in turn, can use the same strategies in their classrooms. The reading for this first workshop, *The Principal*, by Michael Fullan, was used to frame a conversation on the concept of the principal as "lead learner."[6] Fullan argues that principals should use systematic and collaborative approaches to build schoolwide instructional capacity. As lead learners, principals support a culture of continuous improvement by learning alongside staff, rather than micromanaging instructional practice, a philosophical stance consistent with LBUSD's whole-district emphasis on growth mind-set and on leadership development as an extension of teacher professional development.

In discussing *The Principal*, workshop facilitators Kelly An and Kim Dueñas led participants in a Socratic seminar. They explained that their purpose in using the method was to build the leaders' repertoire of strategies to use with teachers, and to model deeper learning teaching practices. Dueñas explained that the Socratic seminar allows teachers "to move beyond 'think, pair, share' and move toward authentic academic discourse." They also provided a protocol with planning tips such as suggestions for creating questions that demand increasingly deeper student thinking.

During the Socratic seminar, Dueñas and An asked participants to apply key concepts from *The Principal* to their roles as assistant principals. They began with a set of warm-up questions: "What makes the principalship such a challenging position? What do you think are the actions effective principals take that set them apart from others?" Aspiring principals drew on their own experiences to start the conversation, with one individual offering, "We're responsible for results. Our results are human beings, and we can't predict human behavior." Another chimed in with "in education, everybody's an expert. How do you move people to 'it's not 50 years ago' while respecting that experience?" As they built on their discussion of the challenges of the

(continues)

principalship, one aspiring principal responded to the idea that constant change is a challenge. "A principal can take lead teachers, instructional leaders, and listen to the struggles they're having and create opportunities where they can work with teachers," she suggested, noting this was an example of "the paradigm shift from the principal being the leader to teachers leading teachers."

The facilitators transitioned to their first core question, beginning with a less demanding recall question, as they would for a K–12 classroom: "What does Fullan suggest is outmoded in terms of how educators have come to define the role of principal as instructional leader?" Participants immediately began citing the text and relating it back to their own contexts. One aspiring principal reflected on Fullan's concept that as lead learners, principals support collaborative learning and growth. She said, "I thought about my one-on-one coaching and being right alongside my *one* teacher, and a shift to a team of teachers. You have to move the group . . . rather than the individual teacher." Another offered, "The principal is not just roaming the hallways. They also have to participate in learning. . . . What's *out* is us being on the outskirts of it." An aspiring principal responded to that idea: "Those tend to be my tendencies, to be a box checker and hold people accountable. It's a wrong driver to be an accountability holder. When I check those boxes, I'm robbing teachers of their professionalism."

The facilitators then asked the participants to consider two sets of "drivers" that Fullan outlines in his book—one virtuous and the other vicious—and to discuss how those personal drivers arise in their daily work. One aspiring principal struggled with the way Fullan categorizes accountability as a vice, as opposed to capacity-building, a virtue. She explained: "When I first stepped into the shoes of [aspiring principal], I looked at my role as an accountability person. Looking to make sure teachers are out in the lines to meet students. Now I'm finding myself smacked with the capacity-building role." Her cohort mate responded with, "I love what Fullan says. 'If we build capacity, accountability comes.' Trusting that with time, accountability comes with those teachers and we are doing less of the micromanaging." Participants nodded in agreement and continued to build on this idea. One aspiring principal suggested, "Extreme pressure leads to dysfunctional behavior. You have to build capacity for people to take responsibility for what we're asking them to do."

Participants also drew on the text and each other to engage in problem-solving. One aspiring principal raised the issue that "with deadlines you get into that vicious cycle." Her cohort mates offered solutions. One suggested that to build the kind of collaborative decision-making processes that Fullan advocates, they should "create a system around collaborating to make decisions. Create documents around those systems. Practice those systems." Another participant cited Fullan: "He says to use the group to change the group, instead of you solving the problem on your own because it's quicker. Once the group is there, it starts to resonate from that group out to the staff. So, that group will be changing on a bigger scale."

By thinking together around an anchor text, participants were able to build a deeper understanding of key leadership concepts, think differently about their roles as leaders, and think about how to adjust their leadership practices in ways that are specific to their own contexts and experience as leaders. Not only did this experience with a Socratic seminar help support their own learning, but it also modeled deeper learning instructional strategies for participants to use with teachers and look for in classrooms.

FIELD ASSIGNMENTS ALLOW PIPELINE PARTICIPANTS TO APPLY THEIR LEARNING. After each workshop, pipeline participants complete a field assignment that requires them to apply what they learned in the session to their current roles as teachers and leaders. Each field assignment is followed up at the next workshop by dedicated time to debrief assignment outcomes. For example, aspiring principals took a personality quiz during one session and were tasked to pay attention to how their personality strengths and challenges affected their work as assistant principals. During the field assignment debrief, one aspiring principal noted that she realized she should work on building relationships. While she found it easy to have patience and empathy with the students in her school, she struggled to do the same with parents and teachers. She set a goal to practice patience and empathy with the adults in her school community. Participants find value in these experiences: 93 percent of participants reported that the field assignment was an excellent learning experience for becoming a principal.

SHADOWING AND MENTORSHIP CREATE LEARNING OPPORTUNITIES FOR ASPIRING LEADERS. The pipeline programs also include shadowing and mentorship. Mentors for future administrators are assistant principals; mentors for aspiring principals are principals. Mentors coordinate four to six shadowing visits at their school sites and connect with their mentees at least once a week over the phone and once or twice a month in person. The LBUSD leadership development team is intentional about matching program participants with mentors who will complement their strengths and needs. Participants can be matched anywhere in the district, allowing them to broaden their range of experience and to prepare for a wider set of placements. Strategic mentorship pairings help participants meet their individual leadership learning goals.

Pipeline participants spoke highly of the shadowing and mentorship. A middle school principal remembered, "It's strategic because they're giving you exposure to different aspects of the campus. Like if there's a school site council meeting, I want you here on this day. If there's a PTA meeting, come on this day." A high school vice principal likewise touted the value of full-day shadowing experiences and "learning all the way through to the end of the day." She also appreciated being able to attend multiple shadowing sessions throughout the year: "Coming at five different times, it was always different . . . I can experience sometimes with disciplining kids, sometimes with walking classrooms, or leading coaching or department meetings."

LEADERS MEET LEARNING GOALS THROUGH OBSERVATION, FEEDBACK, AND REFLECTION. Pipeline program staff perform frequent site visits to observe participants in their day-to-day roles and offer personalized support. During these visits, anchored in a goal-setting process (described in the following section), staff might observe a future administrator teaching a lesson or leading a grade-level meeting. They might observe an aspiring principal facilitating professional development or conducting a classroom observation. After each observation, the participant and the staff member have a reflective conversation, relating the observation to the participant's goals and identifying areas for the participant to work on as they learn to operationalize the district's vision for deeper learning leadership.

Reflection is another key component of the pipeline. The Future Administrators Program requires candidates to work through a series of metacognitive and reflective components during the program, including self-assessments, goal planning, reflective summaries after each shadowing day, and five collaborative logs where the future administrator and the mentor check in on progress toward goals and identify action steps. One of the first activities is a self-assessment based on the leadership Domains and Dimensions. For each leadership area, the candidates classify themselves as unsatisfactory, developing/needs improvement, effective, or distinguished, providing narrative evidence for their score. This self-assessment is the foundation of the goal setting and improvement planning that guides candidates' learning throughout the program. This attention to feedback was reflected in participant survey results: 98 percent of participants reported feeling their program prepared them well or very well to engage in self-improvement and continuous learning.

Once goals are set, each candidate has a conversation with Director Kelly An and Leadership Development Coordinator Kim Dueñas to develop a personalized plan for meeting them. As Dueñas explained, "We look at the goals they have for themselves and the evaluation rubrics very carefully during the process of goal setting so that the goals are carefully tailored for each candidate. . . . Even though the Domains and Dimensions are the same for everyone, they will play out differently at each site."

The goal-setting process exemplifies deeper learning in two important ways. First, it allows pipeline candidates to personalize their learning by initiating metacognitive, reflective activity early on. These goals then become a touchstone for candidates as they intentionally accumulate learning experiences to address their own development. As a middle school assistant principal said, "They push . . . leaders in the direction where they want them to go all while tapping into their individual needs and desires." This self-regulation allows candidates to better monitor their progress, respond more positively to constructive feedback, and seek out support or assistance. Second, it gives pipeline instructors and mentors an understanding of each candidate's needs, making it possible to organize learning experiences in the workshops and during shadowing to facilitate each candidate's growth and development. Goal setting exemplifies deeper learning by modeling the interactions principals can have with teachers when they are administrators. Through their own active engagement in the process, participants learn to facilitate this same metacognitive, reflective, self-regulated, and personalized deeper learning.

District Leadership Expectations and Practices Shape Preparation for Deeper Learning

Deeper learning is infused in the preparation, expectations, and accountability system of LBUSD leaders. The LBUSD Leadership Evaluation Domains and Dimensions are the foundation of leader evaluation in the district, shaping the experiences of aspiring and current leaders in the pipeline. In alignment with these values, pipeline programs equip leaders to provide leadership, development, and growth for their teachers while being held accountable to district expectations.

One part of the annual administrator evaluation cycle is the collaborative inquiry visit (CIV), a cornerstone practice that exemplifies deeper learning principles and cultivates leadership for deeper learning practices. These daylong visits bring district leaders, school leaders, and teachers into the classrooms of their peers at a hosting school site. The purpose is to support school improvement with a focus on teaching and learning. According to the LBUSD *Principal Evaluation Handbook*, CIVs are designed to support professional learning within an individual school and across schools. The CIV protocol guides school and district staff in assessing the school's progress on its goals and determining where the school wants to go next. The classroom walk-through focuses specifically on instructional practice.

Every school in the district hosts a midyear CIV annually and beginning and end-of-year CIVs attended exclusively by district leaders. During midyear CIVs, teachers, principals, and district leaders look at how the Understandings are implemented at the school and think strategically about how the school leader can support teachers in meeting teaching and learning goals. These daylong visits are an important part of the pipeline experience. Future administrators and aspiring principals shadow their mentors on CIV days, gaining a firsthand look at the process and a deep understanding of the connection between school leadership and deeper learning. During a CIV, they observe classrooms and participate in conversations about the quality of teaching and learning alongside teachers and leaders from across the district. Participants also join in, reflecting on the ways in which school and district leaders are working toward their goals and supporting teachers to improve schoolwide instruction.

Collaborative Inquiry Visits

Visitors gathered at one elementary school for a CIV. The visitors—principals and Instructional Leadership Team teachers from two other elementary schools—sat around five sets of tables. At the beginning of the school year, the leaders from the three schools self-selected into a partnership based on their instructional goals for the year. Instructional Leadership Team teachers from the host school split up to sit with their visitors. District leaders made up the final group of visitors, for a total of about twenty-five attendees.

The morning began with a briefing by the host school's principal, a first-year principal who completed the district's Aspiring Principals Program. She began by describing her school, including the student demographics, standardized test score trends, teaching and learning goals, and professional development offerings. Then she introduced the school's theory of action for the year related to the Understanding addressing formative assessment, and informed by Dylan Wiliam's *Embedded Formative Assessment*.[7] Their plan was to embed Wiliam's five strategies for formative assessment into instruction. As stated in the school's theory of action for 2017–18: "If teachers (1) collaboratively plan lessons with clear learning goals and success criteria, design activities to (2) elicit evidence of learning, (3) provide effective feedback, (4) facilitate student to student interaction, and encourage students to (5) take ownership of their learning, then student achievement will increase and the achievement gap for ELLs will narrow."

Next, the host principal previewed the lesson plan structure that visitors would be using while observing in classrooms that day. She expressed that her goal was to build greater instructional consistency across the school: "It's important that at this school, we have common pedagogy. This is a journey. Today is really a baseline for us." Over the course of the day, at least one group of CIV observers visited each classroom, provided baseline data, and supported the host principal in guiding the faculty in a conversation to improve practice. At the end of the briefing, groups of observers made their way to classrooms. Each group spent about ten minutes in each classroom, noting how the teacher used formative assessment strategies.

After visiting several classrooms, it was clear that most teachers were attempting to implement deeper learning formative assessment practices, though to varying levels of success. In an exemplary lower-grade classroom, for example, students were actively engaged and directing their own learning in a math lesson. Students were sitting on the rug in small groups, each with a bucket of objects—cups, water bottles, toys, and classroom supplies. Students worked to measure the height of objects using cubes as a standard unit of measurement. Their learning was self-directed, and they had conversations with their partners to explain their thinking,

(continues)

correct misconceptions, and decide when they were ready to move on. The teacher traveled from group to group observing conversations and offering guidance.

This lesson exemplified both the host principal's expectations for formative assessment and the principles of deeper learning. Students applied their previous learning about units and measurements to a new context. They were involved in a collaborative and productive learning community. They used each other as resources to verify or correct their claims. They watched each other measure as they took turns and helped each other line up cubes to measure accurately. Their learning was personalized through choice; they were able to let their own curiosity and interest guide which objects they would measure and when.

In contrast, after observing another classroom, the host principal noted that "the [teacher's] feedback was about how to do the task, not about what they were learning." Most of the teacher's comments were about where students should be sitting or which boxes they should be filling out in a worksheet, rather than on guiding students toward meaningful learning goals. While the students in that class were sitting together in groups, most worked silently on their own.

When the groups had observed each of the school's twenty-five classrooms, they reconvened and the host principal led a discussion on "stars and wishes," or what they saw that positively reflected the school's theory of action and what staff might continue working on. With the goal to identify opportunities for growth and improvement, the conversation came back to what the host principal might try after the day was over. For example, the host principal shared a comment about one class, and her principal supervisor suggested that she engage in a coaching conversation with that teacher. He also described a strategy that some schools were using to track student learning during lessons to inform planning.

The CIV concluded with a conversation just among the school leaders, as teachers and other staff returned to their day's duties. The visiting principals shared what they had learned and would be taking back to their school sites. The host principal shared some final reflections about how to structure the school's professional learning to get the greatest impact. In particular, she wondered whether she should continue to lead teachers in using formative assessment strategies in isolation, or help teachers apply the strategies to a content area to make them more relevant.

LEADERS LEARN THE VALUES OF COLLABORATION AND CONTINUOUS IMPROVEMENT. In LBUSD, leaders are expected to establish and maintain a collegial and collaborative culture in schools. Preparation for establishing and participating in such collaborative environments begins in pipeline programs. The Leadership Evaluation Domains and Dimensions make direct reference to collaborative work, stating that leaders should "develop and sustain a culture of collaboration and continuous improvement" and "share leadership with their staff." The Understandings, too, communicate the value of collaboration. As a member of the district's Office of Curriculum, Instruction, and Professional Development described, "We really prioritize collaboration, planning, and getting better together, and being learners together." Finally, the district's *Principal Evaluation Handbook* cites a number of assumptions from Bloom and Krovetz's framework for coaching partnerships, including that principals and their assistants work together collaboratively, that they are responsible for growing those around them, and that strong learning organizations have coaching cultures.[8]

This spirit of collaboration is expected of all administrators. As one principal said, "We're always learning as principals just as you would expect teachers and students to continuously be learning and learning side by side, collaboratively." As aspiring administrators work with and shadow their mentors and participate in pipeline program activities, including CIVs, they see this collaboration modeled. A future administrator noted that learning about collaboration in the Future Administrators Program "really was aligning to the work that we do in our district. . . . A lot of it really is the teams sharing their work and the schools learning with and from one another. . . . It's a really kind of awesome way to get that collaboration from the grassroots."

A Future Administrators Program mentor used her own work supporting teachers to model such conversations and engage her mentee in them. The mentor explained that she had experienced pushback from some teachers who felt that releasing the reigns around student talk in the classroom might lead to management issues, and so she was helping to shift teachers' mind-sets around what "quality instruction" looked like. She explained: "The collaborative conversations go hand in hand with getting the results we want. And the kids will be interested if you provide these opportunities and don't just have them sitting in rows and being quiet and still. Plus, it's the expectation so that's what's got to happen." She brought her mentor along as she worked with the teachers, starting with teacher observations. In a follow-up conversation with the mentee, she asked, "Did [the instruction] look right to you? What did you pick up on? Did you see the collaborative conversations?" Her mentee had the opportunity to look for collaboration in classroom instruction, see it modeled as an assistant principal observed teachers as a basis for instructional conversations, and experience it firsthand in her conversations with her mentor.

LEADERS LEARN TO PROVIDE FEEDBACK TO TEACHERS. A key feature of pipeline programs is that leaders learn to provide meaningful feedback to teachers to improve their practice. It is a topic of their workshops, and it is emphasized and modeled during coaching and shadowing. Mentors and mentees discuss in advance what they hope to see in observations, and then afterward they plan the feedback they intend to give to teachers. One Aspiring Principals Program mentor took her mentees to observe a variety of classrooms—that of a struggling teacher, a brand-new teacher, a veteran teacher, and others—without previewing what to expect. After each observation, her mentees discussed what they saw and the feedback they would give the teacher. In the same way that the principal hoped students at her school would have opportunities to discover new learning on their own, she allowed her mentees to develop observation skills without providing her own initial impressions. Through this exercise the mentees built their understanding of what deeper learning practices look like while they also practiced offering targeted, specific feedback to support teachers.

In a related example, a high school vice principal and future administrator mentor had her mentee observe a series of sessions in which she supported a chronically struggling teacher by providing strategies, conversing about the classroom, and observing other classrooms with the teacher. According to the vice principal, her mentee gained valuable insight from these observations over the course of her shadowing visits: "Every time the candidate came to shadow, she could start to see the results of the planning and classroom management." During these visits, the mentor also shared her underlying thinking, the "why" of the strategy, as another opportunity to build the future administrator's skills and knowledge. Through this process, the candidate was learning how to support a teacher and what good teaching looks like. The candidate was also able to calibrate her understanding of the district's instructional expectations—the mentor did not allow the struggling teacher to continue to engage in the same unsuccessful teaching.

Program participants also receive feedback from their interactions with pipeline staff who observe each participant at least once a month. One assistant principal in the Aspiring Principal Program described the support she received from Leadership Development Director Kelly An. As she and An conducted classroom observations together, An asked questions like, "Tell me about the work you're doing with this particular teacher." "Who's your challenging teacher?" "Can I see why?" Then she would dig further. "Can you tell me what you're doing to improve this?" "What's the data showing?" These probing questions helped the assistant principal predicate her leadership development on the on-the-ground realities of her school.

This kind of support exemplifies multiple aspects of LBUSD's approach to leadership. While An helped the aspiring principal improve her practice in explicit ways, she also modeled a coaching approach that the aspiring principal could use with her teachers. The assistant principal remarked that her coaching conversations with An demonstrated "the same level of accountability" that characterized principal-to-teacher coaching. This support also gave the principal the wherewithal to follow through on her ambitious work with staff. Even as she was learning about leadership, she was practicing it and receiving ongoing guidance, feedback, and affirmation about her choices.

LEADERS USE DATA TO DRIVE INSTRUCTIONAL CHANGE. The Domains and Dimensions require that "leaders use data and stakeholder input to shape a shared school vision focused on student achievement."[9] The pipeline programs offer substantial opportunities for participants to develop this skill. Their level of preparation is enabled, in part, by the district's data reporting systems, which allow teachers and principals to generate reports so they can monitor trends and develop responses in a timely fashion. To provide administrators with the skills to create and use data reports, pipeline programs provide hands-on training and practice with the data system. In fact, 90 percent of participants felt their program prepared them well or very well to use student data to inform continuous school improvement.

The data system provides information on a host of indicators, including attendance records, test scores, discipline incidents, AP scores, SAT scores, PSAT scores, graduation status, college admission and attendance, and staff, parent, and student survey data. Recognizing the importance of students' social and emotional well-being, an important component of deeper learning, there are also data on climate, culture, and social emotional measures.[10] Pipeline program participants learn to use this holistic set of data to develop theories of action about student performance and underperformance.

During the Aspiring Principals Program workshop on the teaching and learning domain, one district administrator led a session on using data to drive instructional change. He provided data for "Super Middle School"—a real school that he kept anonymous. Aspiring principals worked in groups to analyze the data and decide where they would focus resources to improve student outcomes. Noting that several student subgroups were not meeting high levels of high school readiness, one group connected high rates of chronic absenteeism to lower readiness, and further connected lower scores on measures of social-emotional learning to absenteeism, forming the basis for a theory of action. Commenting on this lesson, an aspiring principal said she learned that "data should drive the decision that you're going to make" and that she needed to use a wide range of data to focus on addressing root causes, rather than simply focusing on increasing test scores.

ACCOMPLISHMENTS AND DEEPER LEARNING LEADERSHIP IN PRACTICE

The LBUSD Leadership Development Pipeline is designed as an extension of the district's professional development program, and the district has a successful track record of identifying, preparing, appointing, and retaining top principal and administrative talent from within its own teaching ranks. About 92 percent of the district's principals are former Long Beach teachers.[11] Roughly 95 percent of all sitting LBUSD principals and vice principals have gone through the pipeline; the remaining 5 percent are administrators who were hired before the pipeline was established or who completed elements of the workshops as part of their required annual professional development.

District leaders who support principals—including the deputy superintendent of schools, assistant superintendents, and instructional directors—have provided the financial and personnel resources needed to ensure that school leaders in Long Beach are prepared to lead for deeper learning. According to a survey of recent Future Administrators Program and Aspiring Principals Program completers, 88 percent felt well or very well prepared for the principalship. In addition, most agreed that the programs prepared them very well or well with the skills to lead for deeper learning, such as creating collegial and collaborative work environments (90 percent), equitably serving all students (84 percent), and redesigning the school's organization and structure to support deeper learning for teachers and students (81 percent).

A veteran elementary school principal and Aspiring Principals Program mentor shared, "They're very supportive with us in regards to professional development and training, which really helps us. . . . It's a big district, but I feel that all principals are pretty tight." This assessment is borne out by results: of the more than 130 district administrators who entered their positions through the Leadership Development Pipeline over the past twelve years, only two have left the district for reasons other than retirement.

Overall satisfaction of pipeline program participants is high. One high school teacher praised multiple aspects of her preparation in the Future Administrators Program: "I feel like I got a lot of information. It was meaningful. It was substantive. It was interesting. I feel like it improved a lot of my own skill set. It helped me to strengthen areas where I was good at, but it also helped me to look at areas where I know I need help and to move me forward." Her praise extended beyond the substantive aspects of the program to include the work that pipeline program leaders put into providing high-quality experiences. As she noted, "Their organization, the logistics, everything was just top of the line."

An assistant principal had a similarly positive view of the Aspiring Principals Program, explaining: "It's probably the best experience I've had because it allows you to be exposed to other leaders in the district. You're working with other administrators. . . . I'm looking at different dynamics, different demographics, different levels of support. . . . The experience itself, it just gives you a look at what the day-to-day is of being a principal, because it is different than even being an assistant principal."

Another Future Administrators Program mentor said that the program "taught me skills I never knew I needed to have." She attributed the value of that preparation to the types of training she received, including that "they kept it real and didn't sugarcoat the job." She added that the district provides the necessary tools for doing the job and that this continues "even after you've been promoted." She compared her experience with those offered by other districts. "I brag to my brother who is in ABC Unified [School District] and say, 'You know what, ABC can't beat Long Beach in terms of professional development for teachers or for leaders.'" Another Aspiring Principals Program participant said, "I feel bad for administrators in other districts that don't have this internal process," and added, "I don't know how to be better prepared than what the district has done. . . . It's like they invested a lot of time in me and into other candidates that were in my program. I do feel prepared." Another program alumna told us that, in her experience, the pipeline is unique among district leadership development programs: "When I talk to other people that are at different school systems, and they're like 'Wait a minute, you've got that training? Wait a minute, you got this? Wait a minute, you knew this before you went in?' So they've got the training part down. They're asking you to be high quality, so they're giving you high quality." She attributed this difference to the "Long Beach Way," the set of expectations that surrounds leadership preparation, as well as other districtwide initiatives. "It's just the way it's done," she said.

Participants also praised the connection between theory and practice that is evident in the pipeline programs. One program participant who said her pipeline preparation was the "best professional development I've received hands down" attributed the high quality to the connection between coursework and fieldwork. As she described, the training was "not just reading a book but the actual practical, how do you do it, who do you talk to." She elaborated on this, speaking to the applicability of the material from the program: "I can use the stuff they give me. It's not just something I file away and say 'oh well.' It's something I can actually use."

Another participant compared the preparation she received through the Future Administrators Program with the "big picture" view from her administrative credential and doctoral programs, and described how the pipeline emphasized the practical aspects of administration: "The Future Administrators Program did do big picture for sure, but I think it really tried to focus on the actual experiences of the guest speaker, or experiences of your shadowing, or real tangible things. It didn't feel just theoretical, which I think my doctorate program very much did." An aspiring principal likewise reported that her experience in the pipeline was superior to her other preparation experiences and attributed the difference to the theory-practice connection at LBUSD.

Pipeline Participants Lead Deeper Learning Experiences

Pipeline participants also reported that they received strong preparation in how to lead deeper learning experiences. The district's emphasis on continuous improvement, which is conveyed to staff and administrators throughout the professional development system and emphasized in pipeline programs, produces a system in which principals are expected to be learners. As one district administrator explained, "[Professional development] doesn't occur when you're not in the room. It occurs when you're in the room and you sit with your teachers and you learn with them together. And yes, you'll facilitate that work at your school sites as well. So, that's kind of an expectation within our system."

This systemic set of expectations translates into pipeline experiences. One elementary principal noted that the Aspiring Principals Program has "a clear emphasis on the importance of the principal's role as lead learner, the instructional lead for the school site." Eighty-seven percent of pipeline participants reported that the program prepared them well or very well to help teachers improve through a cycle of observation and feedback.

In practice, for example, one principal supported his assistant principals in providing feedback to teachers; his support used strategies that he learned in the pipeline. At the beginning of the year, he conducted classroom observations with his assistant principals and had them write feedback to the teachers. The principal then provided feedback on their feedback with the aim of encouraging his assistant principals to look for evidence of the Understandings in classrooms, including student engagement, collaborative work, and teachers' ability to identify evidence of learning. The assistant principals then conducted observations on their own, which were recorded in a shared document, a source for further collaboration.

LBUSD has created a district-embedded leadership training program that is tightly linked to the district's well-regarded teacher professional development system. In summing up the successes of the LBUSD Leadership Development Pipeline, Director Kelly An spoke to the unique nature of the "Long Beach way" of preparing administrators: "When you think about it, it speaks a lot to the culture we have in our district of high expectations, of continuous learning, and of more of a systematic approach to supporting our students."

Making Deeper Learning Explicit During Professional Development

As part of a district emphasis on math instruction, an assistant principal, also a participant in the Aspiring Principals Program, crafted a hands-on, in-depth lesson study cycle for her kindergarten teachers around teaching students about two- and three-dimensional shapes. First, she modeled a lesson for her kindergarten teachers:

> You want to engage the kids like, "I have this bag of shapes. They're all scattered out and I don't know what to do with them!" You get them excited asking, "Can you help me out? This is what I want you to do. I'd like you to separate these shapes," and then you figure out how the kids are separating them. Some are separating them by color, some are separating them by shape, some are separating them by two dimensional or three dimensional.
>
> You give them time to work. You kind of walk around, you observe. You don't give them any feedback—you don't tell them "this is right" or "this is wrong," because the minute you do that, then it just stops.
>
> [You can] say, "Can you show me another way? Can you tell me more about that? Can you do this?" So you keep them engaged and you walk around, and as you walk around you're note taking about which group or which child you'd like to share out with the class. . . . And then at the end of the lesson you have an idea of where your kids are on this particular skill.

The assistant principal then engaged the kindergarten teachers in a collaborative learning process in which they support each other in trying the lesson she modeled:

> The teachers would then decide who will demonstrate [the next lesson] with their class and we're all going to go in and watch. Then the following day, everyone else teaches [the same] lesson in their class and everyone has at least one colleague watch them. Then the following Thursday at their grade-level meeting, we have a conversation about how teachers felt about the lesson, where their kids are at, what they saw when they observed a colleague. And then we end it with everyone completing a reflection sheet.

Getting her staff to engage in joint lesson planning and receiving real-time feedback from peers was not, however, a simple process. According to the assistant principal, before starting the lesson study process, the instructional culture was very insular. She worked to establish a common purpose in grade-level teaching teams,

(continues)

and by leading demonstration lessons, she could develop an understanding that they are not evaluating one another but rather helping each other move forward. Through this process, teachers were able to come to appreciate that, in the assistant principal's words, "teaching is sharing and sometimes means being vulnerable" and that becoming better at instructional practice requires being open to the learning process as a teacher.

Facilitating this learning for her teachers taught her some valuable lessons as a leader. She explained that "the peer observation part is the most powerful. Sometimes you want to hear from your colleagues more than you want to hear from your assistant principal or principal. And I know from being a classroom teacher that was important to me and I think sometimes [teachers] might take constructive criticism better from a colleague."

FACTORS INFLUENCING SYSTEMIC DEEPER LEARNING LEADERSHIP DEVELOPMENT

The LBUSD Leadership Development Pipeline is an extension of the district's professional development system. This connection means that the pipeline's success is, in part, attributable to the professional development that participants received before they embarked on the administrative track. At the same time, the "Long Beach Way" also creates challenges, such as the complexity of running a program based on collaboration and individualized support and issues that arise with recruiting internal candidates.

District Professional Development Supports Leadership Development

The roots of the pipeline programs are in LBUSD's teacher professional development system. An elementary principal spoke about the strengths of the professional development program, showing how it primes teachers for administrative preparation: "There was an advantage to the [professional development] because each one was specifically tailored to gaining a deeper knowledge and understanding of, not only what's best for students, but also collaborating with my colleagues, understanding the mission and vision of the district, and how our support model and the resources are available to me to support kids, my school, the community."

Dr. Jill Baker also made clear connections between the district's professional development program and the pipeline, emphasizing the pipeline's focus on teaching: "The pipeline programs ... are all centered around teaching and learning. ... We're starting with what works in classrooms and then building, with teaching and learning as the focus, [for] all of our administrative programs and for our sitting principals too." This means that when LBUSD educators enter the pipeline as future administrators, they are already inculcated in the expectations and practices that they will learn to see from an administrator's perspective. This strong link to their previous experiences gives pipeline participants a rich background from which to draw lessons about school leadership.

Connections to Professional Development Create Complexities for Leadership Development

While the strong link to professional development and the emphasis on selecting administrators from the district are assets of the pipeline, they also create challenges. For example, LBUSD's focus on collaboration requires a thoughtful approach to program development. Kelly An, director of leadership development, noted that a key question for pipeline programs is "How do you bring folks together in a very collaborative way, move the work forward, and be supportive of that, not the top-down telling approach?" The struggle, in other words, lies in creating an administrative program that supports the district's high expectations for leadership practice but does so in a collaborative fashion.

Another challenge is providing each participant with preparation focused on meeting their particular needs. This, too, is a commitment rooted in districtwide values. Kim Dueñas, leadership development coordinator, explained how the district vision for student learning is reflected in adult learning: "I feel at the heart of our work as a whole district is really believing that the work that we service for adults really mirrors the philosophy that we have for our students, which is that we really need to meet the learner where they are." She continued, "[We] really try to individualize the learning as much as possible for any age learner, with the understanding that as we are providing that content to our adults, that that immediately translates to the students back at the site."

Combining collaboration with personalization means a high-touch approach in which pipeline program staff work with and get to know participants. Among the challenges of this approach are its time demands, as Kelly An shared when describing her schedule: "In order for me to do site visits with future administrators, site visits with new administrators, site visits with aspiring principals, and site visits with year one principals and year two principals, and then monthly meetings with the new director and aspiring director, that's a lot of site visits."

Internal Recruiting Creates Challenges in Building the Applicant Pool

The high level of selectivity for admissions to the pipeline, while meant to ensure that the right candidates are selected for the right positions, also creates some challenges. The high bar for principals may mean that some teachers are too intimidated to consider a move to administration. Also, because the district seeks out its top teaching talent, some principals may not want to recommend their strongest teachers for the pipeline at the risk of losing them from classrooms.

Another challenge is the makeup of the pipeline candidate pool, particularly its diversity. As Dr. Baker explained, "We feel really good about our pipeline, but then when we go to place people, we realize we don't have enough male leaders. We don't have enough bilingual leaders to do what we want to do. We don't have the diversity of candidates that we want to have in this district. Gender diversity, ethnic diversity, language diversity."

Brian Moskovitz, assistant superintendent of elementary schools, also wondered, "How do we continue to bring in a culturally diverse leadership team that is going to represent students and families in our district?" Because administrators come from the teacher ranks, administrative diversity is directly a result of teacher diversity. As Moskovitz described, "The teachers that are available, people coming out of university . . . are not incredibly diverse. We have a real challenge in bringing in enough teachers to match our demographics . . . because we pull from our teachers into that pipeline. It's really about how do we get those into the teaching profession. Which then gets to how do universities recruit and bring people in?" Even though he recognized that LBUSD had not yet solved this issue, he pointed to district efforts to address it, including expanding teacher programs at Cal State Long Beach and Long Beach City College, and recruiting outside the state to bring in teachers with diverse backgrounds.

KEY TAKEAWAYS

LBUSD's Leadership Development Pipeline programs prepare administrators at all levels to lead for deeper learning. Embedded in the context of the district and built on LBUSD's teacher professional development system, the pipeline programs are aligned with district values and initiatives. Pipeline programs are rooted in mentorship, collaboration, application, reflection, and feedback, with the aim of producing leaders who will work with teachers, and with one another, to realize the district's vision of teaching and learning. Program participants and graduates feel prepared to lead and believe they have the tools to lead for deeper learning. The key takeaways from the program are outlined below.

LBUSD has a context-specific vision for leadership preparation aligned to district deeper learning priorities. The district has developed a clear, coherent vision of leading and teaching that supports deeper learning. This vision is articulated in LBUSD's Understandings Continuum and reinforced through the Leadership Evaluation Domains and Dimensions. The vision is also manifest through districtwide expectations around continuous improvement, learning for leaders, teachers, and students, and the use of data to improve student learning. This vision guides the work of leading and teaching in the district.

LBUSD recruits experienced educators who have demonstrated the ability to teach for deeper learning and are prepared to develop the capacity for deeper learning leadership. LBUSD intentionally builds the skills and knowledge of its teachers and then identifies and recruits experienced teachers with administrative potential. Since the district hires administrators almost exclusively from within, program participants are familiar with the "Long Beach Way." Once in the pipeline, they experience additional high-quality professional development and learn how to lead for deeper learning and to provide deeper learning experiences to teachers.

LBUSD's pipeline programs are anchored in pedagogy and curriculum that exemplify and model deeper learning instructional practice. Pipeline programs are characterized by content and instruction that are contextualized, inquiry-based, and focused on linking theory to specific practices and problem-solving. Preparation for administrators, aligned to district values, is personalized and reflective, enhanced by real-world learning experiences and targeted feedback on leadership expectations, and consistent with deeper learning. Candidates see models of such learning, experience it themselves, and learn to lead it. Additionally, participants collaborate with one another and with experienced colleagues across the district, learning through example and experience to nurture such collaboration among teachers and students.

The district emphasizes continuous improvement in leader preparation, evaluation, and practice and thus helps leaders understand how to use data to create a theory of action based on students' needs. Pipeline programs involve participants in efforts to support improved instruction and student learning, in part through participation in the collaborative inquiry that underlies such efforts. They learn to use a holistic approach that goes beyond standardized test scores to get at deeper issues, while incorporating a whole-child approach that is essential to the growth, learning, and success of students.

CHAPTER 5

STRENGTHENING SCHOOL LEADERS STATEWIDE

Arkansas Leadership Academy's Master Principal Program

The Arkansas Leadership Academy's Master Principal Program (MPP) develops deeper learning–oriented principals throughout the state of Arkansas. As practicing principals, program participants experience deeper learning while applying what they learn in their current schools. The MPP is an example of how an in-service professional learning program can support school leaders in creating equitable, deeper learning environments and drive both school-level and district-level change.

PROGRAM HIGHLIGHTS AND HISTORY

The MPP was established in 2003 by the Arkansas General Assembly to "develop and support leadership capacity across the state that fosters equity and excellence in education."[1] It is a highly selective, three-phase program for public school principals that is designed to expand their knowledge base and leadership skills while catalyzing systems improvement. Participants learn skills while collaborating with school and district stakeholders to create lasting change. Principals progressively build knowledge and skills as they advance through the program's three phases. Phase 1 principals make small changes in their schools to enable an equitable, deeper learning environment. Phase 2 principals focus on using effective leadership skills to collaborate within their schools and districts, empower teachers to become leaders, and use multiple forms of data to drive decision-making. Phase 3 principals work to shift ownership of change efforts and advocate for system improvements beyond their schools or districts, up to the state level.

The MPP, which is free for all principals, serves eighty to ninety principals per year, inclusive of all three phases. About four to six principals go through the Master School Principal designation process annually (see table 5.1). Each

TABLE 5.1   **Overview of Arkansas Leadership Academy's MPP**

Program type	In-service
Mission	Develop and support leadership capacity across the state that fosters equity and excellence in education.
Location	Arkansas (statewide)
Program duration	3 years
Degree or designation conferred	Master School Principal designation
Program highlights	Three-phase program; 3 or 4 residential sessions per phase with readings, activities, and action research projects in between sessions; some coaching in Phase 2
Key staff	MPP staff
Costs and funding supports	No cost to program participants. State of Arkansas allocates $500,000 annually for program administration.

phase runs for a full school year and entails three or four residential sessions. In between sessions, participants complete assigned readings and activities and work on action research projects designed to deepen their knowledge and hone their skills. Principals must apply for each phase, a process requiring them to provide a narrative description of improvements they have made in staff and school culture as well as data that demonstrate student growth on standardized tests. There is no guarantee that principals who complete one phase will be accepted into subsequent phases.

Upon successfully completing Phase 3, principals may apply for designation as a Master School Principal. The designation process requires extensive reviews of school changes and sustained improvement in student outcomes, as well as rigorous assessments of their leadership abilities. Principals who pass the designation process earn the prestigious title of Master School Principal. All designated Master School Principals who remain as full-time principals earn an annual bonus of $9,000 for five years from the Arkansas Department of Education. Those who serve in a high-need school earn an annual bonus of $25,000 for five years.

In 1991, Governor Bill Clinton signed into law the Meeting the National Education Goals: Schools for Arkansas' Future Act, which, among other pieces, directed the establishment of an "Academy for Leadership Training and School Based Management."[2] The purpose of the academy, as described in the bill, was to "provide a variety of training programs and opportunities to develop the knowledge base and leadership skills of school principals, as well as teachers, superintendents and other administrators, and school board members."[3] From this legislation the Arkansas Leadership Academy was established to "develop and support leadership capacity that fosters equity and excellence in education."[4] In 2003, the Arkansas General Assembly introduced a bill entitled "An Act to Improve School Performance by Creating the Master School Principal Program," which expanded efforts to develop school leaders by outlining the details of the MPP.[5] After six months of planning, the MPP accepted its first cohort. The first Master School Principal designation process ran in 2006. The state provides $500,000 annually to fund the MPP.[6]

PROGRAM PHILOSOPHY

The MPP is designed to build leaders' strengths while helping them become continuous learners who create collaborative school environments. The program uses a set of rubrics—the Leadership Performance Strands and Skills—that identify specific skills and structures leaders should develop. Aligned with deeper learning practices, the rubrics create a clear vision for what deeper learning–oriented principals do across five key leadership responsibilities:

- setting clear and compelling direction
- shaping culture for learning
- leading and managing change
- transforming teaching and learning
- managing accountability systems

Setting Clear and Compelling Direction

The first performance strand focuses on developing a mission, vision, and set of core beliefs that can guide practice. Principals are expected to develop a shared purpose and coherent effort through mission, vision, and beliefs; develop, implement, and communicate a results-based strategic action plan; and establish a sense of urgency that leads to action. Principals who have mastered this strand create opportunities for shared decision-making. They engage all stakeholders, employing multiple communication strategies to ensure that all voices are heard. They also create and sustain a sense of urgency and communicate progress to maintain momentum to move ideas to action.

Shaping Culture for Learning

As the mission, vision, and core beliefs are being identified, the MPP also emphasizes the need to create a culture that will be conducive to actualizing that vision. Principals are expected to establish a desired culture through norms, rituals, traditions, common language, and cultural competencies; promote a safe, positive, interactive, and supportive climate; build and sustain collaborative relationships and structures for learning and work; infuse a diversity of people, perspectives, ideas, and experiences into the work; and use skills of influence, persuasion, and advocacy to engage with multiple community sectors as a public leader.

Consistent with deeper learning–oriented schools, principals who master this strand create collaborative learning environments. They regularly include people with diverse perspectives in decision-making and building all aspects of work around the value of cultural diversity and individual identities. Skills associated with this strand include ensuring that all stakeholders believe that all students and adults are capable of success and that the social, emotional, and physical learning environments are safe and risk-free.

Leading and Managing Change

The third performance strand focuses on how to effectively use a systems-thinking perspective to implement meaningful change. MPP participants learn to develop and distribute leadership to sustain a high-performing organization; deploy an integrated management system for systemic results; use individual, group, and organizational change research, processes, and tools; use reflection, inquiry, and assessment practices for continuous learning and improvement; and lead change efforts to scale.

This performance strand emphasizes the importance of collaboratively solving complex problems. Principals who master this strand adopt a model for continuous learning by using reflection, inquiry, and assessment and foster a collaborative schoolwide culture of continuous learning and improvement. This focus on continuous learning is key to deeper learning–oriented schools, which must continuously assess student and teacher needs to best support their learning.

Transforming Teaching and Learning

The fourth performance strand—transforming teaching and learning—is at the heart of the program. Of all the strands, transforming teaching and learning to provide both students and teachers with deeper learning opportunities is the top priority. The MPP focuses on developing principals who expect high-quality teaching and learning; observe teaching practice and provide actionable feedback for professional learning; ensure all learners engage in rigorous, relevant, and student-centered learning experiences; become literate as a leader of digital learning environments; and ensure alignment of standards, curriculum, teaching, assessment, and professional learning.

This performance strand sets the expectation for leaders to shift their understanding of quality teaching from complying with state standards to meeting all students where they are based on their unique learning needs. Leaders who have mastered this strand work with their staff to attend to students' social and emotional competencies, adopt effective deeper learning instructional practices, and develop a culture of collaborative learning.

Managing Accountability Systems

The final performance strand focuses on sustaining the systems and processes that have been created and continuously improving teaching and learning. Principals are expected to use student performance–based accountability systems for decision-making; use adult performance–based accountability systems for decision-making; acquire, allocate, and distribute resources equitably; and embrace implications from emerging knowledge to improve student and adult learning and performance.

Principals develop systems conducive to deeper learning where students often work on long-term projects, solicit feedback from adults or peers, and revise projects based on that input. Leaders who have mastered this performance strand also recognize that each student and adult in the building has unique learning needs, and equitably allocate resources to best support the needs of all students and teachers.

PREPARING DEEPER LEARNING LEADERS

Principals apply to participate in the MPP because they want to improve their leadership skills and better support all teachers and students at their schools. The program is intentionally designed so principals can immediately use what they learn, and the program models specific, collaborative practices principals can take back to their schools. Principals in the MPP also work on long-term action plans and action research projects to solve specific problems of practice in their schools. All program activities are designed to help leaders develop skills and establish school structures that align with the Leadership Performance Strands and Skills, creating the conditions for deeper learning–oriented environments. As leaders engage in deeper learning experiences, they learn how to use their new knowledge to have an impact beyond the school walls.

The MPP Reflects Deeper Learning Principles

The MPP models deeper learning by engaging principals in authentic work. As principals learn and apply new leadership skills, they are putting deeper learning practices in place in their schools.

PRINCIPALS LEARN TO LEAD FOR DEEPER LEARNING BY PRACTICING AND APPLY-ING DEEPER LEARNING–ALIGNED STRATEGIES. One of the MPP's core instructional strategies is to provide space at the residential sessions for principals to engage in and practice activities that create the foundation for deeper learning. The MPP then expects principals to implement these practices in their schools. For example, in Phase 1, leaders participate in an activity intended to model how leaders can collaboratively develop a shared vision and mission in their schools. Leaders respond to a prompt, such as "When it comes to teaching and learning, I believe___," and write their responses on index cards. The facilitator leads an activity in which the principals organize responses to highlight common beliefs. The facilitator then leads a whole-group discussion where participants decide together which ideas are shared by all and should be included in their collaboratively developed mission, vision, and core beliefs. The principals' assignment is to lead the same activity with the staff at their schools.

The MPP employs this idea of learn-practice-apply throughout all program phases, starting with the very first residential session. Kelli Martin, director of teaching and learning at Greenbrier School District and a designated Master School Principal, recalled: "I believe we met in late July for the first institute, and one of our next steps was to begin school differently. It was literally that wide open, but it was based on what you just learned in your first three days of Master Principal. What are you taking away that would make you want to begin school differently this year? Rather than your teachers sitting for three to five hours . . . what can you do differently to start your school year?" The MPP expects principals to return to their schools and engage with their staff differently than they had before, creating the conditions in which teacher knowledge and skills and school structures for deeper learning can develop and thrive.

THE MPP SUPPORTS PRINCIPALS IN ADDRESSING REAL PROBLEMS OF PRACTICE. The MPP engages principals in authentic leadership activities, based on the real-world challenges of their schools, to move their schools toward deeper learning practices. During each program phase, principals develop an action plan to address a need they identify in their schools. For example, Angela Betancourt, a Phase 1 elementary school principal, developed a plan to redesign team meetings so that teachers have specified roles and ownership over the content and functioning of the meetings. Jason Burks, a principal who completed Phase 2, implemented a program to provide individualized student supports as part of the school day. Principals revise their action plans throughout each phase of the MPP, gathering data from their schools, reviewing the success of the plan, and working collaboratively with their cohort members and their school staffs to make improvements. Principals in Phase 3 also conduct an action research project based on a problem of practice. The action research project culminates in a presentation to the Phase 3 cohort, MPP staff, and the principal's superintendent at the final residential session. These presentations serve as a portfolio for the principals, as they share the story of their growth as leaders, their successes, their challenges, and the impact they have had in their schools.

MPP Values Collaborative Learning for Principals

The MPP helps principals understand the importance of creating collaborative environments in their schools by having them participate in and develop their own learning communities. The MPP employs a cohort structure, with participants in each phase attending residential sessions together and completing the same activities in between sessions. The cohort model allows principals to build relationships with educators throughout the state. It also sets up the conditions for leaders to share ideas, experience effective collaboration, and practice giving and receiving useful feedback—key elements of leading for deeper learning.

Typically, MPP staff model or discuss a particular practice, then give participants the opportunity to work together to implement it in residential sessions before trying it in their schools. As Debbie Jones, a Phase 3 graduate, described, "You may be talking about an observation or a scenario that they present to you and then as principals . . . think about how you would solve it. And you talk about it with others." By having principals engage in collaborative exercises, the MPP creates opportunities for participants to learn by working together in a safe space that allows for questioning and fine-tuning of practices before employing these strategies in their schools. As principals make changes in their schools, the MPP also creates opportunities to reflect on their progress with their cohort. Each activity and process that principals implement is followed by an opportunity to reflect with their cohort members and receive valuable suggestions to improve their practice.

The Action Research Project

In a light-filled event space in Petit Jean State Park, Phase 3 principals from across Arkansas waited patiently for their turn to tell the story of their work over the past three years and share their action research projects. At the front of the room, one principal stood with a PowerPoint presentation as his backdrop. The principal began by telling the room that he started his journey in the MPP as a relatively new principal. When he accepted his position at a high-poverty, rural school, he saw the need to help teachers develop their capacity to positively impact how students feel at school. He decided to make it his mission to change the culture in the building, because, he said, "if you can figure out the culture of adults, that'll impact how students feel." He said that his first effort was to build relationships with his teachers, something he learned through MPP is necessary to shape a culture for learning. He then worked with his staff to amend referral polices and think about how student behaviors are often indicative of factors in children's lives outside of school. With limited resources, he pushed his staff to think of alternatives to suspending students, and they created a plan for school nurses and counselors to better support students.

Presenting next was a principal from another district whose action research project focused on the goal of making learning more hands-on, to better engage students. Her presentation included several photos of students sitting in rows of desks and reading, juxtaposed to pictures of those same students collaboratively building a robot. To make this shift, she described how she and her faculty worked together to rethink curriculum, first doing a goal-setting activity like the one she had learned in an MPP session, bringing in the voices and opinions of her entire staff. Over time, she said, they were able to successfully implement project-based learning, and she described students in her school being "engaged for the first time in a long time."

Another elementary school principal described how she led the development of professional learning communities in her school. Teachers now bring student work samples to meetings with other teachers, and all work together to read and then grade student writing, an important process for ensuring alignment across classrooms. The principal shared that she is seeing students take ownership over their own learning.

In addition to fellow cohort members, superintendents sat eagerly in the audience, waiting to hear more about the good work happening at schools in their districts. These presentations are a special opportunity for leaders to engage with their superintendents, share their success stories, and receive recognition for transforming their schools. After the presentations, each superintendent met with their principal(s) to talk about next steps, plans for the next thirty days, and how the superintendents can be supportive. The morning of presentations ended with a lunch for principals and superintendents, another opportunity to build positive relationships and lay the groundwork for continued district buy-in that can lead to systemic change.

In addition, the MPP explicitly recognizes the importance of developing professional learning networks outside of the program. Leaders in Phase 2 are asked to think critically about their professional learning networks, which might consist of other educators whom they are connected to. Principals are asked to reflect on what they would like to learn and who in their network might be able to share their expertise or resources on that topic. They also are asked to reflect on something they might be able to share with others, to spread their knowledge beyond their buildings.

The MPP Helps Principals Focus on Teachers and Instructional Practices

While principals set expectations and create policies and practices to support deeper learning, teachers are ultimately responsible for what occurs in the classroom. In the MPP, principals learn to create conditions in their schools to enable teachers to better meet the needs of all students. The MPP prepares them to use support, collaboration, and distributed leadership to empower teachers to become continuous learners and leaders.

PRINCIPALS LEARN TO REDEFINE THEIR ROLES TO BETTER SUPPORT TEACHERS. The MPP employs a series of activities to help principals broaden their understanding of how to support teachers to implement deeper learning instructional practices. First, principals keep a detailed record of how they spend their time over a one-week period. The result: many principals who self-identify as instructional leaders realize that they spend a majority of their time on noninstructional issues. Next, after logging their time, principals work with their cohort members to analyze these data and discuss changes they can make to become more visible in their schools and better support teachers' instruction.

In Phase 2, principals learn how to use classroom walk-throughs to support teachers in shifting to deeper learning–aligned instructional practices. They also learn how to provide constructive feedback and support teachers' professional growth. As Brenda Tash, an MPP leader, described, "We spend a lot of time talking about classroom walk-throughs, learning walks . . . [and] the impact of those. Who's doing them and why are they doing them? . . . What difference does it make that you're doing that? We work on those kind of processes, and then making sure that they understand why it's important to see what somebody else is doing. . . . Observing teaching practices and providing actionable feedback, we have lots of learning experiences that go around that."

By Phase 3, MPP principals conduct classroom walk-throughs regularly and use the data collected to inform continuous school improvement efforts. In fact, 97 percent of Phase 3 principals reported that the MPP empha-sizes to a moderate or great extent helping teachers improve through a cycle of observation and feedback.

PRINCIPALS CREATE COLLABORATIVE TEACHER ENVIRONMENTS TO SUPPORT DEEPER LEARNING INSTRUCTION. Recognizing that creating a collaborative school culture is a key component of shaping a culture for teacher learning, the MPP models tools for effective teacher collaboration. All—100 percent—of the Phase 3 principals reported that the MPP emphasizes to a moderate or great extent how to create collegial and collaborative work environments.

The MPP teaches specific activities, including simple shifts, that leaders can use in their schools to foster teacher collaboration. For example, in one residential session, principals randomly drew from a hat to determine what table to sit at. Debbie Jones, a Phase 3 graduate, described how this simple activity "taught me about being very conscious of those people that hug the back and how you can make them become part of a meeting by moving them and getting them associated with the right people or being in the right place in the room."

MPP principals also work with their cohort to learn how to work with diverse personalities and leadership styles within their schools. In one Phase 1 activity, for example, principals identify their own leadership style: Do they make swift decisions? Include everyone in decisions? Slow down and learn everything before making any decisions? Reflecting on their own actions helps make the collaboration more successful.

The MPP also encourages the development of professional learning com-munities in schools. Leaders first work with their cohort to develop a shared understanding of the research-based elements of effective professional learn-ing communities. While attending residential sessions, leaders practice facili-tating professional learning communities. As they do so, they share practices they use in their schools and provide ideas and feedback to one another.

PRINCIPALS LEARN TO DISTRIBUTE LEADERSHIP. Developing the capacity for distributed leadership is also a focus throughout each phase of the MPP. Dis-tributed leadership is important for helping teachers take ownership of their own learning and for improving the instructional strategies used in a school. The MPP takes principals through activities that expand their knowledge about distributed leadership and the changes they can make in their schools to implement it. They learn that, by distributing leadership and empowering teachers to become leaders, they can create school environments in which shifts in culture and instructional practice toward deeper learning are driven by many staff members, not just the principal.

A few examples demonstrate the MPP approach. Leaders in Phase 1 read articles focused on distributed leadership, complete a self-assessment of how effectively they delegate tasks, and discuss their current practices, shifts they would like to make, and how to make them with the other principals in their cohort. Other topics for discussion include effective time management and the role of professional learning communities in creating a school culture aligned with distributed leadership. Discussions are guided by key questions such as, Are you the only person who can do this? and What would the other person gain or lose if they fulfilled this responsibility? Similarly, in Phase 3, principals lead small group discussions where they answer questions that spur reflection about specific leadership practices—for example, When should principals lead meetings? When should they be participants? When should they be observers? and When should they not attend at all?

Readings in Phase 3 also address effective staff coaching, and principals have opportunities to practice in role plays with their cohort members. They also choose a teacher for whom they will provide coaching, developing a plan to grow that teacher's leadership capacity using what they have learned.

PRINCIPALS LEARN TO COLLABORATIVELY DESIGN TEACHER PROFESSIONAL DEVELOPMENT. As MPP participants focus more and more on teachers' needs, they also spend time designing supports for them. Indeed, 97 percent of Phase 3 principals surveyed reported that the MPP emphasizes to a moderate or great extent how to design professional learning opportunities for teachers and other staff. In Phase 1, principals create a professional development plan during one of their residential sessions, then take it back to their schools for implementation and iteration over the course of the school year. They make adjustments, gathering more information about teachers' needs through classroom walk-throughs and receiving feedback and ideas from their cohort members. As these plans develop, principals gradually shift responsibility for professional development to the teachers themselves, empowering them to take ownership over their learning. Through this experience, leaders learn how to create a shared vision aligned to deeper learning and how to foster collaborative environments that support this vision.

Reflection, Authentic Assessment, and Feedback Are Core to the MPP

Over the course of the program's three phases, leaders regularly reflect on their current practices, identify their strengths and areas for growth, and make plans to improve their skills enumerated in the Leadership Performance Strands and Skills rubrics.

PRINCIPALS BUILD THEIR STORY OF PERSONAL GROWTH. From the start, MPP requires principals to use the Leadership Performance Strands and Skills rubrics to self-diagnose their strengths and areas for development. The application for each program phase requires principals to provide an extensive description of their competencies, their growth over time, the positive changes they have made in their schools, areas for further development, and plans for change.

Throughout the MPP, principals record their developmental journey in what MPP refers to as the story. The story is not merely an account of what principals have learned but how they have applied their learning in their schools. They reflect on their successes, their failures, and what they learned from both. They describe their reasoning behind, and the outcomes of, those decisions. They also record what they intend to do next to build on their successes and address the areas in which they fell short. Principals share their stories in each phase, and cohort members ask questions and provide feedback to help strengthen them.

As principals self-reflect and build their stories, MPP staff provide substantial, written feedback to each principal through the application process for each phase. The feedback is provided whether or not the applicants are accepted. The feedback allows principals to calibrate their own reflections against those from an external expert. It also provides another perspective on where the principals need to grow. Those who are not accepted into a phase are encouraged to continue developing their practice and reapply in the future.

THE ULTIMATE REFLECTION AND FEEDBACK PROCESS IS THE MASTER SCHOOL PRINCIPAL DESIGNATION. When leaders complete all three MPP phases they are eligible to apply for Master School Principal designation. The application consists of an extensive self-analysis and review process meant to fully evaluate their implementation of the five performance strands and their ability to enact positive change at their schools. Principals begin the process by compiling a portfolio demonstrating their effectiveness as a leader. The portfolio includes a narrative describing their journey to improving student performance, a continuation of their story that includes accomplishments after completing the program. They take a systems-thinking perspective in their narrative, reflecting on the successes and challenges they experienced in their efforts to improve the achievement of all students, improve their own leadership capacity and that of others in their schools, and move effective practices to scale in their schools and district.

Principals also provide evidence of how they have improved student and adult learning in their schools by implementing the components of each performance strand. Principals respond to specific prompts for each of the performance strands, many requiring the principal to provide three specific examples of their efforts or the relevant data. For example, the prompts for shaping a culture of learning include the following:

- Provide three examples of how you continuously promote a safe, positive, interactive, and supportive climate. Share the data you use to assess the effectiveness of your efforts.
- Describe the desired learning culture at your school. Provide three examples of how norms, rituals, traditions, common language, and cultural competencies are being used to continuously reinforce the desired learning culture.
- Provide three examples of how you build and sustain collaborative relationships and structures for student and adult learning and work. Focus one of these examples on your work with community stakeholders.
- Provide three examples of how you infuse diversity of people, perspectives, ideas, and experiences into the work. Focus one of these examples on your work with parents and/or community stakeholders.
- Describe how you, as a public leader, have used skills of influence, persuasion, and advocacy to help community members become social, economic, and political supporters of school and district improvement efforts.

The completed portfolio can be over fifty pages and is intended to be a strong indicator of a principal's ability to effectively lead deeper learning–oriented schools. It is scored by a designation team, which consists of two out-of-state consultants, an accomplished Arkansas educator, and a previously designated Master School Principal, using the Leadership Performance Strands and Skills rubrics. If there is sufficient evidence to score the applicant at a level four or five across all five performance strands, the applicant will move forward to a school site visit.

The site visit is a three- or four-day process to assess the principal's effectiveness. The first day typically entails the principal guiding the designation team through the classrooms of teachers with varying skill levels, from high performers to those needing improvement. These classroom walk-throughs allow the designation team to gauge the principal's understanding of strong instruction and the extent to which it reflects deeper learning principles. Over the rest of the visit, the team visits all classrooms and has conversations with as many stakeholders as possible, including teachers, counselors, custodians, aides, community partners, the superintendent, district administrators, front office staff, parents, and students. In addition, the designation team attends multiple grade-level meetings, vertical team meetings, professional learning communities, and academic coach meetings. They also observe student, parent, and teacher morning rituals and interactions. As one member of the designation team said of the process, "There's no stone that's unturned when we visit a school."

The designation team discusses the evidence collected, details their findings for each performance strand, and provides specific recommendations for continuous improvement, along with the team's decision regarding the Master School Principal designation. All principals receive this feedback regardless of whether they achieve the Master School Principal designation. Those who do not qualify are encouraged to use the feedback to continue improving their practice and reapply for designation in the future.

ACCOMPLISHMENTS AND DEEPER LEARNING LEADERSHIP IN PRACTICE

Since its inception, the MPP has developed a reputation throughout Arkansas as providing some of the best and most rigorous professional development for practicing principals. As of 2019, 705 principals completed Phase 1; of those, 296 completed Phase 2; of those, 175 completed Phase 3. In all, 37 principals have earned the title of designated Master School Principal.

In a survey, principals reported that they gained a lot from their participation in MPP. Nearly all (97 percent of Phase 1 participants and 100 percent of Phase 3 participants) reported that they were very well or well prepared to be a principal. Principals also reported that they were very well or well prepared for a range of deeper learning leadership tasks, including redesigning the school's organization and structure to support deeper learning for teachers and students (94 percent of Phase 1 completers and 96 percent of Phase 3 completers), using student and school data to inform continuous school improvement (92 percent and 96 percent, respectively), and creating collegial and collaborative work environments (97 percent and 96 percent, respectively).

Importantly, MPP principals have successfully made positive changes in their schools, such as creating shared visions, creating cultures of collaboration and learning, empowering teachers as leaders, using data to meet the needs of all students, and changing instruction to reflect deeper learning practices.

Creating Shared Visions as a Foundation for Deeper Learning

MPP's Leadership Performance Strands and Skills emphasize the importance of developing a shared mission, vision, and set of core beliefs among all stakeholders in a school, especially around high-quality, deeper learning instruction. MPP participants have successfully brought their schools together around such visions, crediting the program for providing them with the capacity to do so. In one example, Candie Watts, a designated Master School Principal, used an activity she learned from MPP to create a set of core beliefs for the school. She started the process by having her staff write about their individual beliefs, followed this up with a collaborative discussion, then facilitated a process by which they reached consensus. Watts uses this activity every year to reaffirm staff commitment as well as bring additional voices into the mission, vision, and core beliefs, especially as new staff are hired.

As principals participate in more phases of MPP, they put structures and policies in place that create the enabling conditions for the mission, vision, and set of core beliefs to become a reality in their schools. While mission statements created by MPP principals vary from school to school, many include elements of deeper learning, such as an engaging curriculum, a focus on the whole child, student-centered learning experiences, and a supportive school environment. Examples of school missions include the following:

- Invest in the whole child academically, socially, and emotionally to prepare them for success in their everyday lives.
- Empower students to be successful, productive leaders in society. We are devoted to an engaging and rigorous curriculum, to a safe and student-centered environment, and to innovative teaching and learning that is built on stakeholder collaboration to educate the whole child.
- Empower students to become lifelong learners through a variety of instructional and community-centered experiences that maintain high expectations while incorporating self-motivation and accountability.
- Provide a quality education; use resources through best practices; collaborate with teachers, students, and community partners; ensure a safe and supportive environment.

Creating Collaborative School Cultures Focused on Learning and Continuous Improvement

Professional learning communities are ubiquitous in schools headed by MPP-trained principals. By establishing professional learning communities, principals enable teachers to bring ideas to the table and engage in a process of continuous learning, growth, and instructional improvement. The culture of collaboration is a considerable change for many of the schools. As Watts described, "There were a lot of one-room schoolhouses prior to these experiences that we had together. It was a competitive culture. The culture began to shift to be more collaborative. At this point we are totally okay with learning from each other. We do lots of peer observations. That change has happened over time."

The newly developed professional learning communities focus on understanding student needs and improving instruction to better meet those needs. As principals implement professional learning communities in their schools, they put data in the hands of their teachers and empower them to collaboratively make decisions about improving teaching and learning. One high school, for example, created teams of four core teachers who share the same group of students and a common prep that they use to review the progress of individual students and strategize how to help those who are struggling. A designated Master School Principal similarly changed team meetings in her school to focus on teaching and learning. When teachers started using data to pinpoint where instructional changes were needed, they were able to learn from one another about what changes to make. As the principal described, "The biggest impact on class instruction happened in the team meetings, seeing teachers go back and implement those [instructional strategies] and then bringing their data analysis back in. . . . 'Here's our scores and here's your scores. What did you do differently on that one to teach that skill . . . because mine's not so hot over here?'"

At schools led by MPP-trained principals, teachers, rather than the principal, often led professional learning communities. At one junior high school, a team of teachers was focused on creating a more personalized and supportive learning environment for students. Facilitating a professional development session, this team opened with an activity for teachers to get to know each other better. When the activity was complete, the team transitioned to a conversation about how this activity could be used in classrooms to help students feel more connected to one another. Another segment of the session focused on decreasing student suspensions by helping students navigate difficult situations rather than sending them out of the learning environment.

Empowering Teacher Leaders

As principals create environments where collaboration and learning are valued, they also encourage teachers to become leaders themselves. Distributed leadership helps sustain a high-performing organization focused on strong instructional practices. One principal, for example, implemented the lesson she learned from the MPP about distributed leadership and empowering teachers. "I built just this much of confidence in leaders who were already here. . . . They could run the school. They don't need me to run the school, by any means, and they just needed that boost." Not only did these teachers sustain the organization, but once empowered, they took on projects that improved the school and increased connections with community members. In one such case, a teacher formed a parent advisory council in order to get a more widespread and representative group of parent voices heard at the school.

Empowering teachers to participate in school decision-making allows new voices and new ideas to enter the school. One principal, who described shifts in her conception of leadership during Phase 1, saw this happen when she made changes in her building. Before participating in the MPP, she appointed teachers as permanent members of the leadership team. During her time in the MPP she realized that more of her staff should have greater input into decisions and be heard as leaders. She now has teachers nominate the leadership team, who serve for a year, a change she believes has positively affected her teachers as more have undertaken "more hands-on planning things for the whole building, not just their classroom."

Fostering Deeper Learning Instruction

Many of the early changes evident in schools led by MPP-trained principals—developing a shared mission, creating professional learning communities focused on good instruction, and empowering teachers as leaders—are focused on creating the culture and structures for teachers and other adults to enact deeper learning. As a result of these foundational changes, schools have made good headway on changing instructional practices. A Phase 1 principal described the expectations in place in her school for active instructional strategies:

> All of our teachers . . . know that our expectations are that the teacher
> is always going to be actively engaged with the students. So you

won't see one of my teachers behind her desk. . . . She's always actively involved in the instruction with the kids and what they're doing. . . . You'll see that the teachers are promoting the children to question and question each other and have discussions.

There's a lot of student-led activities in there as well as student choice. They do have choices on the things that they're doing. . . . Students are actively engaged in the learning. It may be that they're using manipulatives in the classroom. It might be that they're doing a science experiment and they have actual things that they're working with. Most of the time our classrooms are not silent. You're not going to go in and see a silent classroom, but the students are talking to each other.

Many of the MPP-prepared principals have established classroom walk-throughs to support this kind of active student engagement. One school created a walk-through tool tailored to the school's instructional vision to help teachers implement new practices. The principal, a designated Master School Principal, described what they look for in classrooms: "We look for elements of respect and rapport between the students and teacher. And between the students themselves. . . . We also focus heavily on student engagement. Is the teacher more the sage on the stage or is she facilitating the learning there? We look for integration of technology, hands-on opportunities. We look for the level of questioning and discussion that is there. And then any differentiation that we might see." School leaders and teachers conduct the walk-through together, all using the same tool. Afterward, they compare notes and have discussions about the instructional strategies they observed.

Another principal described a similar tool that she introduced in her school: "We would look for the level of student engagement, how the students were involved . . . how much student-led teaching was happening in that classroom, or was it all the teacher doing the talking. We listened to how content was presented, was it . . . differentiated among different levels. . . . We looked at peer collaboration for those students, and how the teacher was guiding that collaborative piece, and how she matched some of those students together to work."

By implementing classroom walk-throughs specifically focused on deeper learning instructional practices, leaders ensure that teachers throughout their schools are using these practices, provide scaffolding and support for wider adoption, and identify those teachers who may need additional support.

This kind of instruction is required for designated Master School Principals. For any principal to earn the designation, the preponderance of classrooms in their schools must reflect deeper learning practices. A member of the designation process site visit team said that they look not only at the instructional practices evident in a classroom but also the students' understanding of those practices: "We set this expectation that students are involved in learning. So I'll walk into a classroom and sit down with a group and I'll say, 'Hi guys, how are you doing? . . . What are you up to today?' . . . And the schools we visit, kids have no problem with that. They tell us, 'Yeah, this is what we're doing.' 'Why are you doing this?' And they tell us why they're doing it."

Using Data to Individualize Support for Students and Teachers

Principals who participate in the MPP use multiple forms of data—test scores, teacher observations, conversations with parents, among others—to identify and support the needs of both teachers and students. For example, a high school led by an MPP-trained principal created a class period dedicated to meeting the individual needs of students. Each week, teachers submit a list of students they feel need extra support in a content area. The students then receive that support during the dedicated class period. Students not identified by a teacher sign up for a class they would like extra support in or for an extracurricular activity. This model was so well received by teachers and students that it has been adopted by other district schools.

Principals who participate in MPP also use data to differentiate learning for their teachers. One principal, for example, saw a need to better support her second- and third-grade teams in asking students higher-level questions, so she worked with the teams to develop questions in their lesson plans that they could take back and use in their classrooms. Her fourth-grade team had mastered higher-order questioning but needed support around project-based and problem-based learning, so she made that the focus of their grade-level meetings. Differentiating support for teachers was a notable change for this principal. As she said, "In the past, I haven't really differentiated the learning between the teams. It's always been 'this is what I'm giving everyone' as we go along. And so for this year, that's been the biggest change for me." This example, like the others above, shows how the MPP-prepared principals are practicing deeper learning principles and how they are facilitating, and differentiating, adult learning just as they expect teachers to do for deeper student learning.

Analyzing Data, One Child at a Time

It was a Friday morning at Westside Elementary School in Greenbrier, Arkansas, and grade-level teams were taking turns coming to the staff meeting room to have a group discussion with their principal about student growth over the past quarter. On the Smart Board at the front of the room, the first-grade team projected their check-in agenda, following the protocol that all grade-level teams use to set objectives that guide the content of the meeting.

First on the agenda was discussing the students who were not scoring as well as their teachers expected. A teacher identified one student whom she believed was having trouble reading English and may need to be recommended for special education services. The principal and teachers discussed conversations they had with his parents and their own experiences with him. "We'll keep providing supports," said the principal. "We need to build his confidence and cut through the anxiety." One teacher noted that he did well in after-school intervention time because of the small-group structure. "He's a leader and he's fluent," she said. An intern teacher noted that in class he tries to get out of reading in stations, concluding, "I think he might be shy." His primary teacher decided to engage the student in more small-group activities and follow his progress.

At the second-grade team meeting, the next to have their check-in with the principal, teachers gathered at the assessment wall. The assessment wall was made up of pocket charts filled with student headshots, with each picture placed in one of four color-coded quadrants: high growth and high proficiency (green), high growth and low proficiency (blue), low growth and high proficiency (yellow), and low growth and low proficiency (red). These charts are an effort to make sure that all students are getting the supports that meet their unique needs, and no students are falling through the cracks. As the principal, Angela Betancourt, described, she got the idea for these charts from a designated Master School Principal in her district. As the teachers discussed each student with the principal, they moved their students' pictures between quadrants, based on the growth students demonstrated on interim assessments, and made plans about how to support each of them individually.

Betancourt has used this practice for many years and has improved it each time. One such improvement was moving the practice from the computer to the wall. When the wall was on the computer, "the teachers would tell me where to move the students and I would do it." In contrast, "now the teachers physically take their little card with their little picture and put those kids where they are. They can see every week who is in that bottom club and who is not growing and not performing. They have their little name in their head and their little face. . . . I think it helps them keep more on target of not letting anyone slip. Not that they would ever do that intentionally, but they have a graphic, something right there on the wall that shows them who not to forget or who to make sure that they reach out to that week."

Betancourt has implemented a system in which teachers collaboratively determine the best supports for students based on their needs, using multiple forms of both quantitative and anecdotal data. This holistic view provides a better understanding of how each student's academic and personal life plays into their performance and growth as a learner.

FACTORS INFLUENCING SYSTEMIC DEEPER LEARNING LEADERSHIP DEVELOPMENT

The MPP develops principals' capacity to implement transformational change in their schools and districts. Its success is supported by its commitment to continuous program improvement, ties to other Arkansas Leadership Academy programs, and an expanding network of participants. At the same time, the MPP has experienced challenges such as limited coaching support, principal turnover, and misalignment with state education requirements.

Continuous Improvement Is Expected and Practiced

The Arkansas Leadership Academy is committed to continuously improving the MPP to reflect current research on school leadership and to support the evolving needs of all principals. The Leadership Performance Strands and Skills rubrics, originally developed in 2005, have been amended over the years to reflect changing ideas in educational leadership. Most notably, the rubrics were completely redesigned in 2015 to increase their rigor, make learning their primary focus, and better reflect a systems-thinking perspective. As one staff member described, "We've upped the ante so that we're expecting at the innovative stage a higher level of performance now that is more connected, integrative, innovative, and more complex."

The MPP staff also seek to continuously improve in response to feedback they receive through the designation process. As principals apply to and complete the designation process, the designation team compares their performance with the program's expectations as outlined in the Leadership Performance Strands and Skills rubrics. If the designation team sees any areas in which applicants for designation are struggling, they share that information with the MPP staff. The staff can then adjust the program as necessary to better support the development of those skills. With the designation process occurring annually, the MPP has the opportunity to make adjustments year after year.

Arkansas Leadership Academy Programs Align Change Efforts

The Arkansas Leadership Academy provides seven offerings, in addition to the MPP, that are intended to transform teaching and learning across the state. These programs—Assistant Principal Institute, Executive Leadership Collaborative, Facilitation of Adult Learning Institute, Leadership Team Institute, the Student Voice Initiative, Teacher Leadership Institute, and the School/Organizational Development Program—provide learning opportunities for school and district staff. These programs use the same Leadership Performance Strands and Skills rubrics as those used in the MPP. In fact, to send staff to any academy offering, a school must first have a principal who is currently in the MPP or has completed, at minimum, Phase 1. Blaine Alexander, Arkansas Leadership Academy performance coach, described the MPP as "the gateway" to the academy because of the important role principals play in school transformation. In essence, principals who participate in the MPP are positioned to support others in their schools and districts that participate in academy offerings. In turn, since the other Arkansas Leadership Academy programs use the same language, structures, and processes as the MPP, principals gain colleagues at various levels able to support their transformative efforts toward deeper learning.

Greater engagement in the Arkansas Leadership Academy brings more widespread benefits to districts. District-level participation in academy offerings helps drive the systemic transformation of teaching and learning and helps sustain structures and practices that buoy deeper learning. As Alexander noted, "When you have superintendents who connect with opportunities like the Master Principal Program and they take advantage of it, it just brings an added dimension to their district and building capacity for instructional leadership, and then additional capacity building throughout the buildings." For example, Jerrod Williams, superintendent of Sheridan School District, made it a priority to have staff from all seven district schools participate. As he said, "We thought that was so worthwhile, we brought the academy here and put all of our administrators through it. We put every administrator through Facilitation of Adult Learning [Institute] so everybody could have the same conversation." By aligning more school and district staff to the Leadership Performance Strands and Skills, Williams felt he could drive systemic change and ensure that change efforts across schools were complementary.

MPP Principals Form a Network Throughout the State

Through its cohort model, the MPP has created a network of principals throughout the state who can support each other in the implementation of their deeper learning–aligned change efforts. In this predominantly rural state, many schools are located in small districts or otherwise isolated from one another. By creating a statewide network of principals, the MPP provides opportunities for peer-to-peer learning and support. Kelli Martin, a designated Master School Principal, described the support she felt from this network: "I've gained lifelong personal friends through the networking. . . . I could find someone in every area of the state at this point. That's huge because the principalship is a lonely job. It's lonely, even with an excellent assistant principal. It's still all on your shoulders when it comes down to it, kids, safety, achievement, teachers, health, everything's still on you. But being at the [residential session] and having that network lets you get reconnected and can get you out of a rut . . . or even just being inspired by an idea from another principal."

The network also helps leaders recruit teachers and other staff with deeper learning–aligned visions for teaching and learning. One Phase 1 principal described how she has called on her cohort members when interviewing new teachers: "I just interviewed a teacher that was doing her student teaching at [another school]. Well, [a colleague] is the principal . . . and he's been in my cohort, so I can call him and say, 'Okay, tell me about her. Be honest. Tell me what you really know.'"

In Arkansas, Standardized Test Scores Define Success

Though the Arkansas Leadership Academy and the MPP have successfully improved instructional practices in schools across the state, the state's focus on standardized test scores can limit the implementation of equitable deeper learning environments. Arkansas schools are incentivized to focus on standardized test scores to measure success. For example, the goal of the Reading Initiative for Student Excellence (RISE), a state initiative to promote "a culture of reading" in schools, is to increase the number of students meeting the ACT Aspire reading readiness benchmark.[7] Likewise, schools scoring in the top 10 percent for test scores and/or academic growth qualify for additional per pupil funding through the Arkansas School Recognition Program. While increased funding can benefit teachers and students, the financial incentive could push some schools to focus more on increasing test scores than implementing the personalized, student-centered deeper learning practices encouraged through the MPP.

Coaching Supports Are Inconsistent

In Phase 2, principals receive coaching support to develop their stories. Coaches are assigned regionally, with each coach supporting more than one principal. However, coaching can look different for principals depending on their location and their coach's experience. To become a coach, an individual must be an MPP Phase 3 graduate but does not have to be a designated Master School Principal. They could be an assistant superintendent or a principal, in the same or a different district, with experience at the same school level or not. When asked about coaching, one MPP staff member highlighted it as a challenge for the program:

> I think the biggest challenge that we have is some principals need more support than other principals. If we had the funding to do it, it would be nice to be able to support them better. . . . In [more populated] parts of the state, those principals reach out and help other principals, but then in the rural areas of the state, we don't have quite the saturation. . . . If they don't have a support coach, they don't have anyone at home to help them through some of this. I think it's just the restriction of not being able to provide more personalized coaching for our participants.

In areas where there are more designated Master School Principals or Arkansas Leadership Academy program participants, some principals reported having additional opportunities for coaching or mentorship. For example, one Phase 1 principal had access to support despite being in a phase of the MPP that does not provide coaches. She received support from her district's contracted Arkansas Leadership Academy performance coach and was mentored by a Phase 3 graduate who is also the former principal of the elementary school the principal now leads. The Arkansas Leadership Academy has a total of five performance coaches to support districts through academy programs. Districts must pay a fee for this support, making it less accessible to those with limited funds.

Principal Turnover Affects Program Impact

As principals gain leadership skills through the MPP, they also develop the knowledge and skills that make them well prepared for district office positions, and a portion of the MPP-developed principals do choose that path. Many MPP graduates and designated Master School Principals move to district positions because of their demonstrated leadership abilities, allowing them to have a larger impact in their districts. For example, one principal was immediately hired as a director of teaching and learning in her district once she was designated a Master School Principal. In her new position she made it a goal to have all the principals in her district participate in at least Phase 1of the MPP.

While MPP-trained leaders who move into district positions can influence other principals and have a broader impact, this movement creates leadership turnover in the schools they leave. In some cases, the principal who takes over a school will join the MPP, but that is not a guarantee.

Principal churn can be disruptive to student learning, negatively influence teacher morale, and stall improvement efforts under way.[8]

KEY TAKEAWAYS

Arkansas Leadership Academy's MPP is a highly selective, three-phase, in-service professional development program for practicing principals. It is focused on systems change and builds leadership capacity in five areas—setting clear and compelling direction, shaping culture for learning, leading and managing change, transforming teaching and learning, and managing accountability systems—to foster equity and excellence in education. Principals attend three or four residential sessions per phase, developing skills and enacting policies that enable them to transform teaching and learning. Principals who complete all three phases of the MPP and can demonstrate an impact in their schools, including bringing more personalized, student-centered instructional approaches, are eligible to earn the designation of Master School Principal. The key takeaways from the MPP are outlined below.

The MPP supports principals' deeper learning leadership abilities by providing them with deeper learning experiences. The MPP has a clear vision for what leaders should focus on to transform teaching and learning in their schools, including creating collaborative professional learning communities that support strong instruction and distributed leadership. The MPP models these practices with principals, and principals practice applying these strategies with their cohort members before modeling them with staff and implementing them in their schools.

Principals who participate in the MPP learn by working on real problems of practice. Throughout the MPP, leaders address real problems of practice and engage in long-term projects, including action plans and action research projects, to make real changes in their schools. Leaders also practice reflection and feedback throughout the MPP, improving their practice and adjusting the strategies they implement in their schools to better meet the needs of all students and teachers.

The MPP continuously improves its professional development offerings. In response to changing needs, the MPP has adjusted its tools and practices to better support principals and provide relevant learning opportunities. MPP staff base revisions on current research and on the annual feedback they receive from program applications and the Master School Principal designation process about areas needing additional attention in the program.

A growing network of principals prepared through the MPP enhances the program. Especially in a state with many rural areas, creating a community of practice among principals makes the principalship less isolating. It also provides the opportunity for continued learning among network participants.

Contextual conditions can create challenges for program impact. Limited resources mean the program is unable to create a robust coaching program, and a state that values more traditional teaching and assessment practices works against the program's vision for deeper learning. Despite challenges, the MPP works to overcome barriers and support leaders in their efforts to transform teaching and learning in their schools.

Principals who participate in the MPP learn to create a shared vision in their schools that can set the foundation for deeper learning. Principals have shifted the culture among staff in their schools, creating environments focused on learning and continuous improvement, where all staff work together to achieve a common, collaboratively developed set of goals. Leaders who participate in the MPP empower their teachers to become leaders, and effectively distribute leadership responsibilities in service of the shared vision.

Principals make positive, deeper learning–aligned changes in their schools and districts in each phase of the program. Schools led by MPP-trained principals display evidence of deeper learning instructional practices and staff use multiple forms of data to individualize supports for both teachers and students. Throughout each program phase, leaders make changes in their schools based on the needs of their teachers and students, often differentiating supports to better meet the needs of all learners. Some principals have influenced positive changes at the district level as well.

CHAPTER 6

GOING TO SCALE NATIONALLY

National Institute for School Leadership

The National Institute for School Leadership (NISL) provides research-based, in-service professional learning experiences. NISL equips leaders to be architects of schools that create deeper learning experiences for their students, and does so at scale, providing a useful example of how to move education systems closer to the goal of preparing all students for college and career in the twenty-first century.

PROGRAM HIGHLIGHTS AND HISTORY

NISL strives to enhance participants' leadership skills to improve their practice and boost student achievement. A program of the National Center on Education and the Economy (NCEE), NISL works in close partnership with states and districts to offer learning opportunities for school administrators in all stages of their development. In NISL, cohorts of twenty-five to thirty-two practitioners meet over twelve to eighteen months, spending twenty-four days in workshops led by either national or local NISL-certified facilitators.

The NISL curriculum situates principals as architects who shape the conditions for teaching and learning, think strategically, use data to inform decisions, and build a culture of improvement. Problem-based, deeper learning teaching methods such as group discussions, case studies, role-playing, and a job-embedded action research project require participants to address real problems of practice. Between sessions, participants have access to an online portal with course materials, diagnostic assessments, and message boards shared with peers. Costs range from $5,250 to $13,500 per participant, depending on whether facilitation is provided by national staff or locally certified facilitators. It is a key program feature that these costs are covered by district, state, federal, or philanthropic funds (see table 6.1).

NISL operates in states and districts across the country. In some cases, NISL has worked with policy makers to make the program available to

TABLE 6.1   **Overview of NISL**

Program type	In-service
Mission	Helping districts and states create school and district leaders capable of designing and leading high-performance education systems
Targeted places	Districts in 25 states
Program duration	12–18 months
Degree or designation conferred	In some cases, completion fulfills district or state requirements for licensure or continuing education.
Program highlights	12 two-day intensive workshops facilitated by certified instructors, supplemented with session prework and engagement with online portal; action research project
Key staff	Certified NISL facilitators
Costs and funding supports	$13,500 per participant for a national facilitator; $5,250 per participant for a local facilitator. Funding is provided by districts, states, federal agencies, and philanthropic organizations.

school leaders statewide. For example, NISL forms the core of the Pennsylvania Inspired Leaders program, a state-approved pathway for principals and assistant principals to earn Level II certification, required within five years of becoming a school administrator. In other cases, NISL is implemented on a more localized basis, as in California, where it has been picked up by individual districts, such as Bakersfield City School District, as a professional learning opportunity for their school leaders.

NCEE first piloted NISL in 2003. That year, the Carnegie Corporation of New York and other charitable foundations turned to NCEE to learn what would be needed to create a top-level development program for school leaders. Josh Tucker, national director of scale-up at NISL, noted that the intent was "to create a program that was of the same caliber as leading business schools and military leadership preparation programs in order to impact student learning and achievement." NCEE undertook an intensive process of research, piloting, and field testing in developing its approach, drawing on more than $11 million in support from philanthropy and its own investments.[1] In 2005, NISL became its own division of NCEE, formed to oversee the implementation and scale-up of the program.

Since its beginning, NISL has been implemented in districts across twenty-five states, and in 2016, sixty-five cohorts completed the program.[2]

Over the course of its history, more than 15,000 school leaders have partici-
pated in NISL.[3]

PROGRAM PHILOSOPHY

With deep roots in research, the NISL curriculum emphasizes learning about
and applying evidence-based best practices to create powerful deeper learning experiences. This application of research-based practice is carried out in
the context of NISL's commitment to make changes at scale in schools, districts, and states.

Deeper Learning for All

NISL embodies a strong vision for providing deeper learning opportunities for students, and this drives its approach to leadership development.
Equity—ensuring all students receive appropriate opportunities and supports
to excel in their learning—is an inextricable component of this vision.

DEEPER LEARNING ANCHORS NISL. The organizational vision that drives the
NISL approach is centered on enhancing student learning. NISL's vision
statement articulates what it means for students to be prepared for college
and career, identifying academic development and the acquisition of social-
emotional and civic skills as essential for students' long-term success. It is an
ambitious statement:

> We want, *at a minimum*, to be sure that high school graduates are
> ready to succeed in the two-year and four-year college programs that
> will prepare them for both work and further education.
>
> But that is not all we want. We want students whose mastery of
> the subjects they have studied runs deep—they have the kind of deep
> understanding of those subjects that will enable them to learn other
> things easily when they need to and to apply what they have learned
> creatively and effectively to a wide range of problems and challenges.
> We want them to be able to synthesize what they have learned from
> many domains as they address those challenges and to analyze the chal-
> lenges they face so that they can address them. They will have to be
> very good communicators, in many mediums. They will need to be both
> disciplined and creative at the same time.
>
> But we want far more than that for our students. They need to
> learn how to lead and how to be good team members. We want them
> to set high standards for themselves and to be prepared to work hard

to achieve them. Their character matters a lot to us. We want them to know right from wrong and to do the right thing when it is not easy to do. We want them to take pleasure from serving others and being a contributing member of society. We want them to be tolerant and inclusive. We want them to be tough and kind.[4]

Connections between this description of desired outcomes and the tenets of deeper learning are easy to pick out. NISL's vision statement encompasses deep mastery of subject matter knowledge, creative problem-solving, effective communication skills, skillful collaboration, and learning how to learn. Furthermore, this commitment applies to all students, reflecting the essential connection between deeper learning and equity.

EQUITABLE ACCESS TO DEEPER LEARNING IS A CENTRAL TENET OF NISL. NISL seeks to establish equity as an inherent part of school systems. The program's conception of equitable education is summed up in the three words often repeated by those knowledgeable about the program: "all means all." NISL expects schools to hold all students to rigorous standards and marshal the school's resources to support all students in meeting that bar. Larry Molinaro, NISL's director of curriculum and operations, elaborated: "You really do have to believe that all students can learn, . . . that these students actually can do the work. And by the work we mean really high-level work. . . . If you believe that, then the rest of what you need to do is to organize your building so that you are making sure that all students get what they need to hit those qualifications."

According to the NISL philosophy, creating conditions for equitable and rigorous learning requires strategic decision-making by school leaders, particularly regarding the allocation of resources to support student learning. Realizing this vision of equity often requires a mind-set shift, a recognition that some students will need more or different resources than others to graduate prepared for college and career, whether that is more time, tailored instructional materials, or more experienced teachers.[5] Program participants learn to identify and implement strategies to disrupt status quo inequities and make real progress toward deeper learning for all.

School Leaders as Architects of Deeper Learning

NISL's view of education leadership positions principals as leaders of learning who facilitate the creation of rich and engaging school environments. According to an NISL administrator, this focus on the principal as an instructional leader has long been a hallmark of NISL's work: "When

NISL got started, the focus in education leadership was much more about being a chief administration officer. Somebody whose job was to make sure that the buses run on time, that the master schedule worked, that food services were negotiated. We were, at that time, very much on the cutting edge, if not the bleeding edge, of thinking about the principal's job as an instructional leader."

Reflecting this orientation, NISL emphasizes the role of principals as strategic thinkers, team builders, instructional leaders, and the drivers of equitable results.[6] Ann Borthwick, learning systems architect at NISL, agreed that NISL "helps develop school leaders as people who see themselves as leaders of learning and as learners themselves." NISL acknowledges the importance of applying sophisticated disciplinary knowledge to achieve high-quality instruction but views teachers as the professionals most directly tasked with that responsibility. Effective school leaders, in contrast, are charged with creating motivating and supportive environments in which professional educators can effectively teach and their students can learn. Dougal described the role that principals can play in creating the conditions for highly effective school systems: "It's not just as simple as a philosophy about instruction and learning. It's about the structures of the school day and the way in which you empower teachers to use time effectively with each other so that they can spend time discussing individual students, discussing their courses, discussing their subject matter . . . that takes time. That is what leadership is about: It's about providing those opportunities, which involves structures and incentives."

NISL's philosophy about how to develop administrators with the capacity to effectively lead schools for deeper learning is instantiated in three research-based conceptual frameworks that are meaningfully reflected in the curriculum: NCEE's 9 Building Blocks for a World-Class Education System, the NISL Wheel, and NISL's Conceptual Framework for Leadership.

NCEE's *9 Building Blocks for a World-Class Education System* articulates the features of top-performing school systems around the world:

- provide strong supports for children and their families before students arrive at school
- provide more resources for at-risk students than for others
- develop world-class, highly coherent instructional systems
- create clear gateways for students through the system, set to global standards, with no dead ends
- assure an abundant supply of highly qualified teachers

- redesign schools to be places in which teachers will be treated as professionals, with incentives and support to continuously improve their professional practice and the performance of their students
- create an effective system of career and technical education and training
- create a leadership development system that develops leaders at all levels to manage such systems effectively
- institute a governance system that has the authority and legitimacy to develop coherent, powerful policies and is capable of implementing them at scale[7]

The building blocks emerged from an analysis of practices common to education systems that rank highly on international student assessments. They point to the importance of providing rigorous and equitable learning opportunities that are supported by highly skilled teachers and leaders and overseen by thoughtfully designed systems of governance and accountability. The research also underscores that "a key reason the top performers have succeeded is the emphasis they put on the way the whole system is designed—how all the parts and pieces and those systems work in harmony, with a particular emphasis on the levers of structures, incentives, and feedback loops."[8] This systems thinking reflects the program's intent to prepare leaders who are capable of designing school systems that drive toward deeper learning for teachers and students.

NISL's vision for how the features of top-notch education systems manifest in individual schools is expressed through a second framework: the NISL Wheel (see figure 6.1). The NISL Wheel is centered on a single objective: "getting all students to the point where they are genuinely ready to be successful in college, if they choose to attend, and in the careers they choose for themselves."[9] The concentric circles radiating from that central goal describe the principal's toolbox for achieving meaningful learning for all students.[10]

The innermost ring highlights the factors that leaders are able to directly influence ("three keys to success"): high-quality aligned instructional systems, high-quality teachers and teaching, and high-performance organization and management. Achieving high quality across these three areas demands thoughtful decision-making from school leaders around learning standards, curriculum, student assessment, teaching quality, professional learning for educators, and continuous improvement efforts. The outer rings of the Wheel acknowledge the importance of equitably distributed resources; easily accessible, relevant data; positive school culture; and out-of-school factors in creating the conditions for deeper learning.

FIGURE 6.1

Source: National Center on Education and the Economy, *The NISL Wheel: A Guide for School Leaders* (Washington, DC: National Institute for School Leadership, 2016), 5.

Principals' control is more diffuse, and the pathways for altering these characteristics are less direct than in the inner tiers.

Finally, NISL describes the type of leader that is capable of shaping a school that reflects its vision through its Conceptual Framework for Leadership. Whereas the Building Blocks and the Wheel are based on an examination of the practices of top-performing education systems, the Conceptual Framework for Leadership is based on best practices in leadership development across industries, including business, the military, and education. The Framework articulates eight dimensions of effective leadership:

- Student of learning: Education leaders understand how people learn.
- Strategic thinker: Leaders have and apply a framework for strategic decision making to bring their vision to life.
- Advocate for change: Leaders must have the ability to get others on board for their vision.
- Builder of teams: Leaders develop a team that participates in leadership and decision making in meaningful ways.
- Creator of learning culture: Leaders create organizational culture aligned with their desired results.
- Ethical decision maker: Moral leadership is crucial to developing thriving schools.
- Communicator: Leaders communicate well with stakeholders.
- Driver of equitable results: Leaders believe "all means all" and act to support all students in meeting high standards.[11]

NISL was developed to prepare leaders to fulfill this vision of effective school leadership. These three frameworks—the Building Blocks, the Wheel, and the Conceptual Framework for Leadership—express how NISL's philosophy is instantiated at different levels of the education system. In short, NISL's philosophy is that principals who apply key leadership competencies to build school environments aligned with the vision outlined in the Building Blocks and the Wheel will realize equitable and excellent education for all students.

PREPARING DEEPER LEARNING LEADERS

Much like the deeper learning that NISL seeks to facilitate for students, the program pairs mastery of rigorous academic content with active and experiential learning experiences for participants. This combination supports participants in developing key dispositions, knowledge, and skills to lead for deeper learning. In doing so, NISL models deeper learning for participants, enhancing their preparation for effective school leadership.

Supporting Mastery of Deeper Learning Principles

One of the core ways that NISL equips leaders to build deeper learning schools is through its research-based curriculum. The curriculum is designed to build leaders' capacity to ascertain the need for systems change, act as instructional leaders, promote excellence in instruction across content areas, implement a system of high-quality, standards-based instruction, and

TABLE 6.2   **NISL curriculum overview**

Course 1: World-Class Schooling: Vision and Goals	Course 2: Focus on Teaching and Learning	Course 3: Sustaining Transforming Through Capacity and Commitment
Unit 1: The Educational Challenge	Unit 4: Foundations of Effective Learning	Unit 8: Promoting the Learning Organization
Unit 2: The Principal as Strategic Thinker	Unit 5: Leadership in the Instructional Core—English Language Arts and History	Unit 9: Teams for Instructional Leadership
Unit 3: Elements of Standards-Aligned Instructional Systems	Unit 6: Leadership in the Instructional Core—Science and Mathematics	Unit 10: Ethical Leadership for Equity
	Unit 7: Coaching for High-Quality Teaching	Unit 11: Driving and Sustaining Transformation
		Unit 12: Final Case Simulation and Presentations

provide coaching for teachers.[12] Participants' engagement with the NISL curriculum instills a vision for effective teaching and deeper learning and prepares leaders to formulate strategic decisions aimed at bringing that vision to life.

The curriculum is divided into three courses, each composed of three to five units (see table 6.2). Each unit is the focus of a two-day, in-person workshop. Course 1 introduces context surrounding global education and the global economy, as well as the importance of strategic thinking in effective leadership. Course 2 is an intensive examination of high-quality teaching and learning with an explicit focus on deeper learning. Course 3 explores the role of school leaders in managing and sustaining school transformation, building organizational talent and capacity, and developing caring and just communities that facilitate deeper learning for all. The curriculum is housed on an online portal and includes course readings and session plans, as well as diagnostic assessments, message forums, and videos.

COURSE CONTENT INSTILLS LEADERS WITH A VISION AND MOTIVATION FOR SYSTEMS CHANGE. From the earliest units, the curriculum establishes a vision for effective teaching and learning through exposure to the research-based conceptual frameworks developed by NCEE and NISL. Participants read NCEE's *9 Building Blocks* in preparation for the opening unit and later engage with *The NISL Wheel*. Both documents resurface throughout the program as touchpoints for leaders as they dig deeper into different dimensions of teaching, learning, and leadership. Throughout Course 1, participants consume research on global economic and education trends that conveys an urgent need for change in American schools. Participants study how American schools perform against their international counterparts and examine how other nations' school systems are structured to prepare students for life after graduation. A national NISL administrator elaborated, "We really push leaders to recognize that the design of their system is for an antiquated economy, that a majority of the students that are being prepared in that way will not actually be able to earn a living wage by and large in the new economy." One participant noted that this stage setting became an important take-home message: "By placing those pieces in front of us at the very beginning of the course, it [gave] me a deeper purpose to the work that I'm doing." Another participant noted, "There is no time to waste. That charge is what really resonated with me."

THE CURRICULUM EQUIPS LEADERS WITH A RESEARCH-BASED UNDERSTANDING OF DEEPER LEARNING. The curriculum is also designed to support participants in developing a solid grounding in learning theory. Course 2 dives into the program's vision of equitable and excellent schools by engaging participants with theory and research on deeper learning. For example, participants read research on the science of learning and development, including sections of the seminal 2000 report *How People Learn: Brain, Mind, Experience, and School* from the National Research Council. Later, participants discuss the concept of deeper learning and are introduced to evidence-based instructional strategies for promoting the deep content mastery and well-rounded skill development that defines it. Participants then explore the application of those principles for teaching and learning in core subject areas.[13]

NISL's objective in introducing participants to the science of learning is to provide the foundation for a coherent theory of learning to inform their practice as instructional leaders.[14] NISL's perspective is that when schools lack this sort of unified theory, it inhibits the alignment of education standards, curriculum, instruction, and assessment that characterizes the highest-performing education systems.[15] Principals, as instructional leaders, must bring those elements into alignment to support educators in teaching for deeper learning. In fact, nearly all participants (98 percent of those surveyed) noted that the program emphasized how to redesign a school's organization and structure to support deeper learning for teachers and students. Most (88 percent) felt the program prepared them well or very well to lead such a reorganization themselves, even though many survey respondents had not yet completed the full program.

EQUITY IS WOVEN THROUGHOUT THE CURRICULUM. Equity is a central component of NISL's vision for deeper learning schools, and the notion of "all means all" is interwoven throughout the curriculum. The equity conversation starts in the first unit when participants read *Leading for Equity: The Pursuit of Excellence in the Montgomery County Public Schools*, a text that explores one district's efforts to close opportunity and achievement gaps associated with race and class.[16] Participants return to the story of Montgomery Country throughout the program. Many other courses incorporate various dimensions of equity. As Tim Schneider, Louisiana state coordinator, said, nearly every session asks, "How does 'all means all' apply to what we're learning right now?"

Participants also complete a unit that focuses specifically on equitable, ethical, and just education leadership. The unit explores the notion that equitable, ethical, and moral leadership is an important part of ensuring all students meet high standards, which requires leaders to create a safe learning environment—academically, socially, emotionally, physically—and allocate resources in an equitable manner. The unit dives into ideas such as cultural competence and returns to international comparative examples of equitable school structures. During the unit, participants complete an assessment to understand their school's culture and an equity autoethnography to reflect on the lenses that they bring to this dimension of leadership.

THE CURRICULUM PREPARES LEADERS TO STRATEGICALLY ADVANCE A VISION OF DEEPER LEARNING FOR ALL. The curriculum identifies strategic thinking as the key vehicle through which effective principals can advance equitable and meaningful change in their schools. Schneider described it this way: "If your vision is going to be 'all means all,' what does that really look like to you? We teach our participants to think strategically, how to analyze situations, how to overcome barriers in that first course."

Participants are introduced to the NISL's framework for strategic thinking during Course 1. Their starting point is the development of a thorough, data-driven analysis of current conditions in the school. Lisa Bastion, an NISL alumna and current facilitator, described how the program "is structured in a way that really makes you think through processes . . . reflecting on your practices, seeing what it [education] should look like versus what it's looking like right now." Leaders then develop a specific vision to guide their actions, select strategies to achieve that vision, and take action to make change.[17] Throughout the program, participants practice strategic thinking by engaging in hands-on learning activities and grappling with real problems of practice.

COURSE CONTENT IS INTENTIONALLY SCAFFOLDED TO DEEPEN LEADERS' LEARN-ING. The NISL curriculum is intentionally scaffolded so that important concepts and themes recur and deepen over time. Molinaro, NISL's director of curriculum and operations, described how this structure helps to develop leaders with the skills and knowledge to make transformational change: "It's structured that way so they look first [at] this idea of systems thinking, the idea of strategy in Course 1. They then get into the research on how people learn, which is really getting into the classroom as a system. Then unit 7 is sort of a pivot point into this idea of how you actually build capacity within your organization to do all the things that you've identified in the first six units." Janice Case, California state coordinator, agreed that the curriculum is scaffolded such that leaders are confident in their ability to make change by the end of the course: "So much of the learning throughout Course 3 is very much about what they can do. They feel very much like they can control much of it, so it's a great way to take all the learning from those first seven units and then build on it in a way that there's a lot of confidence." Participants, too, noted that the recurrence of content and themes helped them create connections and adopt a systems-thinking mind-set.

Fostering Learning Communities

The NISL groups participants in cohorts that advance through the program collectively. As with many facets of the program, this is an intentional design choice rooted in research about the value of professional learning communities in supporting adult learning.[18] Josh Tucker, national director of scale-up, explained, "All of our programs have been developed with a strong foundation of research. That's not just the content area[s], that's [also] the pedagogical approaches that we use [including] the fact that we're cohort based, which is often novel for a lot of these principals. . . . They're actually part of a cohort and sharing. Not just learning from us, but from their peers." The cohort structure fosters learning communities among participants and supports the development of long-lasting professional relationships.

NISL USES A COHORT STRUCTURE TO PROMOTE THE FORMATION OF LEARNING COMMUNITIES. NISL is strategic in helping participants engage with and build relationships with their peers. Each of the program's face-to-face sessions includes interactive pedagogies such as pair work, group discussions, and hands-on learning activities, which enable participants to work together and learn collaboratively. Facilitators use techniques such as randomly assigning partners for activities to ensure that participants have opportunities to collaborate with all of their cohort peers.

As a result of these strategies, by the later units, "cohorts are true learning communities," said Schneider. "They know each other well, they've built a trust in the room, they're willing to share in ways they would not share at unit 1." One participant, a vice principal, described how his initial trepidation gave way to a sense of community: "When we first all came in, I think I knew everybody's name . . . but I didn't know them at all. I never worked with them. . . . I don't feel that way anymore in our cohort." Another member of the same cohort agreed that the cohort had developed a positive learning climate: "It's a comfortable setting. I don't feel like I'm criticized when I may say something dumb."

LEARNING COMMUNITIES BENEFIT LEADERS' DEVELOPMENT. Program staff and participants alike report that the relationships that develop within cohorts create a basis for participants to support each other's learning. As one participant explained, "We're sitting at a table with the mix of people and so when we're sharing something that's happened [in your school], people will say, 'Oh, well how'd you handle that?'" Another participant said, "It's the people for me that's the most appealing part. [It's] collaborating and having real conversations about real schools and real kids that we see on a daily basis." Another participant echoed, "People coming from different school backgrounds and contexts, that's been very helpful. I think the cohort is an essential part of it. I don't think I would've gotten nearly as much out of it if I hadn't been with a cohort."

Some networks offer support even after participants complete the program. That was the experience that Bastion, chief academic officer for Lincoln Parish School Board in Louisiana, had with her cohort: "Some of us that went through the program together from other districts email each other. We call each other. 'What are you doing about this? Did you see this new law change? What are you all doing?' . . . We have continued to be a close group." When Louisiana introduced a new set of student assessments, Bastion connected with several members of her cohort to discuss how they planned to use the assessments in their schools.

DISTRICTS AND STATES CONFIGURE COHORTS TO ADVANCE THEIR GOALS FOR NISL. There is intentionality in how states and districts implementing NISL construct cohorts of learners. In Bakersfield City School District, for example, the cohort was chosen to be diverse by role and years of experience, including principals and vice principals, new administrators and veteran ones. Mark Luque, assistant superintendent for educational services in Bakersfield City School District, explained that the district felt this blend of experience would foster more learning than a more homogenous group. In contrast, Louisiana's Lincoln Parish School Board opted to support the participation of secondary principals one year and elementary principals the next, with the aim of promoting collaboration across buildings.

Creating Experiential and Authentic Learning

NISL is structured to promote deeper learning among participants by incorporating engaging learning activities focused on real problems of practice and on personalized learning experiences informed by formative assessment. These experiences impart a sophisticated understanding of deeper learning and effective school leadership, preparing leaders to create rich learning environments for both adults and students in their buildings.

WORKSHOPS ARE DESIGNED FOR INTERACTION. NISL is structured to foster meaningful, interactive engagement with course materials to enhance the learning of participants. This is an intentional choice based on research about how people learn. As Molinaro explained, "We look at these key practices that the research shows apply across disciplines, the idea of . . . using multiple and varied representations of concepts or tasks; encouraging elaboration, questioning, and self-explanation; engaging learners in challenging tasks with supportive guidance and feedback; teaching with examples in cases; priming student motivation, partly getting to some of the preconceptions, and then using formative assessment as part of the instructional paradigm."

To promote this type of authentic engagement, much of the time participants spend together is structured around interactive, problem-based learning opportunities. Participants engage in small- and large-group discussions, analyses of case studies, simulations and role plays, and hands-on projects. As one participant described, "It's not like a sit-and-get; there's interaction, and there's a lot of time for collaborative conversations."

Practicing to Lead

The classroom is abuzz on a Saturday morning as a national facilitator leads a cohort through a workshop on coaching teachers. More than twenty school administrators—all active principals or assistant principals in an urban district—gather around four clusters of tables intently reading background information for the activity. After reading about the context for the role play, participants identify volunteers to play two roles: principal and teacher.

At one table, a first-year assistant principal prepares to play the role of a principal concerned to learn that one of her teachers perceives English language learner status as a disadvantage. The principal's observation notes, provided as background materials for the exercise, mention that the teacher focused on managing student behavior at the expense of meaningful content learning in his classroom. Hesitating, the participant expressed uncertainty about how to begin the conversation. One of her peers assured her that the group is a safe space to "try out" one of the hardest and most important parts of a principal's job and suggested she take a few moments to write down some coaching questions before diving in. Another suggested she try to anchor the role of the teacher to a person she's met in real life to make it easier to engage in the role play.

After taking a few moments, the participant started her "debrief" with the teacher, using the questions she wrote down as a guide to elicit reflections from her role-playing partner. Meanwhile, the other members of the group quietly observed the interaction, taking notes and scanning the guiding questions laid out in their course materials.

After the role play concluded, the group conducted its own debrief. One member noted that she liked one of the questions that the principal had asked and suggested another as a follow-up. Meanwhile, the NISL facilitator stopped by the table, quietly observing the conversation, and asked whether the participants thought having a coach with expertise working with multilanguage learners might be helpful. A number of participants nodded, noting that the coach's expertise would be helpful in addressing the concerns with this teacher's practice. The group continued to discuss and debrief, sharing their expertise and experiences with one another.

NISL PARTICIPANTS GRAPPLE WITH AUTHENTIC PROBLEMS OF PRACTICE. NISL participants have opportunities to apply new concepts learned in the program to real-world problems of practice. Tucker explained that NISL's focus on applied learning is reflected in "everything from the use of case studies within our program to the participants' using the diagnostics to bring information from their school back into the room." This reliance on problem-based and practical activities creates authentic learning opportunities as participants practice real leadership competencies in a feedback-rich environment supported by NISL facilitators and their cohort peers.

Participants also apply what they learn in the program to problems of practice in their own schools through the Action Learning Project, another vehicle for practicing strategic thinking and decision-making. NISL participants create a foundation for their projects in the first unit by completing NISL-designed diagnostic assessments about their school's context. These diagnostics generate data about areas of strength and potential areas for improvement and are designed to help participants adopt a data-focused mind-set for analyzing their schools. Janice Case, California state coordinator, explained the process: "They [participants] use the data from the series of diagnostics they take with us, and we walk them through the process of how to analyze the reports they get. It's an actual step-by-step walkthrough of it, which models for them how you look at data. And the idea is that they use what they learn from that series of diagnostics, coupled with the rest of their context, to identify a vision that they want to tackle." NISL encourages participants to focus their action learning project on a goal to improve instruction, but each participant selects a specific focus in response to their analysis. Examples of projects include supporting elementary teachers in teaching writing and working with middle school teachers on providing timely and important feedback to students.

As leaders progress through the action learning project, they develop strategies to achieve their vision and create a plan for carrying out those strategies in their buildings. Each unit of NISL incorporates a relevant piece of this process. There are numerous opportunities for participants to receive feedback during workshop sessions and, on an individual basis, from NISL facilitators. At the culmination of the project, participants engage in a structured evaluation and reflection about the process. This engagement with real problems of practice is intended to create authentic learning environments bridging coursework and participants' work in schools.

Personalizing Learning Through Formative Assessment

Formative assessment is an integral part of how NISL defines effective and equitable instruction. "Good instruction requires constant formative assessment," explained a national NISL administrator. This principle applies to students sitting in schools and to the adults with whom NISL works, explained Case: "At the heart of equitable practice is each person getting what they need. That includes the adults. So, if you're working really hard on trying those equitable practices with the kids, but you've ignored the fact that you're not giving more resources to some teachers who need more resources in order to be at the level you need them to be at, then we have a breakdown in our equitable practices."

NISL courses include frequent opportunities for formative assessment. There are two facilitators at each course meeting who listen, guide conversations, and offer feedback. One participant reported that her facilitators "really do model what good teaching is in a classroom," providing on-the-spot feedback and directing discussion. Participants are also supported with opportunities to assess their own learning and performance throughout the program. They complete diagnostic assessments throughout the program to reflect more generally on their practice and the needs of the students and teachers in their schools.

Surfacing participants' knowledge through formative assessment allows facilitators to adapt course sessions to better support participant learning. To ensure participants fully grasp key concepts, facilitators might slow down an activity, provide individual support, strategically pair participants for small-group activities, or shift their approach to ensure learning objectives are met.

Modeling Deeper Learning

Modeling deeper learning is another way that NISL strives to prepare leaders to recognize and enact deeper learning tenets in their schools. By using active and experiential learning experiences, NISL models deeper learning in action. These models support participants in developing a vision of what effective instruction looks like and introduces strategies that participants can apply in their own practice. Todd Baldwin, Kentucky state coordinator for NISL, explained that experiencing deeper learning equips leaders with a vision for their schools: "If I, the leader, don't know what [deeper learning] looks like for me, then there's no way that I'm going to be able to re-create the environment and conditions in which that can happen for my kids in my building. . . . Likewise, if I don't know what [deeper learning] looks like for me, I can't create those conditions for that to happen in my building for the teachers."

Although school leaders typically are not directly responsible for teaching students for deeper learning, NISL equips them with a robust understanding of effective instruction so they are able to create the conditions where such teaching is expected and supported. For example, one science activity required participants to show a representation of the sun, the earth, and the moon, develop a formula to find the distance between the objects, and explain their process. In this activity, the participants experienced hands-on learning and group discussion, and they practiced metacognition, communication, and collaboration. Essentially, they experienced deeper learning. While the participants were engaged in hands-on instruction, the facilitator made the modeling explicit by asking questions such as, "What did you see?" "What strategies did you notice that I made you do?" "What type of conversation skills did you practice?"

This immersion in deeper learning and the modeling approach are designed to seed effective practices. As Case explained, "If I'm going to bring this learning back to my school, to teachers and then ultimately to kids, I have to understand it well enough to do it, and I have to model the heck out of it. So we spend a lot of time reinforcing the idea that every time you stand in front of your staff, every time you talk to an individual teacher, you have to be modeling those principles behind how people learn."

NISL ACCOMPLISHMENTS AND DEEPER LEARNING LEADERSHIP IN PRACTICE

That NISL has been implemented at such a large scale—serving dozens of cohorts per year and graduating thousands of school leaders—and in a variety of states and districts makes it a compelling model. This is particularly so given the program's documented successes.

Several evaluations have shown positive associations between school leaders' participation in NISL and student achievement. One, a 2011 study in Pennsylvania, found that student achievement in schools led by NISL principals improved at a greater rate than at similar schools over a period of four years. The evaluation compared student performance on state reading and math assessments across elementary, middle, and high schools with similar student demographics and past test scores. In both subjects and across grade levels, schools led by NISL participants demonstrated significantly larger gains in the proportion of students achieving proficiency.[19] Another study in Massachusetts compared elementary and middle schools led by NISL graduates with schools matched on key student and school features.[20] Again, researchers observed significant positive associations between student achievement in reading and math and principal participation in NISL. A third study of the NISL's effectiveness, in Milwaukee Public Schools, also found small but statistically significant benefits for students' reading and math performance on state assessments.[21] These studies provide compelling evidence of NISL's effectiveness in improving student learning outcomes.

In addition to these formal studies of student achievement, the effectiveness of the program is evident in the deeper learning–aligned practices of its graduates. NISL graduates leave the program able to create collaborative learning environments for teachers, act as instructional leaders, and use

Inquiry-Based Learning Across Content Areas

It is morning at Cato Middle School, one of three middle schools in Bakersfield City School District. Principal Brooke Smothers-Strizic walks through the sprawling campus during one of her twice-daily rounds. On her walk, she encounters a circle of seventh graders dancing outside with their history teacher. These students have worked with their teacher to learn a vintage dance as part of their study of American history and are spending today's class session practicing for a showcase where they and other classes will perform. The teacher gives her a brief update on the class's progress as students partner up and restart the dance, unphased by the principal's presence.

Moving on to a sixth-grade science classroom, Principal Smothers-Strizic greets one of the students by name and stoops down by his desk to discuss today's inquiry, an experiment to test which way of folding an aluminum foil boat maximizes the weight it can hold. The teacher, Smothers-Strizic later explained, got the idea for the lesson from a special professional learning workshop that she attended last summer.

Standing up, Principal Smothers-Strizic quietly asks the teacher about grades for two eighth-grade students who are on the verge of earning honors, confirming the information in the school's data system. Earlier that morning, the principal had analyzed end-of-year grade data for nearly all of the students in eighth grade to prepare for a big end-of-year assembly and celebration and would, over the course of the day, caucus with a number of her teachers about questions that arose from that analysis.

On this brief morning walk, other classes, too, were engaged in inquiry-based deeper learning activities across multiple content areas. As Principal Smothers-Strizic observed these activities, she continued to check in with teachers about the performance of individual students, applying her data analysis and demonstrating the keen awareness of teachers and students necessary for deeper learning leadership.

data for improvement. They understand effective deeper learning instruction and know how to support it. In Louisiana and Bakersfield, California, participants reported that the program prepared them well or very well to be a principal (94 percent and 83 percent, respectively). Further, they reported being prepared for deeper learning leadership, in particular. For example, they felt very well or well prepared to lead instruction that focuses on how to develop students' higher-order thinking skills (94 percent of Louisiana participants; 87 percent of Bakersfield participants) and redesigning the school's organization and structure to support deeper learning for teachers and students (94 percent of Louisiana participants; 83 percent of Bakersfield participants).

With the district's first cohorts just over halfway through their NISL experience, administrators in Bakersfield City School District reported already seeing the benefits. Diane Cox, assistant superintendent of human resources, reported an increase in confidence and engagement from leaders participating in the program, and particularly among newer principals. She also described how NISL "opened the flood gate up" for new types of collaboration and learning, from Twitter chats to book studies. Mark Luque, assistant superintendent, also noted the increased engagement and networking among staff participating in the program: "It's resulted in principals at varying levels taking these topics back to their school sites and having in-depth, engaging conversations with their principals and their teachers."

FACTORS INFLUENCING SYSTEMIC DEEPER LEARNING LEADERSHIP DEVELOPMENT

NISL's preparation of leaders to build deeper learning schools is supported by broader investments in systems and infrastructure that enable NISL to offer executive learning consistent with its vision. Specifically, NISL's investments in facilitator development and support, partnerships with participating districts and states, and its own continuous improvement efforts all make possible the creation of deeper learning experiences for leaders, preparing them to create systemwide change to benefit teachers and students.

Ensuring Facilitation Capacity

The success of NISL rests on the skills of national and local facilitators who deliver the program. At the time of writing, NISL had 39 national facilitators; these are NISL employees and contractors deeply versed in the NISL curriculum who travel throughout the country running NISL programming. There were also 366 local facilitators prepared through NISL's Facilitator Certification Institute to lead programs in their district or state, as well as 250 or so facilitator candidates completing certification. This large and growing network of trained and certified facilitators is central to achieving the program's goals of effective and widespread implementation.

NISL facilitators must have a high level of comfort with the program materials and with facilitation in order to create deeper learning experiences for leaders. Schneider noted that facilitation is very demanding: "The material in the [program] is very comprehensive and you need to have very deep understanding in order to facilitate properly, which can be very different than just teaching a class." In addition to having deep content knowledge, Case noted that facilitators must display a high level of competence in working with adult learners, figuring out how to support learning "in a way that's almost like self-discovery, versus just being told." NISL's facilitator training and certification ensure that the corps of facilitators are well equipped to lead NISL along both of these dimensions.

FACILITATOR CERTIFICATION FOLLOWS A CONSISTENT, INTENTIONAL PROCESS. The process of cultivating a skilled group of facilitators begins in NISL itself. All facilitators first participate in NISL, giving them firsthand knowledge to draw on. Once aspiring facilitators complete the program, they apply to NISL's Facilitator Certification Institute—a six-day intensive program of study broken into two, three-day sessions. The application requires aspiring facilitators to reflect on their learning from NISL, including their action learning project, and describe the ways that they have applied that learning to their practice. NISL has found the application process useful for identifying candidates likely to succeed at the institute. This intentionality at the beginning of the process is crucial, as Case explained, because it sets applicants up for success. While there "could certainly be a counseling out," she explained, "it's rare because our front-end process is so strong."

The institute builds on aspiring facilitators' experience in NISL with deeper dives into key content areas and instructional techniques. The institute emphasizes themes and tactics used throughout the program, giving facilitator candidates a chance to think about the curriculum through a facilitator's lens. The centrality of equity in NISL's philosophy also shows, as Sharon Brumbaugh, director of quality support, described: "The theme of equity runs through everything that we do. It runs through the whole [program] and we drive that home to them on the first day of the institute." In the institute, facilitator candidates also become thoroughly familiar with NISL diagnostics and action learning projects. Throughout, facilitator candidates practice facilitation with the support of institute leaders and peers—just as NISL participants are supported in practicing key skills within their cohorts.

In the final step of the facilitator certification process, aspiring facilitators complete a video-based performance assessment in which they review a video of their facilitation, reflect on their performance, and identify areas where they see evidence of NISL's facilitation competencies. NISL certifiers evaluate the assessment, considering both the quality of the facilitation and the candidate's reflections on their performance. The importance of reflection underscores how seriously NISL takes continuous improvement.

One relatively new development is the adoption of a formal career ladder for facilitators that articulates different competencies across a continuum of development. The career ladder offers an example of NISL "walking the walk" of research on high-performing systems, explained Larry Molinaro, director of curriculum and operations. "We built a whole certification and credentialing process that actually allowed facilitators to grow and take on different roles." As with NISL as a whole, research plays a key role. For facilitators, Molinaro explained, "We tried to model the research from high-performing organizations."

FACILITATORS RECEIVE TOOLS AND SUPPORTS TO DEVELOP THEIR PRACTICE. After certification, NISL continues to support facilitators to ensure that they are equipped to implement the program well. Facilitators are provided with materials and tools including facilitation guides with detailed learning objectives, advice for facilitation, sample prompts, and additional information about the research that informs the curriculum. These materials help facilitators implement the curriculum well while allowing for a level of flexibility. Brumbaugh described this approach: "It's not an instructor guide where you've got to go step by step. . . . We want you to use our curriculum, we want you to make sure that you're hitting the major themes, but we want to also see how you think about delivering that."

All facilitators also receive ongoing support from national staff after they begin to work with cohorts. This support follows an individualized and developmental approach, the same one facilitators use with participants. As Case explained, "Our responsibility is to meet a facilitator where they are and get them to the place that we need and expect them to be." NISL often scaffolds the experiences of new facilitators by pairing them with more veteran staff. In California, local facilitators first cofacilitate with an experienced national facilitator before leading their own cohort, a form of built-in support that doubles as quality assurance. Josh Tucker, director of national scale-up, noted that this mirrors NISL's philosophy about best practices to support learning for teachers and students: "It's very much how we believe schools should work with students. . . . You want everybody achieving at a high level. The support you provide to get them there and the time required to get there might change, but your goal is the same high standard at the end."

For all facilitators, ongoing support continues even after their initial forays into facilitation. This, too, can vary depending on the needs identified. Staff from the national office might travel to observe a unit and provide on-site support, or they might connect virtually to provide advice on logistics or troubleshooting for tricky units. NISL also records videos of veteran facilitators and makes the footage available as a model for others. At a larger scale, NISL convenes both national and local facilitators at conferences that take up important questions around facilitation techniques, new relevant research, and the NISL's ongoing tweaks to the curriculum. The conferences are biennial, with a national meeting one year and regional meetings the next. Finally, as Laura Groth, field research analyst, noted, facilitators help one another to grow. "They share a lot of their own materials. They can say, 'This is how I customized this. This wasn't working for me, so I did this instead.'" These informal and ongoing supports complement more formal learning opportunities.

Creating State and District Partnerships
Because NISL is committed to scaling its approach to achieve maximum impact on student learning, replicating the program with quality and fidelity is crucial. Close relationships between NISL and the districts and states that implement the program create an infrastructure for growing the program without sacrificing rigor or quality.

Working with states and districts is an important mechanism for NISL to influence school leadership and promote widespread system change. At the most basic level, districts and states are indispensable partners in the sustainability of the program because they typically fund NISL participation for their school leaders. A national NISL administrator acknowledged that implementing NISL requires a significant investment and that, typically, "schools and districts just don't spend that type of money on professional development for principals." Tim Schneider, Louisiana state coordinator, noted that although the cost can be a barrier for some partners, "on a scale, it's a bargain."

Once a district or state has adopted the program, it has an important role in shaping the way the program is deployed. It works hand in hand with NISL to make strategic choices about which geographic areas to target, which educators are eligible or encouraged to apply, and which are ultimately selected for participation in NISL and Facilitator Certification Institutes. Districts and states advertise opportunities to potential participants and help to generate participant buy-in for the experience. Active engagement and support from state or district leadership can signal to participants that NISL is a priority worth their time and effort.

Coherence and alignment between the NISL philosophy and state and district policies are important for enabling deeper learning in schools, another reason meaningful partnerships are important for the program's success. For example, a heavy focus on test-based accountability may be perceived as at odds with providing individualized deeper learning opportunities, discouraging leaders from focusing on the creation of a standards-aligned instructional system emphasized through the program. Mark Luque, assistant superintendent in Bakersfield City School District, reflected that efforts to bring about deeper learning "only [work] when there is complete alignment within the district. NISL by itself is a very good quality tool to improve leadership development, but you have to have synergy and alignment from your board, your superintendent, your district staff. Without that, any program doesn't work."

Because NISL believes that system-level alignment matters greatly in developing deeper learning environments, the organization has expanded its offerings in recent years. It has piloted a Superintendent's Academy (a two-year professional development series for district leaders) and the Teaching for Effective Learning Series (a two-year series for educators working in schools led by principals who have completed NISL).

Investing in Continuous Improvement

NISL is committed to continuously refining and improving the program to enhance its efficacy in preparing leaders for deeper learning. This commitment is manifest in its investment in internal research and evaluation capacity. In recent years, staff have been recruited to help manage federally funded evaluations of the program. Groth explained that NISL has begun to ask questions such as, "When it's working, why is it working?" "What does it look like?" "When people are struggling what does that look like?" End-of-course evaluations are one area of focus for this early effort; NISL's research staff have been engaged in exploring how the daily evaluations submitted by participants can inform efforts to support facilitators and improve the curriculum.

Likewise, NISL's dedication to its identity as a learning organization is manifest in its investment in the development and capacity of its national staff. For example, national facilitators and staff are encouraged to participate in NCEE-U, an ongoing learning series that deepens staff knowledge of high-performing international systems. The series helps to inform NISL staff members' work on the program, with its focus on the features of exemplary systems. State coordinators have monthly phone calls to share information and learn from each other, and report that national staff—right up to the CEO—are readily available to support their work and learning.

NISL's commitment to continuous improvement is evident in its constant refinement of the curriculum. Tucker said that NISL is "very, very intentional about looking for what the latest research is." While avoiding "chasing the research and going after every fad," he explained, the organization "make[s] a point of reviewing content, delivery, and quality assurance along the way." Ann Borthwick, learning systems architect, likewise notes, "We're in a kind of constant process of revision and rethinking of how to sharpen its focus and make it more effective. . . . Nothing's ever finished."

The commitment to ongoing refinement and improvement is well illustrated in the substantial revisions NISL made to the curriculum in 2015 and 2016. The revisions incorporated recent benchmarking research from NCEE, refined the program's conceptual framework around leadership development, and created a flexible digital platform to house course materials. The core themes of NISL did not shift significantly during this revision, but the underlying research base and the organization of the courses did. For example, the units focused on teaching and learning were tied more closely to research on the science of learning, and the later units of the course focus more tightly on how to organize a school environment to drive high-quality teaching. The curriculum also was winnowed from four courses to three in 2016 to foster a more coherent philosophy around instructional leadership. As one national NISL administrator said, "It wasn't until the new curriculum in 2016 that we were able to intertwine [a philosophical approach to leadership] with what we were seeing in the highest-performing education systems in the world."

Along with revisiting the conceptual and theoretical underpinnings of the courses, curriculum developers sought to ensure that NISL's learning activities were structured and facilitated in ways that provided deep engagement with content. One important shift in the 2016 revision was an evolution in NISL's use of case studies to reflect a more analytic approach. As Molinaro explained, "When I talk about case study, I mean it's a case that gives you enough data so that you know what the scenario is, and then it talks about the decisions that were made. It's really murky and oftentimes ambiguous. The idea is to say, what were the decisions? How do I evaluate the decisions? Were they right? Do I think they were right? There's no clear-cut answer. We changed our cases to be much more along those lines."

This approach to case analysis is consistent with the principles of learning theory that NISL has built into other activities, and it provides participants with an applied opportunity to practice the diagnostic thinking they will need as school leaders.

KEY TAKEAWAYS

The NISL program is a case of developing capacity for deeper learning leadership at scale through evidence-based, in-service programming that serves school administrators at all stages of their development. Even as NISL continues to refine its approach to preparing leaders for deeper learning, the program has already reached more than 15,000 practicing administrators across twenty-five states with its unique approach to executive development for school leaders. NISL has equipped current and aspiring school leaders with the knowledge, skills, and dispositions to lead for deeper learning and, in doing so, has contributed to school systems' efforts to align themselves toward such learning. Through their engagement with research-based concepts and models in a supportive environment, leaders in NISL experience rich, authentic learning for themselves so that they, in turn, are able to provide leadership for such learning in schools. The key takeaways from the program are outlined below.

NISL operates in a wide variety of contexts but maintains a consistent, specific, and research-based vision for high-quality teaching, learning, and leadership that is informed by research from multiple disciplines. NISL seeks to deliver deeper learning for all students by developing principals equipped with the skills to create aligned and high-functioning school systems as instructional leaders. Its frameworks articulate NISL's philosophy on the features of high-performing education systems, excellent and equitable schools, and effective school leadership. They serve as the foundation for all program learning opportunities.

NISL provides a scaffolded curriculum and authentic learning activities undertaken in intentionally crafted cohorts. These program elements prepare leaders for the complex work of crafting environments capable of producing deeper learning among students. The cohesion among program elements extends participants' learning by modeling deeper learning, contributing to the development of leaders capable of designing systems and enacting practices that promote powerful learning experiences among staff and students in schools.

NISL has created a careful and consistent process for developing and supporting facilitators, leveraging close partnerships with states and districts that implement the approach, and engaging in continuous improvement. These efforts support the development of systems and infrastructure that facilitate the creation of deeper learning experiences for leaders. Consistent with its research orientation, NISL is committed to continuous improvement that promotes iteration and refinement of its approach over time.

CHAPTER 7

DEEPER LEARNING
LEADERS

Dimensions of Practice and Preparation

To provide equitable access to deeper learning for all students, school leaders must mobilize the collective resources of a school community with intentionality and skill. Enacting preparation and professional development to foster these capacities in school leaders is an analogous process. It requires intentionality and skill to translate programs' priorities and commitments into effective learning opportunities and experiences. In our close examination of school leader preparation and development programs, we aimed to conceptualize the dimensions of deeper learning leadership and illuminate promising strategies for developing these dimensions in aspiring and experienced principals.

The programs described in the cases differ in their structures, practices, participants (preservice or in-service), administrative entities (university, nonprofit, district), size, and geographical scope (district, region, state, nation). Still, their common commitment to a vision of leadership preparation for deeper learning and their shared methods of implementing this commitment in practice outweigh their differences. This commonality conveys a broader understanding: leadership preparation for deeper learning can come in many forms so long as key commitments and dimensions are in place.

It is to these key commitments and dimensions that we now turn. We began our analytical process by looking across programs to describe the dimensions of leadership for deeper learning as defined and enacted by the programs, their candidates, and graduates. This emergent conception of school leadership is intended to encompass the spectrum of knowledge, skills, and dispositions required to lead for deeper learning and equity in twenty-first-century schools. After we laid out these dimensions, we identified the program features and practices associated with each. Table 7.1 summarizes both the dimensions of leadership for deeper learning and their aligned program features. In the rest of this chapter we explore these

TABLE 7.1   **Dimensions of leadership for deeper learning and aligned program features**

Dimensions of leadership for deeper learning	Aligned dimensions of leadership preparation for deeper learning
Leaders follow and share a vision for deeper learning	Programs follow a vision centered on deeper learning
Leaders prioritize equity	Programs align leadership priorities with equity and social justice
Leaders build collaborative communities of practice	Programs create communities of learning and practice and emphasize collaboration and distributed leadership
Leaders provide deeper learning opportunities by creating developmentally appropriate and improvement-focused staff supports	Programs use and model instructional strategies for leaders to experience deeper learning
Leaders adopt a contextualized approach for systemic alignment for deeper learning	Programs prepare leaders to think strategically about, and create supportive systems for, deeper learning

dimensions and features at a level of detail useful to educators and other stakeholders interested in implementing leadership preparation for deeper learning in their local contexts.

WHAT DOES IT MEAN TO LEAD FOR DEEPER LEARNING?

Creating deeper learning environments requires a new conception of effective school leadership. In our study, this conception is laid out in the visions, goals, and priorities each program sets, and realized through program structures and practices. Through a comparative analysis of the programs, we identified five dimensions of leadership for deeper learning:

- *Leaders follow and share a vision for deeper learning.* Deeper learning leaders adopt a vision focused on developing students' deeper learning competencies. They follow that vision in their actions and intentionally build systems, culture, and norms to enact it in schools. Leaders' system building enables teachers to provide deeper learning opportunities for students.
- *Leaders prioritize equity.* Deeper learning leaders prioritize equity and social justice. They know the social, historical, economic, and political contexts of their communities. They understand how race,

class, gender, religion, sexual orientation, and other factors shape student learning. They believe that all students are capable of learning and achieving at high levels, and they structure opportunities to enact that belief while seeking out, and working to resolve, opportunity gaps.

- *Leaders build collaborative communities of practice.* Deeper learning leaders enact leadership as a collaborative endeavor with teachers. They create the time and structures to enable collaboration. They distribute leadership responsibilities and decision-making, relinquishing some control to foster deeper engagement from fellow educators, make good use of their expertise, and empower them with opportunities to be change agents.
- *Leaders provide deeper learning opportunities by creating developmentally appropriate and improvement-focused staff supports.* Deeper learning leaders provide staff members with developmentally grounded and personalized learning opportunities, reflecting the opportunities they expect teachers to provide in classrooms. They understand staff members' abilities and focus professional development on the skills and knowledge needed to create deeper learning classrooms. Deeper learning leaders also orient teacher accountability systems through a holistic, data-informed approach explicitly focused on continuous improvement and empowerment.
- *Leaders adopt a contextualized approach for systemic alignment to deeper learning.* Deeper learning leaders take a systems perspective to school change grounded in their local context. They know the potential levers for lasting change and how to use them strategically, based on the understanding that deeper learning carries over from leaders to teachers to students. They think about improvements to individual classrooms and to the whole school. They are diagnosticians, able to use a wide array of data to understand strengths and areas for development as they strive for continuous improvement.

This new conception of leadership for deeper learning is necessary to provide leaders the capacity to redesign schools and manage change, organize adult learning, connect to communities, and support rigorous, relevant learning for all students. For such leaders, deeper learning is a guide and a goal, driving them to create opportunities for both teachers and students to experience deeper learning in supportive environments.

WHAT PROGRAM FEATURES PREPARE LEADERS FOR DEEPER LEARNING?

Just as leading for deeper learning requires a new conception of leadership, supporting school leaders in learning to lead in this fashion requires new models of preparation and development. A cross-program analysis revealed program features aligned with each dimension of deeper learning leadership. Stated differently, there are five dimensions of leadership preparation for deeper learning:

- To develop leaders' capacity to follow and share a vision centered on deeper learning, *programs follow a vision centered on deeper learning.*
- To develop leaders' capacity to prioritize equity, *programs align leadership priorities with equity and social justice.*
- To develop leaders' capacity to build collaborative communities of practice in their schools, *programs create communities of learning and practice and emphasize collaboration and distributed leadership.*
- To prepare leaders to provide deeper learning opportunities by creating developmentally appropriate and improvement-focused staff supports, *programs use and model instructional strategies for leaders to experience deeper learning.*
- To prepare leaders to adopt a contextualized approach for systemic alignment to deeper learning, *programs prepare leaders to think strategically about, and create supportive systems for, deeper learning.*

A Vision Centered on Deeper Learning

To develop deeper learning leaders, it is important to articulate a vision for teaching, learning, and leadership that embraces the principles of deeper learning. Either explicitly through program planning documents or implicitly through the leaders' focus of study, deeper learning sits at the center of programs' work and informs the structures and practices of leader development. Furthermore, programs seek to enable leaders to similarly develop and enact their own visions in schools.

The Arkansas Master Principal Program (MPP) uses a set of rubrics aligned with deeper learning practices that embody the MPP's vision for what principals need to do to transform their schools. These rubrics focus on five key leadership areas—setting clear and compelling direction, shaping culture for learning, leading and managing change, transforming teaching and learning, and managing accountability systems—and provide leaders with a road map for developing and sustaining productive, collaborative deeper learning school environments. Of these focus areas, "transforming teaching and learning" is identified as the core business for students and adults, reflecting the centrality of the learning environment and opportunities in schools.

The Long Beach Unified School District (LBUSD) Leadership Development Pipeline is embedded in a whole-district system of teacher and leader development and thus is grounded in the instructional vision of the district, the Understandings Curriculum. The Understandings, which shape the practices of district leaders and teachers, are aligned with deeper learning. They emphasize meaning-making, conceptual understanding, differentiation, and collaboration. Because LBUSD recruits administrators almost exclusively from within the district, candidates in the leadership pipeline are already steeped in the Understandings from their previous professional development. In the pipeline, they experience the Understandings from the perspective of instructional leaders or "lead learners," keeping deeper learning–aligned instructional values centered in their work. Furthermore, leaders' learning and evaluation are guided by the Domains and Dimensions of Leadership Evaluation, which enable leadership for deeper learning through their focus on collaboration, continuous improvement, providing learning opportunities for staff, and meeting the needs of each student.

The National Institute for School Leadership (NISL) focuses on a holistic conception of student learning that emphasizes college and career readiness for all students, socioemotional and academic development, and deep understanding, synthesis, and collaboration. NISL's vision is captured in the NISL Wheel, which puts student learning at the center of a system of leader actions and institutional supports. This guidance is further distilled in NISL's Conceptual Framework for Leadership, which lays out a deeper learning–aligned set of dimensions of effective leadership. NISL incorporates this vision, and the theory and research behind it, into course content and other program resources. NISL's curriculum is designed to provide leaders with both the vision and the motivation to pursue deeper learning in their buildings.

The Principal Leadership Institute (PLI) at the University of California, Berkeley, conceives of strong leadership primarily in terms of student-centered and relationship-based concepts. This conceptualization encompasses both practical and theoretical aspects of the principal role and is grounded in empirical evidence about how social justice leaders enact equity-oriented agendas. This notion of leadership is operationalized by five core values that cut across all program aspects: engaging in reflective practice; fostering strong relationships through collaboration; embracing distributed leadership to effect change; taking a systems perspective; and disrupting inequity and striving for social justice in structures, practices, and policies.

These core values show up as consistent drivers of the program's design and are reflected in the Leadership Connection Rubric used to coach, support, and assess leaders.

The University of Illinois Chicago (UIC) conceptualizes strong principals as those who are change agents capable of leading underserved urban schools to improve learning outcomes. The program's vision for transformational leadership includes expertise in instructional leadership, organizational leadership, and practitioner inquiry. The program's focus on deeper learning is prominent throughout coursework and practice-based program elements. Participants learn to create school cultures with high expectations for all students, foster collaborative learning environments for teachers and students, and engage key staff in instructional leadership roles. The program emphasizes active and project-based learning from the principal to the teachers and students. UIC participants become proficient in conducting cycles of inquiry—the collaborative, data-based routines of diagnosis, planning, implementation, and assessment—that promote adult learning to improve deeper learning–aligned instructional practices and student learning.

Priorities Aligned with Equity

Deeper learning leadership development programs share an emphasis on equity and providing experiences that prepare leaders to make it a priority. Leaders learn to provide deeper learning experiences for all students, considering issues such as institutionalized inequities and distribution of resources, and use their position to shape policy and enable change. Programs recruit candidates from diverse backgrounds and experiences who have the dispositions to engage with and confront inequities. They then provide them opportunities to do so through coursework and field experiences.

UIC prioritizes issues of equity throughout the program. It recruits participants who demonstrate a commitment to social justice and constructs cohorts to reflect the racial and ethnic diversity of the Chicago Public Schools (CPS) student population. UIC infuses equity throughout all courses to provide multiple, scaffolded opportunities for participants to reflect and strategize. Also, UIC places residents in schools that prioritize equity, immersing them in the challenges and strategies of addressing educational inequalities. The learning community at UIC fosters candidates' engagement in equity issues through coaching and cohort relationships that enable difficult conversations and mutual support.

A core value of UC Berkeley's PLI is disrupting inequity and striving for social justice. The PLI demonstrates these values beginning with recruitment and admissions practices to build racially, ethnically, socioeconomically, and professionally diverse cohorts, prioritizing applicants with clear commitments to equity and demonstrated leadership capacity. The PLI also brings a social justice lens to each course with assignments like the community-mapping project, in which candidates learn how to identify and leverage community assets to benefit students. This lens encourages candidates to develop local partnerships, and PLI students have worked with community colleges, Boys and Girls Clubs, police departments, and youth councils. The PLI also partners with AileyCamp to model how leaders can work toward social justice and to expand candidates' understanding of what socially just instruction looks like.

The core values of LBUSD's Leadership Development Pipeline include an equity focus. Both the Understandings, which underlie district instruction and professional development, and the Leadership Evaluation Domains and Dimensions emphasize educating all students equitably. Equity is central to the district's professional development system, and since LBUSD does most of its recruiting internally, candidates are steeped in these values before they enter the pipeline.

NISL is committed to providing all students with deeper learning experiences. The program's conceptual framework states that a leader is a driver of equitable results who supports all students in meeting high standards. The notion of "all means all" is a mantra of NISL, interwoven throughout the program. NISL's vision of leadership practice acknowledges resource equity as a key enabler of learning and recognizes that equitable, ethical, and just leadership plays a key role in ensuring high standards for all students.

Collaborative Communities of Learning and Practice
Collaborative communities of practice represent both the means and the ends for leadership development for deeper learning. Learning communities convey important lessons about leadership for deeper learning. At the same time, the experiences leaders have within these communities, and the benefits they produce, have the pedagogical purpose of demonstrating the value of the structures and practices. Programs frequently employ cohorts for both purposes.

PROGRAMS PLACE LEADERS INTO COHORTS TO ENHANCE LEARNING. As a means, communities are a tool for instruction, reflection, learning, and development. Programs place candidates into cohorts to enable shared inquiry, create safe environments to propose ideas and ask questions, and provide opportunities to collectively grapple with what it means to lead for deeper learning. These communities of practice help leaders build on each other's knowledge and provide academic and social-emotional support to one another.

In the Arkansas MPP, participants progress through each program phase as a cohort, attending residential sessions and working together to complete the activities between sessions. This component sets up the conditions for leaders to practice key elements of leading for deeper learning as they share ideas, collaborate, and practice giving and receiving useful feedback. Participants learn new processes by practicing with their cohort before trying them in their schools. Activities are followed by opportunities for shared reflection and problem-solving through which cohort members improve their practice. The cohort structure also creates a statewide network of principals, providing additional opportunities for peer-to-peer learning and support and promoting continuous learning after the program.

At UIC, the collaborative nature of the cohort fosters strong relationships, enabling participants to challenge one another and provide alternative perspectives. The cohort is strengthened by the program's emphasis on admitting participants with shared values such as commitments to advance social justice and work collaboratively. The coursework builds on cohort collaboration, giving participants opportunities to hear multiple viewpoints and to prepare for a variety of school environments. The bonds developed—among cohort members, across cohorts, and between participants and coaches—create networks of support that last for years. The growing network of UIC alumni provides increasing numbers of UIC-prepared principals to serve as mentors and model the program's values.

Heeding the research on effective practices in adult learning, NISL creates professional learning cohorts and builds peer relationships during in-person workshops. Cohorts facilitate shared reflection and deepen learning experiences, and facilitators draw on cohort members' strengths to enhance each other's learning. These relationships often continue beyond the program as cohort members stay in touch and provide ongoing support to each other.

UC Berkeley's PLI also uses a cohort model, but it further divides cohorts into workgroups of four or five candidates. Workgroups are intentionally selected to represent candidates with different backgrounds and skills. Groups complete structured assignments that scaffold their growth, moving them from group work to collaborative practice. Having opportunities to collaboratively build skills and make mistakes creates a rich learning space.

LEARNING COMMUNITIES MODEL AND TEACH COLLABORATION AND DISTRIBUTED LEADERSHIP. Along with being a means of learning, communities of practice represent a goal of that learning. As participants experience collaborative learning, they develop the capacity to create and use similar collaborative structures. Being part of a community of practice helps participants see the advantages of distributed leadership in their schools even as they acquire the knowledge and skills to implement it.

Distributed leadership is one of the foundational ideas behind the PLI's philosophy, grounded in empirical evidence about the benefits of shared governance. The PLI encourages its principals to adopt distributed leadership models and collaborative work environments. Participants learn to do this through their engagement with PLI faculty and coaches, who model the program's vision of collaborative leadership in their check-ins, discussions, and monthly coaching seminars as well as in PLI workgroups, where candidates develop the skills and mind-sets of collaborative leaders.

LBUSD has created a de facto districtwide learning community through its professional development efforts. LBUSD describes principals as "lead learners" who learn alongside teaching staff, adopt inclusive decision-making models, and seek the perspectives of community members. Prospective principals know these expectations from their experience as teachers, and the LBUSD leadership pipeline models collaboration through administrator-run workshops, mentoring from practicing administrators, collaborative inquiry and evaluation visits, and participation in school instructional leadership activities. Furthermore, the Leadership Evaluation Domains and Dimensions focus on "a culture of collaboration and continuous improvement" and also "collective professional learning opportunities." Evaluation is seen as a collaboration for shared learning and the improvement of practice beginning in pipeline programs and continuing into administrators' practice.

Developing the capacity for distributed leadership is a focus throughout each phase of the Arkansas MPP. Principals learn how to create a shared vision of teaching and learning among their staff, guided by the stated expectation in the Leadership Performance Strands and Skills that leaders "develop and distribute leadership to sustain a high-performing organization."[1] The MPP takes principals through activities that expand their knowledge about distributed leadership and identify changes they can make in their schools to enact it. In one assignment, leaders complete a self-assessment of their effectiveness at delegation and work in small groups to identify shifts they can make to more effectively share tasks. Through this and other assignments, principals learn to create school environments where shifts toward deeper learning are driven by many staff members, not just the principal.

Distributed leadership is similarly emphasized in UIC's program. For example, UIC candidates receive coaching about gradually releasing responsibilities across a range of leadership areas, from designing and directing professional development to developing the policies for a school's multitiered system of supports. Principals learn that a sense of ownership among teachers is closely linked to teachers' deep engagement. Additionally, UIC participants focus on developing collaborative teacher teams capable of directing their own learning and supporting each other's. Mentor principals in residency schools use collaborative, distributed leadership models that prioritize teachers' instructional leadership and create a collective commitment to instructional improvement. They serve as models of effective practice.

The Use and Modeling of Deeper Learning Instructional Strategies

Programs incorporate deeper learning instructional strategies in multiple ways. They utilize coursework and clinical experiences to show leaders, through example and participation, how to use these strategies. Programs also emphasize developmentally grounded and personalized instruction in coursework, coaching, professional development, and assessment. These instructional strategies are employed in the context of authentic learning opportunities focused on real-world problems in schools.

PROGRAMS USE DEEPER LEARNING–ALIGNED INSTRUCTIONAL STRATEGIES AND MODELS. By modeling deeper learning instructional strategies in courses, the programs enable participants to experience this type of learning. As program participants shadow mentor principals, immerse themselves in their residencies, and work through realistic scenarios and case studies of exemplary leadership practices, they both observe and participate in leadership for deeper learning. These models and experiences help them to better understand what deeper learning leadership looks like in practice.

NISL uses problem-based teaching methods to prepare participants to recognize and enact deeper learning tenets in their schools. Participants practice strategic decision-making and other leadership competencies through case studies, simulations, and role plays. These active and experiential learning opportunities support participants in developing a vision of effective instruction while introducing strategies to apply in their own practice. The exercises allow leaders to practice leading for deeper learning in a supportive and feedback-rich environment with facilitators and their peers as the curriculum supports their learning through intentional scaffolding, with important concepts and themes recurring and deepening over time. Content-focused units also highlight what deeper learning–aligned instruction looks like. For example, during the unit on deeper learning in science, participants create models of the solar system, experiencing instructional strategies as students before discussing the benefits of such strategies.

The Arkansas MPP models strategies that leaders can use to build relationships in their schools and to support their teachers in employing deeper learning–aligned instruction. Similarly, leaders in the LBUSD pipeline experience deeper learning when they shadow experienced administrators who model deeper learning and include them in collaborative learning opportunities. Both programs include opportunities to practice deeper learning leadership followed by field assignments with reflective components that facilitate conceptual understanding.

Berkeley PLI staff focus course content, assignments, and assessments on the application of theory to a real-world context. The community-mapping project is one such assignment, allowing candidates to deepen leadership competencies in collecting, analyzing, and gaining insights from data, applying them in action, and reflecting on outcomes and implications in a cycle of inquiry. As theories of data gathering and analysis play out in practice, participants experience deeper learning themselves. AileyCamp also models deeper learning and enables participants to experience deeper learning from the student perspective.

UIC also provides participants with models of deeper learning. Residents work in schools that value and model the principles of deeper learning, where they can see firsthand the structures and supports that principals must establish to enable deeper learning environments and support inquiry-based instructional practices and performance-based assessments. UIC also enacts deeper learning principles through assessment and evaluation practices aligned with deeper learning, including ongoing formative assessments as well as a summative "juried review," a compilation of artifacts and reflection completed at the end of the residency.

PROGRAMS PROVIDE LEADERS WITH DEVELOPMENTALLY GROUNDED AND PERSONALIZED LEARNING. Among deeper learning instructional strategies, one of the most prominent is developmentally grounded and personalized instruction. Programs provide such instruction to their participants through a combination of assessment practices, mentoring and coaching, individualized planning and goal setting, and opportunities for leaders to reflect and self-assess. These practices enable programs to tailor their instruction and support to candidates' strengths and needs. Programs also facilitate leaders' development of the skills and knowledge that enable these practices in schools.

LBUSD's leadership pipeline prepares leaders through a series of experiences in which they receive individualized support. They are assigned mentors who complement their skills and areas for development. Mentors support leaders to reflect on their needs in relation to the district's Leadership Evaluation Domains and Dimensions and model effective approaches. For example, participants and mentors conduct classroom walk-throughs together and then collaboratively produce feedback for the teacher.

NISL's curriculum includes reflective components such as diagnostic self-assessments and reflections during workshops. Reflecting on their learning and examining their roles as leaders prepares leaders to think systemically and strategically. Courses include frequent opportunities for formative assessment, with two facilitators listening, guiding conversation, and offering feedback. Formative assessment allows facilitators to adapt course sessions to better individualize and support participant learning.

The Arkansas MPP also requires principals to self-diagnose their strengths and areas for development based on the Leadership Performance Strands and Skills rubrics. Principals record their developmental journey through "the story," in which they document what they have learned, how they have applied their learning, their failures and successes and what they learned from both, and their plans for building on successes and addressing areas for growth. The story is required in the application for all program stages and the Master School Principal designation. MPP staff provide substantial written feedback for each phase, even for unsuccessful applicants.

At UIC, mentoring by the on-site principal at the residency school and coaching by UIC clinical faculty contribute to individuals' learning. Residents work with UIC coaches to develop and continually revise personalized professional development plans. UIC coaches conduct weekly site visits and provide feedback on issues of practice. Residents' progress is assessed in monthly "triad" meetings of the resident, mentor principal, and coach and follows cycles of inquiry focused on candidate growth, goals, and plans. Aspiring leaders in the PLI also benefit from coaches who conduct observations and provide support as candidates become fluent in the daily exercises of school leadership. Coaches observe as leaders conduct observations and conferences with teachers, providing immediate, individualized feedback afterward.

PROGRAMS PROVIDE JOB-EMBEDDED LEARNING OPPORTUNITIES FOCUSED ON REAL PROBLEMS OF PRACTICE. Another deeper learning instructional strategy is authentic, job-embedded learning. Leaders focus on real problems of practice in learning experiences that are engaging and applicable to the challenges they will face as administrators.

The Berkeley PLI designs assignments that are extensions of candidates' daily work at their schools. Assignments push candidates to apply theory to their work, collect data at their schools, and conduct analyses through action research. Likewise, each phase of the MPP requires principals to identify a need in their school and develop an action plan to address it. They revise the plans throughout the MPP, gathering data, reviewing implementation progress, and working with their cohort and school faculty to foster improvements. Phase 3 adds another authentic learning opportunity, an action research project based on a real problem of practice.

UIC's coursework embodies frequent intersections between theory and practice. Course topics, assignments, and discussions are deliberately linked to the residency as course-embedded, clinically enacted tasks. In the doctoral phase of the program, candidates continue their learning through multiple cycles of practice, assessment, and reflection. The capstone thesis, too, is based in real problems of practice, requiring participants to document their cycles of inquiry and improvement as they work to build the organizational capacities of their schools.

NISL, likewise, provides principals with authentic learning opportunities to engage with real problems of practice. The Action Learning Project is a vehicle for practicing strategic thinking and decision-making. It takes participants through a cycle of inquiry in which they gather data on the school context, identify a problem, and develop a strategy to address it. Participants progress through this cycle in successive units of the program, creating a well-scaffolded research process with numerous opportunities to receive feedback, input, and guidance.

In LBUSD's pipeline programs, connections to practice are frequent and clear. Workshops, run by practicing administrators, include presentations, work-throughs of real administrative issues, and discussions applied to practice. Participants work with the district data system and have opportunities to reflect, share, and discuss connections to the context of LBUSD schools. Shadowing practicing administrators and working with mentors, candidates see and participate in school and instructional leadership while applying their learning in real-world applications.

Preparation to Create Supportive Systems for Deeper Learning

Leadership for deeper learning means working within systems, including classrooms, schools, and districts. Therefore, programs that prepare administrators to lead for deeper learning include a focus on systems change and strategic thinking. Leaders learn to create supportive environments for change, lead and participate in inquiry around system performance and improvement, and work collaboratively to implement decisions. This emphasis on strategic and systemic thinking and action gives leaders the tools to support and incentivize the deeper learning practices they are being prepared to lead.

The Berkeley PLI frames schools as systems, each steeped in its own culture, norms, and beliefs, which require a leader who can understand this complexity, navigate the development of teachers and students, and create learning opportunities that are deep, meaningful, and personalized. In coursework, instructors highlight specific systemic change strategies that leaders can employ to increase equitable outcomes for all students. In assessment center sessions, candidates engage in simulated scenarios where they provide instructional leadership, interpret data for school improvement, and analyze levers for systemic change. Additionally, the Leadership Action Research Project assesses candidates' ability to identify an equity issue in their school and lead cycles of inquiry to analyze, strategize, implement, and adapt systemic approaches to school improvement.

NISL's theory of action focuses on systems change at scale, and the program prepares school leaders to create and maintain change to support deeper learning for all students. The program's vision, rooted in research on successful education systems globally, positions principals as strategic thinkers who "understand the differences between strategy and tactics and have a framework within which to approach decisions in a strategic way."[2] Program assignments reflect this view, as exemplified by the action research projects, in which participants develop a vision for student learning in their school community and create an action plan to achieve that goal.

The Arkansas MPP focuses on systems change by building leaders' capacity to think systemically, collaborate with school and district stakeholders, and drive change. One of the program's performance strands requires that leaders "deploy an integrated management system for systemic results."[3] A related substrand tasks leaders to "lead change efforts to scale," in part by fostering a "systems perspective on how to leverage systems change."[4] Principals are required to demonstrate that they can implement systems improvement as they progress through the program. Participants record this process in their ongoing narratives of their change efforts.

The preparation of leaders to think in terms of systems is also evident at UIC, a program built on the idea that schoolwide improvement occurs through organizational learning. The program's organizational strand examines the history of schools as organizations, theories of organizational change, and practical applications for facilitating educator development, building parent and community support, and implementing supportive learning environments. Cycles of inquiry are a signature program pedagogy and a primary mechanism for cultivating organizational learning. Through repeated cycles, participants learn how to analyze student data and find patterns, and how to organize and mobilize teachers around shared learning using data.

For LBUSD, systemic thinking is embedded in Leadership Development Pipeline programs, which themselves are part of a districtwide learning and professional development system. Because LBUSD recruits and prepares administrators internally, they are already familiar with LBUSD's strong emphasis on shared, districtwide practice that aligns classrooms and schools to central office initiatives. LBUSD prepares them to lead teacher professional development in their schools. In this sense, a systemic approach is built into LBUSD's pipeline.

WHAT FACTORS SUPPORT SYSTEMIC DEEPER LEARNING LEADERSHIP DEVELOPMENT?

To successfully implement the dimensions of leadership preparation for deeper learning, programs give significant attention to their own structures and systems. Doing so makes leadership preparation for deeper learning possible and creates the conditions in which the leaders they prepare can enact deeper learning in schools. Programs, thus, engage in improvement efforts, make investments to build internal capacity, and work to support systemic change at the state and district levels.

A Culture of Continuous Improvement

Just as programs teach leaders to embrace continuous improvement, program staff engage in continuous learning for program improvement. They conduct cycles of data collection, analysis, and reflection to enhance their own capacity to build candidates' deeper learning leadership capabilities. They work to revise and update their practices to better meet the needs of their candidates and to advance leadership for deeper learning.

The strength of UIC's program is due, in part, to its commitment to continuous self-improvement. Five full-time doctoral-level research staff study program impact using a comprehensive participant data tracking system. UIC has demonstrated a commitment to improvement through multiple rounds of program redesign. Through these efforts, UIC has revamped academic courses, improved tools and protocols, enhanced collaboration with CPS, bolstered funding streams, and focused EdD program completion on the improvement of organizational capacity and performance.

NISL was established through an intensive process of research, piloting, and field testing. The curriculum is the subject of constant refinement, as shown in the substantial revisions that incorporated benchmarking research from the National Center on Education and the Economy, refined the program's conceptual framework around leadership development, created more connections across units, and shifted case studies to a more analytic approach. Moving forward, NISL has invested in its internal research capacity, hiring staff to carry out a formative evaluation effort to support facilitators and improve the curriculum, while engaging with external evaluators to understand the program impact and inform its improvement efforts.

The Arkansas Leadership Academy completely redesigned its Leadership Performance Strands and Skills to focus on learning and systems change rather than on management. The revised rubrics incorporated a higher standard of rigor and connections to other leadership programs in Arkansas and to state and national standards. The MPP also engages in ongoing improvement efforts using feedback received through the Master School Principal designation process. The team that assesses applicants for the designation shares information about principals' skill development, including trends that highlight gaps in performance. The MPP uses this information to adjust programming to better support principals' learning.

Internal Capacity Building

Programs also take steps to build internal capacity to support leadership preparation for deeper learning. Efforts include developing staff and making connections that strengthen the program and its impact. The Berkeley PLI builds program capacity through its intentional recruitment, training, and support of coaches. The PLI combines a rigorous, multistage hiring process for coaches with intensive training and monthly collaborative seminars. Coaches have opportunities to seek guidance from one another and to participate in peer coaching sessions. NISL also invests in staff development and has created a thorough and consistent process for preparing and supporting program facilitators. Potential facilitators must apply to NISL's Facilitator Certification Institute, complete the six-day program, and prepare a video-based performance assessment. After certification, NISL facilitators regularly complete formative assessments to support their development, and all facilitators receive ongoing support from national staff and through conferences.

Other programs build capacity through internal collaboration. At UIC, collaboration is a key structural feature, and this extends to the relationship between the leadership program and the UIC College of Education. The

College of Education has supported the program by establishing and funding the Center for Urban Education Leadership, funding faculty positions for leadership coaching, paying resident salaries, and securing research grants. At LBUSD, the capacity of the Leadership Development Pipeline is enhanced by connections to the districtwide professional development system. The pipeline is built on, extends, and is supported by this system. District professional development serves as a route for identifying experienced, high-performing teachers as potential school leaders. Once in the pipeline, leaders sustain school- and districtwide leadership capability.

Systemic Change Efforts at District and State Levels

Programs that prepare leaders for systems change also work to support change at state and district levels. District-level change is facilitated through partnerships. UIC's yearlong residency is made possible by its mutually beneficial partnership with CPS, based on a shared understanding of what good leadership looks like. Through the partnership, UIC collaborated with CPS and other local programs to develop the district's principal competencies. Additionally, CPS has provided financial support for the program since its inception, and UIC has, in turn, hired a formal liaison to the district. Likewise, UC Berkeley's PLI leverages its partnerships with four nearby districts to strengthen recruitment and assemble racially diverse and talented cohorts. The partner districts benefit over time as nearly half of the program's almost 600 graduates have gone to work in them.

The Arkansas Leadership Academy takes a different tack, working beyond the MPP to spark systemwide educational improvements. The MPP is one in a suite of offerings by the Arkansas Leadership Academy, including programs for assistant principals, teacher leaders, school leadership teams, district administrators, and others. These programs, all based on the Strands and Skills, work together to support the transformation of teaching and learning and provide opportunities for school and district personnel to collaboratively build a foundation for deeper learning. District-level participation in academy offerings drives the systemic transformation of teaching and learning and can help ensure that structures and practices that advance deeper learning are sustained over time.

NISL focuses on school leaders as change agents as part of a strong commitment to promoting systems change at scale. In pursuit of this goal, NISL has been implemented across twenty-five states in an array of contexts, both urban and rural, serving student bodies of varying demographics. The program may be implemented statewide or in individual districts. The goal of large-scale systems change to make an impact on student learning, however, brings with it concerns for program quality and fidelity. NISL has created an infrastructure to support rigor and quality by building close relationships with the districts and states that implement the program.

FINAL THOUGHTS ON LEADERSHIP PREPARATION FOR DEEPER LEARNING

As we have described, leadership preparation for deeper learning takes many forms, though its core elements can be described succinctly: follow a deeper learning vision, align priorities with equity, create and emphasize learning communities, model the instruction leaders should promote, and teach systemic thinking. To implement these dimensions, program designers need to consider their own capacity, local context, the history and resources of the local schools and districts, the experiences and skills of the school leaders and educators, and the students being served. The examples laid out here are a starting point for program planning and implementation, which itself must entail a process of deeper learning.

While these dimensions may appear similar to popular conceptions of school leadership and preparation, it is their laser focus on deeper learning principles that sets them apart. While it is expected that school leaders have a vision, deeper learning leaders center that vision on active learning pedagogies, equity, and educating the whole child. While all school leaders develop their staff, deeper learning leaders do so in a way that reflects deeper learning for adults and builds staff capacity to enact the same practices in classrooms. Likewise, the features of the programs we studied are not unique, but their focus on deeper learning content and pedagogical strategies is. Many preparation and development programs require internships and residencies. However, in these programs, clinical experiences are completed in deeper learning–aligned schools and focused on developing the knowledge and skills to create and sustain such schools.

In other words, the visions, structures, and practices described here enable the programs to develop not just high-quality principals but high-quality principals able to promote deeper learning and equity. Such school leaders are needed to support teachers who enact deeper learning in their classrooms. These leaders and teachers, working together and with other educators, administrators and staff, and communities and families, can create deeper learning schools and districts. The unique focus of the programs described here, and of the leaders they prepare and develop, is what enables them to be part of the work of transforming education systems to provide all students with access to deeper learning experiences.

CHAPTER 8

POLICIES FOR LEADERSHIP DEVELOPMENT

For educators and stakeholders who share the goal of transforming education systems to make deeper learning opportunities available for all students, the features and practices of the leadership development programs described here can provide ideas and guidance for program development and improvement. Yet, program-level efforts are not carried out in a vacuum; they succeed or fail in the context of education systems shaped by federal, state, and local policy. Therefore, even though program-level efforts are essential, attention to these systems and their requirements, incentives, and barriers is necessary to enact transformative change. Just as school leaders create environments in which deeper learning can thrive, policy makers construct supports and incentives for deeper learning leadership preparation and development programs while also removing barriers that stand in their way.

To aid them in doing so, we have identified six policy priorities:

- define and operationalize high-quality leadership practice
- incorporate performance assessments to evaluate principals' effectiveness
- provide funding and supports for high-quality clinical partnerships
- create pipelines for promising candidates
- encourage targeted recruiting of leadership candidates
- underwrite leader training

DEFINE AND OPERATIONALIZE HIGH-QUALITY LEADERSHIP PRACTICE

A key feature of the leadership development programs highlighted here is their articulation and enactment of a vision aligned to deeper learning. States seeking to enable programs to formulate and enact such a vision should consider the role of state standards in making this possible. Across the programs studied, the standards, rubrics, and assessments through which they operationalized their priorities were informed by and aligned with state school leadership standards. For example, the Arkansas Master Principal Program (MPP) articulates its vision in its Performance Strands and Skills and accompanying rubrics. These, in turn, are aligned to the standards for the Arkansas Leader Excellence and Development System and to the Interstate School Leaders Licensure Consortium Standards, which the Arkansas Department of Education has adopted.

Other examples show that aligning programs to state standards can go hand in hand with local design efforts. The Berkeley Principal Leadership Institute (PLI) Leadership Connection Rubric, which guides the coaching, support, and assessment of program participants, made use of the California Professional Standards for Educational Leaders, such that the rubric "aligns with and encompasses" the standards, but "with a specific emphasis on equity and social justice."[1] At the Long Beach Unified School District (LBUSD), the Leadership Evaluation Domains and Dimensions, which lay out what leaders should know and be able to do in the Leadership Pipeline programs, draw on state and national standards.

Because state school leader standards have significant potential to influence leadership development programs, the content of these standards matters. States should consider the degree of alignment between their standards and leadership for deeper learning. While this book can help the process of alignment, states can also look to innovative programs within their own borders, as illustrated by University of Illinois Chicago (UIC). Illinois sponsored a series of state initiatives, including the creation of the Illinois School Leader Task Force, chaired by UIC's Steve Tozer. The task force's recommendations were shaped in part by UIC's earlier program revisions and called for new standards, selective admissions, residencies, and partnerships between districts and leadership preparation programs. The result was a revision to state program accreditation standards.

Through standards, requirements, and expectations for school leaders, states can incentivize and support leadership preparation programs' adoption and enactment of visions aligned with deeper learning. Importantly, the incorporation of state-level standards and expectations does not preclude efforts to design programs responsive to local needs. Indeed, the relationship between state agencies and leadership development programs can be two-way, with innovative programs informing state systems, which can then support broader innovation as state standards are operationalized across programs.

INCORPORATE PERFORMANCE ASSESSMENTS TO EVALUATE PRINCIPALS' EFFECTIVENESS

Performance assessments can authentically measure candidates' leadership capacity, inform the personalization of candidates' support, and create connections between program learning opportunities and the work of school leadership. Because of these multiple uses, state and program adoption of performance assessments aligned with deeper learning leadership can be a compelling driver for program change. Performance assessments can both influence program design and ensure program completers have the requisite knowledge and skills to lead for deeper learning.

The Berkeley PLI illustrates the multiple roles of performance assessments. Throughout the program, candidates complete case studies, presentations, group work, and action research projects. Such assessments help gauge candidates' development of the skills and competencies set forth in the Leadership Connection Rubric. Performance assessment is perhaps best exemplified by the program's assessment centers, in which candidates work through real-world scenarios and receive immediate feedback.

UIC also incorporates performance-based assessments at multiple points, providing rich information about candidate learning. A key assessment is the "juried review" that participants complete at the end of their residencies, for which they compile artifacts, complete a written reflection, and present their work to program faculty. Data from this review provide deep insights on candidate development.

Performance-based rubrics can support the design and scoring of performance assessments. At LBUSD, the Leadership Evaluation Domains and Dimensions are used across the leadership pipeline to assess performance through observations, reviews of leaders' work, artifacts of practice, and school data. Similarly, the Arkansas Leadership Academy's Performance Strands and Skills identify deeper learning–aligned, critical skills against which MPP candidates are assessed. The MPP makes use of these rubrics in leaders' self-diagnoses of their strengths and areas for development, particularly in the applications for each program phase and for Master Principal designation.

PROVIDE FUNDING AND SUPPORTS FOR HIGH-QUALITY CLINICAL PARTNERSHIPS

Support for clinical partnerships between programs and districts can ensure that internships and residencies—critical features of high-quality preparation—become universal and sustainable. Partnerships between leadership preparation programs and K–12 districts that include joint financial support, design input, and responsibility can ensure a clear and consistent vision for deeper learning. They also can link preparation to local contexts and connect initial preparation, early career support, and ongoing professional development.

Partnerships are essential to both preservice and in-service programs. At Berkeley, the PLI has developed strong relationships with four partner districts. These partnerships support candidates' clinical placement and coaching, strengthen recruitment, and create extended communities of practice among teachers and administrators who have completed the program and share its mission. Likewise, many of UIC's features—the yearlong residency, connections between coursework and practice-based requirements, mentorship and coaching, integration of academic and site-based faculty— are implemented through the robust partnership between the program and Chicago Public Schools (CPS).

Even for programs not based in districts or institutions of higher education, district partnerships prove to be important. The Arkansas MPP goals for leaders are only possible with the support of districts; superintendents are necessary to support principals' program participation and enable them to attend residential sessions. The Arkansas Leadership Academy tightens relationships with districts by making schools' participation in other academy offerings contingent on their principals' current or past participation in the MPP. This requirement enables MPP principals to work in concert with school teams that attend academy trainings and share a deeper learning vision. Partnerships with districts and states allow the National Institute for School Leadership (NISL) program to function. Districts and states typically fund leaders' participation in the program, and they work with NISL to publicize the program, choose district sites, and make eligibility determinations and selection decisions. It is this collaboration that enables the large-scale replication of the program with quality and fidelity.

While much of the work of establishing and maintaining partnerships happens in programs and districts, states interested in incentivizing and supporting leadership preparation for deeper learning should take note of the indispensable role partnerships play in it. There are a variety of ways that states can create the conditions for successful partnerships. States can be collaborators and funders, as in the case of NISL. They can also develop requirements, like those in Illinois, mandating formal partnerships between preparation programs and school districts, including supervised internships for participants.

CREATE PIPELINES FOR PROMISING CANDIDATES

Leadership pipelines that start with recruiting deeper learning–oriented teachers and support their preparation, induction, and professional learning opportunities serve multiple roles. They improve the practice of individuals, create an ongoing supply of qualified leaders, and, in doing so over time, contribute to systemic change.

The LBUSD Leadership Pipeline is an example of a comprehensive preservice and in-service program for school and district leaders at all administrative levels. The pipeline is the primary route to leadership positions in LBUSD—from staff interested in becoming assistant principals, to aspiring principals, to school- and district-level administrators. Administrators further along the pipeline serve as mentors for those in the earlier stages, creating consistency in vision and priorities across the district.

Other programs, while not full pipelines, also provide a learning progression. UIC is both a preparation and an induction program. The preparation stage includes coursework and a residency leading to certification. The induction stage includes more coursework, in-service coaching, and a doctoral capstone project. Many program graduates serve as mentor principals. The Arkansas MPP is set up in three phases that progressively build on participants' knowledge and skills as they work toward the Master Principal designation. Principals work within their schools in Phase 1, expand their leadership skills to engender collaboration and make data-driven decisions in Phase 2, and advocate for system improvements in Phase 3. In addition to the MPP, the Arkansas Leadership Academy has eight programs that provide learning opportunities for teachers, assistant principals, principals, district staff, state administrators, and others, using the Leadership Performance Strands and Skills rubrics and many of the same practices as the MPP, supporting systemwide improvement. At NISL, where the theory of change depends on wide engagement with districts and states, program offerings have been expanded to support superintendents and teachers in states and districts where NISL is active. These offerings make NISL's work with school principals part of a broad approach that encompasses all system levels.

ENCOURAGE TARGETED RECRUITING OF LEADERSHIP CANDIDATES

Targeted recruitment allows schools, districts, and programs to identify candidates with deeper learning leadership potential and those who represent historically underserved populations, rather than choosing leaders from self-selected candidates who can afford the time and expense of leadership training.

At Berkeley, the PLI's selection process emphasizes a commitment to equity, demonstrated leadership capacity, and cohort diversity. The process begins with extensive outreach to generate interest and demystify the application process, particularly for nontraditional applicants. Nearly half of the applicants come to the program through alumni referrals. Its performance-based selection process includes a full day of interviews and group discussions, during which PLI staff assess applicants' interaction skills, ability to collaborate, and willingness to dialogue about social justice.

The LBUSD pipeline programs are integrated into the district's professional development system, providing a pool of interested and qualified applicants. Still, admission into the pipeline is selective and requires both written and performance-based tasks. The intensity of the process speaks to the weight that LBUSD places on recruiting, preparing, supporting, and retaining the right leaders for the district. Furthermore, while applicants can self-select, the district tasks current principals with identifying strong teachers with leadership potential.

UIC, too, boasts a rigorous, highly structured recruitment and selection process. Cohorts are intentionally recruited to increase the racial and gender diversity of CPS school leaders. The application process is comprehensive and includes the submission of materials and in-person tasks and interviews. The admissions panel uses an extensive rubric to judge an applicant's strengths as a learner in the context of urban schools and diversity; personal commitment to equity and educational excellence; presence and attitude as a leader; collaborative orientation in working with and leading adults; culturally responsive and deep instructional knowledge; educational systems management expertise; and ethical conduct and leadership.

UNDERWRITE LEADER TRAINING

Significant financial investments and ongoing support make possible the program features and practices highlighted here. This is true for candidates as much as for programs. Funding for tuition expenses, along with paid internships and residencies, can enable high-quality candidates to complete preparation programs and enter school leadership without going into debt. It also makes it feasible for candidates to take the necessary time for robust clinical placements that characterize deeper learning–aligned programs. Removing or mitigating financial constraints can make leadership preparation more accessible to a broader range of applicants.

Funding for candidates to participate in leadership programs stands out as a feature of deeper learning–aligned programs. The Arkansas MPP is funded by the state at no cost to participants, while the cost of NISL's Executive Development Program is covered by district, state, federal, or philanthropic funds. At LBUSD, all programs are free to participants apart from the Clear Administrative Credential program, which costs $3,500 per year to cover coach stipends and Association of California School Administrators program fees. Berkeley's PLI uses scholarships to offset costs and relies on a mix of UC and philanthropic funding to provide partial scholarships to meet program goals around candidate diversity. At UIC, the paid, full-year residencies are partly funded by CPS while the program actively helps other participants secure full-time, nonteaching positions offering clinical experiences comparable to funded residencies.

CONCLUSION

Leadership preparation and development programs aligned to deeper learning can be encouraged, incentivized, and supported by policy makers, particularly at the state level. *Defining and operationalizing high-quality leadership practice* can orient programs toward practices consistent with preparing leaders for deeper learning. Some states may need to update their standards, perhaps in partnership with innovative preparation programs within their own borders. Other states that already have deeper learning–aligned standards may face challenges putting standards into practice. These states can work with local preparation programs to build local buy-in, meet community needs, and effect school transformation.

States can also *incorporate performance assessments* to provide authentic measures of candidates' skills and capacities while giving programs information they can use to meet candidate needs and pursue programmatic improvement. Such assessments can also be aligned to state leadership standards to promote well-aligned transformation at scale. *Providing funding and supports for high-quality clinical partnerships* makes possible the internships and residencies that are critical features of leadership preparation for deeper learning. Support for partnerships contributes to their sustainability while creating shared practices and expectations across program and district contexts focused on authentic, job-embedded clinical experiences.

Other recommendations focus on leadership candidates. *Pipelines for promising candidates* provide a career path and ongoing development for school and district leaders, keeping strong candidates engaged and building individual and local capacity. *Targeted recruiting* opens school leadership to a wide pool of qualified candidates who have the potential to lead for deeper learning, while giving schools and districts the opportunity to pick candidates who will meet their local needs. Finally, *underwriting leader preparation* provides financial support for program participants to undertake their preparation and professional development while receiving loans, scholarships, or funded residency placements, enabling both robust clinical experiences and the targeted recruiting of promising candidates.

In closing, principals who lead for deeper learning build systems and support teachers so that students develop the knowledge and skills they need to be successful in today's world. Yet, there are few programs designed to prepare leaders for these new roles. The case studies in this book offer valuable lessons for policy makers, principal preparation and professional development program staff, and district administrators. They provide examples and guidance, as well as ideas and inspiration, for creating and sustaining programs that focus on the knowledge and skills preservice and in-service principals need to lead for deeper learning. The dimensions of leadership preparation for deeper learning derived from these case studies, and laid out here, conceptualize this vision of leadership so it can be operationalized in programs and districts and supported by policy.

As more programs are structured according to these dimensions and adopt the priorities and features highlighted here, more leaders will enter the field with the capacity to build educational environments conducive to deeper learning. More teachers will be empowered to create deeper learning classrooms. More students will have the opportunity to experience deeper learning and develop the knowledge and skills they need to thrive. Ultimately, fulfilling the promise of deeper learning teaching and leadership means transforming schools so that all students have equitable access to these opportunities.

METHODOLOGY AND SURVEY RESULTS

This study sought to deepen the field's knowledge of deeper learning leadership and the key design features of leadership preparation and professional development programs that prepare participants to lead for deeper learning. To achieve these aims, we used a multiple case study approach examining five models of leadership preparation and development.

CASE SELECTION

To identify programs to serve as case study sites, we first asked experts in the field of school leader development to recommend exemplary programs for consideration, using a snowball sampling technique to generate a list. We also conducted a scan of programs that were past recipients of the University Council for Educational Administration's Exemplary Educational Leadership Preparation Program Award, adding these to our list.

The research team chose the five case study sites from this list through a rigorous and iterative process. We started with background research on each nominated program's design and outcomes, including conversations with program leaders to learn more about each program's model. We were seeking out leadership preparation and development programs that met most or all of the following criteria:

- Coursework explicitly models project-based learning and authentic performance-based assessments for candidates.
- Coursework is integrated with field experiences.
- There is an explicit focus on equity-centered pedagogy.
- Clinical placements are located in schools that are highly collaborative, focus on personalization, provide authentic curriculum and assessments, and are responsive to students' needs.
- Coursework and clinical experiences emphasize developing relationships with students, their families, and communities.

These criteria were modeled on *Preparing Teachers for Deeper Learning*; a similar set of criteria was used to identify the features of programs that prepare teachers to create equitable deeper learning for students.[1] The final sites were chosen to ensure program diversity along several metrics—program size, participants (preservice or in-service), administrative entity (university, nonprofit, state, or district), and geographical scope (district, region, state, nation)—to reflect the range of approaches operating in the field, enable us to identify a set of broadly applicable findings, and provide clear connections between our work and an inclusive spectrum of leadership preparation and development program models.

DATA COLLECTION AND ANALYSIS

We conducted case studies between the spring of 2017 and the spring of 2018 using a multimethod research design that included several data sources.

Interviews of key stakeholders. We conducted semistructured interviews with program faculty, mentors and coaches, current program participants, program graduates, district leaders, community organizations, and others involved in program development and implementation. Interviews covered program design, local partnerships, political context, factors that support or hinder implementation, evidence of effectiveness, and participant experiences. In total, we conducted 124 interviews (see table A.1).

Surveys of program participants. We surveyed program participants and recent alumni about their experiences with core program components and with program outcomes. Overall, 248 participants and graduates responded, for a response rate of 69 percent (see table A.2).

Observations of program components and program participants. We observed course sessions, coaching meetings, and other core program components. We also shadowed program participants and recent alumni in their schools or field experiences (see table A.3).

Document review. We analyzed a wide variety of documents, including publicly available materials as well as internal program materials. These included websites; admissions forms; research, evaluations, or publications about the program; program handbooks; course materials and syllabi; and data on participant experiences, demographic characteristics, and outcomes.

Analysis. We reviewed and coded transcribed interviews, observation notes, and documents to identify key topics and emergent themes. We analyzed survey data to produce frequencies and means for each question. Our analyses sought to triangulate data from all sources, seeking confirmatory and disconfirmatory evidence to identify key findings and themes and determine which were specific to particular sites and which were cross-cutting.

FULL SURVEY RESULTS

Table A.4 provides the full survey results. Note that there is a small amount of variation in response rates by individual question. We only report *N* size for individual questions if more than 10 percent of participants in a given cohort did not respond to a question.

TABLE A.1 **Interview sample**

	Arkansas MPP	LBUSD	NISL	Berkeley PLI	UIC	All sites
Program staff and affiliates	6	4	11	19	7	47
Participants	3	6	11	6	11	37
Other district administrators	4	2	4	1	1	12
Other school staff	2	6	1	16	3	28

TABLE A.2 Survey sample overview

Total sample

	Arkansas MPP	LBUSD	NISL	Berkeley PLI	UIC	All sites
Total number in sample	106	83	64	24	81	358
Total number responded	65	62	43	21	57	248
Response rate	61%	75%	67%	88%	70%	69%

Cohorts sampled

	MPP		LBUSD	NISL		PLI	UIC	
Cohort name	Phase 1 (P1)	Phase 3 (P3)	LBUSD	Bakersfield (B)	Louisiana (L)	PLI	Residency Completers (RC)	EdD Completers (EdD)
Number in sample	69	37	83	25	39	24	31	50
Number responded	39	26	62	23	20	21	17	40
Response rate	57%	70%	75%	92%	51%	88%	55%	80%

TABLE A.3   **Observations conducted**

Arkansas MPP	LBUSD	NISL	Berkeley PLI	UIC
• Phase III residential session • 5 school visits • 2 school faculty meetings	• Aspiring Principals workshop • 2nd year principal meeting • Continuing Future Administrators meeting • Collaborative inquiry visit • 4 coaching observations	• Course module • 2 school visits	• Course • AileyCamp lesson • Assessment center • School visit • District faculty meeting • 2 coaching sessions	• Course • Chicago Leadership Collaborative professional development session • 3 school visits • School staff development meeting • 2 triad meetings • Coaching session

TABLE A.4 Full survey results

Percentage of participants reporting their program had the following qualities

	AR MPP (P1) N = 39	AR MPP (P3) N = 26	LBUSD (LDP) N = 54	NISL (B) N = 23	NISL (L) N = 18–19	UCB (PLI) N = 21	UIC (RC) N = 15	UIC (EdD) N = 35	All sites N = 231–232
The program uses problem-based learning approaches, such as action research or inquiry projects	100% (100%)	100% (100%)	87% (67%)	100% (100%)	100% (100%)	100% (100%)	100% (100%)	100% (97%)	97% (92%)
The program uses field-based projects in which you apply ideas from your coursework to your experience in the field	100% (100%)	100% (100%)	93% (87%)	100% (96%)	100% (100%)	100% (90%)	100% (93%)	100% (97%)	98% (95%)
You are in a student cohort—a defined group of individuals who began the program together and stay together throughout the courses	100% (98%)	100% (96%)	96% (96%)	100% (100%)	95% (95%)	100% (100%)	100% (100%)	97% (86%)	98% (96%)

Note: The top number indicates the percentage of participants who reported their program had these qualities "somewhat" or more, and the number in parentheses under each percentage indicates the percentage of participants who reported their program had these qualities to a "moderate" or "great extent."

(continues)

TABLE A.4   (continues)

Percentage of participants reporting their program emphasized leading instruction

	AR MPP (P1) N = 39	AR MPP (P3) N = 26	LBUSD (LDP) N = 54	NISL (B) N = 23	NISL (L) N = 18	UCB (PLI) N = 21	UIC (RC) N = 15	UIC (EdD) N = 35	All sites N = 231
The program emphasizes instructional leadership focused on how to develop students' higher-order thinking skills	100% (92%)	100% (96%)	98% (80%)	100% (100%)	100% (100%)	90% (67%)	93% (80%)	97% (80%)	98% (86%)
The program emphasizes instructional leadership focused on raising schoolwide achievement on standardized tests	100% (90%)	96% (85%)	96% (81%)	70% (43%)	100% (100%)	76% (38%)	100% (80%)	97% (91%)	90% (82%)
The program emphasizes how to select effective curriculum strategies and materials	97% (79%)	92% (81%)	89% (65%)	83% (65%)	100% (89%)	86% (48%)	87% (47%)	91% (51%)	87% (70%)
The program emphasizes how to lead instruction that supports implementation of new state standards	92% (85%)	92% (81%)	94% (78%)	91% (65%)	100% (89%)	81% (33%)	87% (60%)	91% (66%)	87% (76%)

Note: The top number indicates the percentage of participants who reported their program emphasized leading instruction "somewhat" or more, and the number in parentheses under each percentage indicates the percentage of participants who reported their program emphasized leading instruction to a "moderate" or "great extent."

Percentage of participants reporting their program emphasized leading and managing school improvement

	AR MPP (P1) N = 39	AR MPP (P3) N = 26	LBUSD (LDP) N = 54	NISL (B) N = 23	NISL (L) N = 17–18	UCB (PLI) N = 20	UIC (RC) N = 15	UIC (EdD) N = 35	All sites N = 229–230
The program emphasizes how to use student and school data to inform continuous school improvement	100% (97%)	100% (100%)	100% (96%)	100% (74%)	100% (100%)	100% (100%)	100% (93%)	100% (97%)	100% (95%)
The program emphasizes how to lead a schoolwide change process to improve student achievement	100% (100%)	100% (100%)	98% (94%)	96% (96%)	100% (100%)	100% (100%)	100% (100%)	100% (100%)	99% (98%)
The program emphasizes how to engage in self-improvement and your own continuous learning	100% (100%)	100% (100%)	100% (96%)	100% (91%)	100% (100%)	100% (100%)	100% (87%)	97% (94%)	100% (97%)

Note: The top number indicates the percentage of participants who reported their program emphasized leading and managing school improvement and the number in parentheses indicates the percentage of participants who reported their program emphasized leading and managing school improvement to a "moderate" or "great extent."

(continues)

TABLE A.4 (continues)

Percentage of participants reporting their program emphasized shaping teaching and learning conditions

	AR MPP (P1) N=39	AR MPP (P3) N=25–26	LBUSD (LDP) N=54	NISL (B) N=23	NISL (L) N=17–18	UCB PLI N=20	UIC (RC) N=15	UIC (EdD) N=35	All sites N=229–230
The program emphasizes how to create collegial and collaborative work environments	100% (100%)	100% (100%)	100% (94%)	96% (87%)	100% (100%)	100% (95%)	87% (87%)	97% (97%)	98% (96%)
The program emphasizes how to work with the school community, parents, educators, and other stakeholders	100% (100%)	100% (100%)	100% (93%)	79% (39%)	100% (100%)	100% (100%)	80% (73%)	97% (89%)	96% (89%)
The program emphasizes how to lead schools that support students from diverse ethnic, racial, linguistic, and cultural backgrounds	97% (92%)	100% (88.47)	98% (94%)	100% (87%)	100% (100%)	100% (100%)	80% (60%)	94% (74%)	97% (90%)
The program emphasizes how to lead schools that support students' social and emotional development	97% (92%)	100% (85%)	96% (93%)	83% (57%)	100% (94%)	100% (95%)	53% (47%)	83% (54%)	91% (80%)
The program emphasizes how to develop systems that meet children's needs and support their development in terms of physical and mental health	92% (77%)	96% (85%)	96% (87%)	61% (22%)	94% (89%)	100% (75%)	53% (40%)	80% (40%)	87% (61%)

The program emphasizes how to create a school environment that develops personally and socially responsible young people and uses discipline for restorative purposes	92% (69%)	81% (65%)	94% (85%)	52% (22%)	94% (89%)	100% (90%)	60% (40%)	71% (34%)	83% (64%)
The program emphasizes how to redesign a school's organization and structure to support deeper learning for teachers and students	100% (100%)	100% (100%)	94% (87%)	100% (96%)	100% (100%)	100% (90%)	93% (87%)	100% (94%)	98% (90%)

Note: The top number indicates the percentage of participants who reported their program emphasized shaping teaching and learning conditions "somewhat" or more, and the number in parentheses under each percentage indicates the percentage of participants who reported their program emphasized shaping teaching and learning conditions to a "moderate" or "great extent."

(continues)

TABLE A.4 (continues)

Percentage of participants reporting their program emphasized developing people

	AR MPP (P1) N = 39	AR MPP (P3) N = 26	LBUSD (LDP) N = 53–54	NISL (B) N = 22–23	NISL (L) N = 17–18	UCB PLI N = 19–20	UIC (RC) N = 15	UIC (EdD) N = 35	All sites N = 228–230
The program emphasizes how to design professional learning opportunities for teachers and other staff	100% (100%)	100% (96%)	98% (96%)	100% (91%)	100% (100%)	100% (100%)	93% (87%)	100% (94%)	99% (96%)
The program emphasizes how to help teachers improve through a cycle of observation and feedback	100% (97%)	100% (96%)	100% (98%)	100% (70%)	94% (94%)	100% (95%)	93% (73%)	97% (94%)	99% (92%)
The program emphasizes how to recruit and retain teachers and other staff	95% (74%)	85% (69%)	77% (53%)	52% (17%)	100% (94%)	90% (60%)	67% (53%)	91% (66%)	83% (61%)
The program emphasizes how to manage school operations efficiently	95% (87%)	92% (81%)	94% (83%)	87% (65%)	100% (100%)	90% (70%)	60% (40%)	91% (60%)	91% (76%)
The program emphasizes how to invest resources to support improvements in school performance	97% (87%)	88% (81%)	91% (70%)	77% (45%)	100% (100%)	100% (79%)	67% (33%)	89% (66%)	90% (72%)

Note: The top number indicates the percentage of participants who reported their program emphasized developing people "somewhat" or more, and the number in parentheses under each percentage indicates the percentage of participants who reported their program emphasized developing people to a "moderate" or "great extent."

Percentage of participants reporting their program emphasized meeting the needs of all learners

	AR MPP (P1) N = 38–39	AR MPP (P3) N = 26	LBUSD (LDP) N = 54	NISL (B) N = 23	NISL (L) N = 18	UCB PLI N = 20	UIC (RC) N = 15	UIC (EdD) N = 35	All sites N = 229–230
The program emphasizes how to meet the needs of English language learners	85% (56%)	81% (54%)	94% (74%)	74% (39%)	89% (83%)	100% (85%)	60% (47%)	83% (23%)	85% (57%)
The program emphasizes how to meet the needs of students with disabilities	87% (55%)	81% (50%)	94% (69%)	65% (39%)	94% (89%)	100% (95%)	60% (53%)	86% (23%)	86% (57%)
The program emphasizes how to equitably serve all students	95% (85%)	96% (85%)	98% (90%)	96% (65%)	100% (100%)	100% (100%)	80% (60%)	91% (60%)	95% (81%)

Note: The top number indicates the percentage of participants who reported their program emphasized meeting the needs of all learners "somewhat" or more, and the number in parentheses indicates the percentage of participants who reported their program emphasized meeting the needs of all learners to a "moderate" or "great extent."

(continues)

TABLE A.4 (continues)

Percentage of participants reporting their program prepared them to lead instruction

	AR MPP (P1) N = 36	AR MPP (P3) N = 25	LBUSD (LDP) N = 48-49	NISL (B) N = 23	NISL (L) N = 18	UCB (PLI) N = 19	UIC (RC) N = 15	UIC (EdD) N = 35	All sites N = 219-220
Lead instruction that focuses on how to develop students' higher-order thinking skills	94% (75%)	100% (84%)	94% (71%)	100% (87%)	100% (94%)	95% (47%)	86% (86%)	97% (80%)	96% (77%)
Lead instruction that focuses on raising school-wide achievement on standardized tests	97% (81%)	100% (76%)	94% (76%)	96% (48%)	100% (94%)	100% (47%)	100% (87%)	97% (89%)	97% (75%)
Select effective curriculum strategies and materials	94% (69%)	96% (64%)	92% (79%)	83% (48%)	100% (94%)	100% (53%)	73% (60%)	94% (48%)	92% (65%)
Lead instruction that supports implementation of new state standards	94% (75%)	96% (76%)	92% (78%)	91.3% (52%)	100% (89%)	95% (42%)	86% (73%)	94% (60%)	94% (69%)

Note: The top number indicates the percentage of participants who reported their program prepared them "adequately" or better, and the number in parentheses under each percentage indicates the percentage of candidates reporting their program prepared them "well" or "very well."

Percentage of participants reporting their program prepared them to lead and manage school improvement

	AR MPP (P1) N = 35–36	AR MPP (P3) N = 25	LBUSD (LDP) N = 49	NISL (B) N = 23	NISL (L) N = 18	UCB (PLI) N = 19	UIC (RC) N = 15	UIC (EdD) N = 35	Al sites N = 219–220
Use student and school data to inform continuous school improvement	97% (92%)	100% (96%)	100% (90%)	91% (57%)	100% (83%)	100% (95%)	100% (93%)	100% (97%)	99% (89%)
Lead a schoolwide change process to improve student achievement	100% (94%)	100% (88%)	98% (86%)	100% (78%)	100% (94%)	100% (100%)	100% (93%)	100% (97%)	99% (91%)
Engage in self- improvement and your own continuous learning	100% (97%)	100% (96%)	100% (98%)	100% (87%)	100% (94%)	100% (100%)	93% (93%)	97% (97%)	99% (96%)

Note: The top number indicates the percentage of participants who reported their program prepared them "adequately" or better, and the number in parentheses under each percentage indicates the percentage of candidates reporting their program prepared them "well" or "very well."

(continues)

TABLE A.4 (continues)

Percentage of participants reporting their program prepared them to shape teaching and learning conditions

	AR MPP (P1) N = 36	AR MPP (P3) N = 24–25	LBUSD (LDP) N = 48–49	NISL (B) N = 22–23	NISL (L) N = 18	UCB PLI N = 19	UIC (RC) N = 15	UIC (EdD) N = 34	All sites N = 217–219
Create collegial and collaborative work environments	100%	100%	96%	100%	100%	100%	93%	100%	99%
	(97%)	(96%)	(90%)	(78%)	(100%)	(100%)	(80%)	(85%)	(91%)
Work with the school community, parents, educators, and other stakeholders	100%	100%	100%	83%	100%	100%	73%	94%	95%
	(97%)	(96%)	(86%)	(39%)	(100%)	(100%)	(60%)	(68%)	(82%)
Lead schools that support students from diverse ethnic, racial, linguistic, and cultural backgrounds	97%	100%	100%	100%	100%	100%	66%	97%	97%
	(86%)	(80%)	(86%)	(70%)	(100%)	(100%)	(53%)	(68%)	(81%)
Lead schools that support students' social and emotional development	94%	92%	94%	86%	100%	100%	47%	88%	90%
	(83%)	(76%)	(80%)	(41%)	(89%)	(95%)	(47%)	(50%)	(71%)
Develop systems that meet children's needs and support their development in terms of physical and mental health	94%	92%	98%	74%	94%	100%	53%	79%	88%
	(64%)	(72%)	(69%)	(30%)	(89%)	(79%)	(47%)	(47%)	(62%)

Create a school environment that develops personally and socially responsible young people and uses discipline for restorative purposes	92% (64%)	92% (64%)	98% (78%)	65% (39%)	100% (83%)	100% (89%)	53% (47%)	82% (41%)	88% (63%)
Redesign the school's organization and structure to support deeper learning for teachers and students	100% (94%)	100% (96%)	98% (81%)	100% (83%)	100% (94%)	100% (95%)	100% (93%)	100% (82%)	99.5% (88%)

Note: The top number indicates the percentage of participants who reported their program prepared them "adequately" or better, and the number in parentheses under each percentage indicates the percentage of candidates reporting their program prepared them "well" or "very well."

(*continues*)

TABLE A.4 (continues)

Percentage of participants reporting their program prepared them to develop people

	AR MPP (P1) N = 37	AR MPP (P3) N = 25	LBUSD (LDP) N = 48–49	NISL (B) N = 23	NISL (L) N = 17	UCB (PLI) N = 19	UIC (RC) N = 14	UIC (EdD) N = 34	All sites N = 217–218
Design professional learning opportunities for teachers and other staff	100% (97%)	100% (96%)	98% (88%)	100% (83%)	100% (88%)	100% (95%)	86% (79%)	97% (82%)	98% (89%)
Help teachers improve through a cycle of observation and feedback	97% (95%)	100% (96%)	96% (88%)	96% (65%)	100% (94%)	100% (100%)	86% (86%)	100% (91%)	97% (89%)
Recruit and retain teachers and other staff	92% (65%)	96% (68%)	81% (60%)	48% (13%)	100% (94%)	89% (53%)	64% (43%)	88% (62%)	82% (58%)
Manage school operations efficiently	95% (86%)	96% (80%)	96% (73%)	74% (52%)	100% (94%)	95% (53%)	50% (36%)	94% (59%)	90% (69%)
Know how to invest resources to support improvements in school performance	97% (76%)	96% (76%)	94% (65%)	65% (43%)	100% (94%)	100% (79%)	64% (50%)	94% (71%)	91% (69%)

Note: The top number indicates the percentage of participants who reported their program prepared them "adequately" or better, and the number in parentheses under each percentage indicates the percentage of candidates reporting their program prepared them "well" or "very well."

Percentage of participants reporting their program prepared them to meet the needs of all learners

	AR MPP (P1) N = 37	AR MPP (P3) N = 25	LBUSD (LDP) N = 49	NISL (B) N = 23	NISL (L) N = 18	UCB (PLI) N = 19	UIC (RC) N = 15	UIC (EdD) N = 34	All sites N = 220
Meet the needs of English learners	92% (43%)	84% (64%)	92% (59%)	83% (35%)	89% (67%)	100% (68%)	47% (40%)	74% (18%)	85% (48%)
Meet the needs of students with disabilities	92% (43%)	88% (60%)	94% (61%)	65% (39%)	100% (61%)	100% (89%)	47% (40%)	76% (24%)	85% (51%)
Equitably serve all students	95% (68%)	92% (80%)	100% (84%)	96% (78%)	100% (83%)	100% (100%)	80% (47%)	91% (56%)	95% (75%)

Note: The top number indicates the percentage of participants who reported their program prepared them "adequately" or better, and the number in parentheses under each percentage indicates the percentage of candidates reporting their program prepared them "well" or "very well."

(continues)

TABLE A.4 **(continues)**

Percentage of participants reporting their program prepared them to be a principal

	AR MPP (P1) N = 37	AR MPP (P3) N = 25	LBUSD (LDP) N = 49	NISL (B) N = 23	NISL (L) N = 18	UCB PLI N = 19	UIC (RC) N = 15	UIC (EdD) N = 35	All sites N = 221
Overall, how well do you feel your leadership program prepared you to be a principal?	100% (97%)	100% (100%)	98% (88%)	100% (83%)	100% (94%)	100% (95%)	93% (87%)	100% (97%)	99% (93%)

Note: The top number indicates the percentage of participants who reported their program prepared them "adequately" or better, and the number in parentheses under each percentage indicates the percentage of candidates reporting their program prepared them "well" or "very well."

NOTES

CHAPTER 1

1. Pamela Cantor, David Osher, Juliette Berg, Lily Steyer, and Todd Rose, "Malleability, Plasticity, and Individuality: How Children Learn and Develop in Context," *Applied Developmental Science* 23, no. 4 (2019): 307–337, https://doi.org/10.1080/10888691 .2017.1398649; Linda Darling-Hammond, Lisa Flook, Channa Cook-Harvey, Brigid Barron, and David Osher, "Implications for Educational Practice of the Science of Learning and Development," *Applied Developmental Science* 24, no. 2 (2020): 97–140, https://doi.org/10.1080/10888691.2018.1537791; Linda Darling-Hammond and Channa Cook-Harvey, *Educating the Whole Child: Improving School Climate to Support Student Success* (Palo Alto, CA: Learning Policy Institute, 2018), https://doi.org/10 .54300/145.655; National Academies of Sciences, Engineering, and Medicine, *How People Learn II: Learners, Contexts, and Cultures* (Washington, DC: National Academies Press, 2018), https://doi.org/10.17226/24783; David Osher, Pamela Cantor, Juliette Berg, Lily Steyer, and Todd Rose, "Drivers of Human Development: How Relationships and Context Shape Learning and Development," *Applied Developmental Science* 24, no. 1 (2020): 6–36, https://doi.org/10.1080/10888691.2017.1398650.
2. Darling-Hammond et al., "Implications for Educational Practice"; David F. Labaree, "School Syndrome: Understanding the USA's Magical Belief That Schooling Can Somehow Improve Society, Promote Access, and Preserve Advantage," *Journal of Curriculum Studies* 44, no. 2 (2012): 143–163, https://doi.org/10.1080/00220272.2012 .675358; David B. Tyack and Larry Cuban, *Tinkering Toward Utopia* (Cambridge, MA: Harvard University Press, 1995), 85.
3. Anna Brown, "Key Findings About the American Workforce and the Changing Job Market," Pew Research Center, October 6, 2016, http://www.pewresearch.org/fact -tank/2016/10/06/key-findings-about-the-american-workforce-and-the-changing -job-market/; National Research Council, *Education for Life and Work: Developing Transferable Knowledge and Skills in the 21st Century* (Washington, DC: National Academies Press, 2012), https://doi.org/1017226/13398; Thomas J. Donohue, *Building a 21st Century Workforce*, U.S. Chamber of Commerce, August 28, 2017, https:// www.uschamber.com/series/your-corner/building-21st-century-workforce; Joergen Oerstroem Moeller, "Struggle to Prepare the Workforce for a Fast Changing World" (presentation, 6th Asian-Europe Foundation Conference, Singapore, October 9–13, 2017), https://yaleglobal.yale.edu/content/struggle-prepare-workforce-fast-changing -world-0.
4. David H. Autor, Frank Levy, and Richard J. Murnane, "The Skill Content of Recent Technological Change: An Empirical Exploration," *Quarterly Journal of Economics* 118, no. 4 (November 2003): 1279–1333, https://doi.org/10.1162/003355303322552801.
5. *A Time for Deeper Learning: Preparing Students for a Changing World* (Washington, DC: Alliance for Excellent Education, 2011), https://all4ed.org/wp-content/uploads /2013/06/DeeperLearning.pdf; Barnett Berry, *Teacher Leadership and Deeper Learning for All Students* (Carrboro, NC: Center for Teaching Quality, 2016), https://www

.teachingquality.org/wp-content/uploads/2018/03/DeeperLearning_CTQ.pdf; Linda Darling-Hammond, *The Flat World and Education: How America's Commitment to Equity Will Determine Our Future* (New York: Teachers College Press, 2010), https://doi.org/10.1177/003172171009100403; Rick Mintrop, Elizabeth Zumpe, Kara Jackson, Drew Nucci, and Jon Norman, *Designing for Deeper Learning: Challenges in Schools and School Districts Serving Communities Disadvantaged by the Educational System* (Stanford, CA: Carnegie Foundation for the Advancement of Teaching, 2022), https://www.researchgate.net/profile/Elizabeth-Zumpe/publication/360529326_Designing_for_Deeper_Learning_Challenges_in_Schools_and_School_Districts_Serving_Communities_Disadvantaged_by_the_Educational_System/links/627c2535107cae29199e3b47/Designing-for-Deeper-Learning-Challenges-in-Schools-and-School-Districts-Serving-Communities-Disadvantaged-by-the-Educational-System.pdf; Pedro Noguera, Linda Darling-Hammond, and Diane Friedlaender, *Equal Opportunity for Deeper Learning* (Boston, MA: Jobs for the Future, 2015), https://files.eric.ed.gov/fulltext/ED560802.pdf; Diane Ravitch, *The Death and Life of the Great American School System: How Testing and Choice Are Undermining Education* (New York: Basic Books, 2010).

6. Pedro A. Noguera, *Taking Deeper Learning to Scale* (Palo Alto, CA: Learning Policy Institute, 2017), 26, https://learningpolicyinstitute.org/sites/default/files/product-files/Taking_Deeper_Learning_Scale_REPORT.pdf.

7. Darling-Hammond et al., "Implications for Educational Practice"; Linda Darling-Hammond, Lisa Flook, Abby Schachner, Steve Wojcikiewicz, Pamela Cantor, and David Osher, *Educator Learning to Enact the Science of Learning and Development* (Palo Alto, CA: Learning Policy Institute, 2021), https://learningpolicyinstitute.org/sites/default/files/product-files/Educator_Learning_for_SoLD_REPORT.pdf, https://doi.org/10.54300/859.776; Linda Darling-Hammond, Jeannie Oakes, Steve Wojcikiewicz, Maria E. Hyler, Roneeta Guha, Anne Podolsky, Tara Kini, Channa Cook-Harvey, Charmaine Mercer, and Akeelah Harrell, *Preparing Teachers for Deeper Learning* (Cambridge, MA: Harvard Education Press, 2019); Noguera et al., *Equal Opportunity for Deeper Learning*.

8. Kyla L. Wahlstrom, Karen Seashore Louis, Kenneth Leithwood, and Stephen E. Anderson, *Learning from Leadership: Investigating the Links to Improved Student Learning* (New York: Wallace Foundation, 2010), http://www.wallacefoundation.org/knowledge-center/school-leadership/key-research/Documents/Investigating-the-Links-to-Improved-Student-Learning.pdf; Kenneth Leithwood and Doris Jantzi, "Transformational School Leadership for Large-Scale Reform: Effects on Students, Teachers, and Their Classroom Practices," *School Effectiveness and School Improvement* 17, no. 2 (2006): 201–227, https://doi.org/10.1080/09243450600565829; Kenneth Leithwood and Carolyn Riehl, "What We Know About Successful School Leadership," in *A New Agenda for Research in Educational Leadership*, ed. William A. Firestone and Carolyn Riehl (New York: Teachers College Press, 2005), 22–47; Jason A. Grissom, Anna J. Egalite, and Constance A. Lindsay *How Principals Affect Students and Schools: A Systematic Synthesis of Two Decades of Research* (New York: Wallace Foundation, 2021), https://www.wallacefoundation.org/knowledge-center/pages/how-principals-affect-students-and-schools-a-systematic-synthesis-of-two-decades-of-research.aspx; Leib Sutcher, Anne Podolsky, and Danny Espinoza, *Supporting Principals' Learning: Key Features of Effective Programs* (Palo Alto, CA: Learning Policy Institute. 2017), https://learningpolicyinstitute.org/product/supporting-principals-learning-key-features-effective-programs-report.

9. Linda Darling-Hammond, Michelle LaPointe, Debra Meyerson, Margaret Orr, and Carol Cohen, *Preparing School Leaders for a Changing World: Lessons from Exemplary Leadership Development Programs* (Stanford, CA: Stanford University, Stanford Educational Leadership Institute, 2007), https://www.wallacefoundation.org/knowledge-center/pages/preparing-school-leaders.aspx; Mark A. Smylie and Joseph Murphy,

"School Leader Standards from ISLLC to PSEL: Notes on Their Development and the Work Ahead," *UCEA Review* 59, no. 3 (Fall 2018): 24–28, http://www.npbea.org/wp-content/uploads/2018/10/Smylie-Murphy-2018-School-leader-standards-from-ISLLC-to-PSEL-UCEA-Review-article-only.pdf.

10. National Policy Board for Educational Administration, *Professional Standards for Educational Leaders* (Reston, VA: National Policy Board for Educational Administration, 2015), http://npbea.org/wp-content/uploads/2017/06/Professional-Standards-for-Educational-Leaders_2015.pdf.

11. Jeannie Oakes, Martin Lipton, Lauren Anderson, and Jamy Stillman, *Teaching to Change the World* (New York: Routledge, 2018), https://doi.org/10.4324/9781351263443.

12. John D. Bransford, Ann L. Brown, and Rodney R. Cocking, eds., *How People Learn: Brain, Mind, Experience, and School* (Washington, DC: National Research Council, 2000), https://doi.org/10.17226/10067.

13. Bransford et al., *How People Learn*.

14. Lauren B. Resnick, Mary Catherine O'Connor, and Sarah Michaels, *Classroom Discourse, Mathematical Rigor, and Student Reasoning: An Accountable Talk Literature Review* (Pittsburgh, PA: Learning Research Development Center, 2007); Roland G. Tharp and Ronald Gallimore, *Rousing Minds to Life: Teaching, Learning, and Schooling in Social Context* (New York: Cambridge University Press, 1988), https://doi.org/10.1017/CBO9781139173698.

15. Bransford et al., *How People Learn*; Noguera et al., *Equal Opportunity for Deeper Learning*; K. Brooke Stafford-Brizard, *Building Blocks for Learning: A Framework for Comprehensive Student Development* (New York: Turnaround for Children, 2015), https://www.turnaroundusa.org/wp-content/uploads/2016/03/Turnaround-for-Children-Building-Blocks-for-Learningx-2.pdf.

16. Hanna Melnick, Channa Cook-Harvey, and Linda Darling-Hammond, *Encouraging Social and Emotional Learning in the Context of New Accountability* (Palo Alto, CA: Learning Policy Institute, 2017), https://learningpolicyinstitute.org/product/encouraging-social-emotional-learning-new-accountability-report.

17. Cantor et al., "Malleability, Plasticity, and Individuality"; Darling-Hammond et al., "Implications for Educational Practice"; Linda Darling-Hammond and Channa Cook-Harvey, *Educating the Whole Child: Improving School Climate to Support Student Success* (Palo Alto, CA: Learning Policy Institute, 2018), https://learningpolicyinstitute.org/sites/default/files/product-files/Educating_Whole_Child_REPORT.pdf, https://doi.org/10.54300/145.655; National Academies of Sciences, Engineering, and Medicine, *How People Learn II*; Osher et al., "Drivers of Human Development."

18. Darling-Hammond et al., "Implications for Educational Practice"; Darling-Hammond et al., *Educator Learning*.

19. Darling-Hammond et al., *Preparing Teachers for Deeper Learning*.

20. Rebecca Goldring and Soheyla Taie, *Principal Attrition and Mobility: Results from the 2016–17 Principal Follow-up Survey* (Washington, DC: US Department of Education, National Center for Education Statistics, 2018), https://nces.ed.gov/pubs2018/2018066.pdf.

CHAPTER 2

1. Shelby Cosner, Steve Tozer, Paul Zavitkovsky, and Samuel P. Whalen, "Cultivating Exemplary School Leadership Preparation at a Research Intensive University," *Journal of Research on Leadership Education* 10, no. 1 (2015): 11–38, https://doi.org/10.1177/1942775115569575.

2. 96th Illinois State Legislature, *Public Act 096-0903* (Springfield: 96th Illinois State Legislature, 2010), https://www.ilga.gov/legislation/publicacts/fulltext.asp?Name=096-0903.

3. Chicago Office of the Mayor, "Mayor Emanuel and CPS CEO Brizard Announce Chicago Leadership Collaborative to Foster New Generation of Leaders at CPS,"

August 15, 2011, https://www.chicago.gov/city/en/depts/mayor/press_room/press
_releases/2011/august_2011/mayor_rahm_emanuelandcpsceojean-claudebrizardann
ouncechicagolead.html.

4. Chicago Public Schools, "Chicago Leadership Collaborative," accessed January 8, 2018, https://www.cps.edu/careers/school-leadership/principal-quality/principal-pipeline/.

5. University of Illinois Chicago, Center for Urban Education Leadership, "Overview: EdD Urban Education Leadership," 2013, https://education.uic.edu/academics /student-resources/doctoral-student-resources/doctoral-student-handbook/overview -doctoral-programs/overview-edd-urban-education-leadership/.

6. University of Illinois Chicago, Center for Urban Education Leadership, "Overview: EdD Urban Education Leadership."

7. University of Illinois at Chicago College of Education, *Illinois Board of Higher Education 8 Year Review Self-Study* (Chicago: UIC College of Education Department of Educational Policy Studies, EdD in Urban Education Leadership Program, 2016), 12.

8. University of Illinois at Chicago College of Education, *8 Year Review Self-Study*.

9. Historically, CPS has provided full-time residencies for the majority of UIC participants. In one recent year only about 65 percent of UIC participants received the residency stipend; the other participants completed their leadership residency while also engaged in other funded activities. For example, in one exceptional case, a participant was teaching four math classes in addition to fulfilling his instructional leadership role for his residency; another participant served as a program manager in her school. This was a year in which the state and CPS budgets were at their nadir. Under such circumstances, the program is actively involved in helping its participants secure full-time nonteaching positions that offer clinical experiences as rich as CPS-funded residencies.

10. University of Illinois at Chicago College of Education, *8 Year Review Self-Study*, appendix C.2.13, 8.

11. University of Illinois at Chicago College of Education, *8 Year Review Self-Study*, appendix C.2.13, 1.

12. Eduardo Bonilla-Silva, *Racism Without Racists: Color-Blind Racism and the Persistence of Racial Inequality in America* (Lanham, MD: Rowman & Littlefield Publishers, 2021).

13. Alliance for Excellent Education, *A Time for Deeper Learning: Preparing Students for a Changing World* (Washington, DC: Alliance for Excellent Education, 2011), 3; Barnett Berry, *Teacher Leadership and Deeper Learning for All Students* (Carrboro, NC: Ford Foundation, n.d.); Pedro Noguera, Linda Darling-Hammond, and Diane Friedlaender, *Equal Opportunity for Deeper Learning [Executive Summary]*, Students at the Center: Deeper Learning Research Series (Boston: Jobs for the Future, 2015).

14. University of Illinois at Chicago College of Education, *8 Year Review Self-Study*, 3.

15. University of Illinois Chicago, Center for Urban Education Leadership, "Recognitions," accessed December 26, 2018, http://urbanedleadership.org/impact/recognitions/.

16. University of Illinois at Chicago College of Education, *8 Year Review Self-Study*.

17. Cosner et al., "Cultivating Exemplary School Leadership."

18. Cosner et al., "Cultivating Exemplary School Leadership."

19. University of Illinois at Chicago College of Education, *8 Year Review Self-Study*.

CHAPTER 3

1. University of California, Berkeley, Graduate School of Education, Principal Leadership Institute, "Our Mission," accessed December 12, 2018, https://bse.berkeley.edu /academics/professional-programs/principal-leadership-institute.

2. Gray Davis, "State of the State Address," California State Library, January 7, 1999, http://governors.library.ca.gov/addresses/s_37-davis1.html.

3. Legislative Analyst's Office, "Teacher Quality," California State Legislature, Legislative Analyst's Office, 1999, https://lao.ca.gov/analysis_1999/education/education_depts2 _anl99.html.

4. University of California, Berkeley, Graduate School of Education, Principal Leadership Institute, "Frequently Asked Questions," accessed January 2, 2019, https://gse
.berkeley.edu/academics/professional-programs/principal-leadership-institute/faq.
5. Data Reporting Office, "DataQuest 2018–19 Enrollment by Ethnicity, Berkeley Unified Report (01–61143)," California Department of Education, 2019. https://dq.cde
.ca.gov/dataquest/dqcensus/enrethlevels.aspx?agglevel=District&year=2018-19&cds
=0161143; California Department of Education, "District Profile: Berkeley Unified,"
2019, https://www.cde.ca.gov/sdprofile/details.aspx?cds=01611430000000; California Department of Education, "District Profile: Oakland Unified," 2019, https://www
.cde.ca.gov/sdprofile/details.aspx?cds=01612590000000; California Department of
Education, "District Profile: San Francisco Unified," 2019, https://www.cde.ca.gov
/sdprofile/details.aspx?cds=38684780000000; California Department of Education,
"District Profile: West Contra Costa Unified," 2019, https://www.cde.ca.gov/sdprofile
/details.aspx?cds=07617960000000.
6. Kyla L. Wahlstrom, Karen Seashore Louis, Kenneth Leithwood, and Stephen E.
Anderson, *Learning from Leadership: Investigating the Links to Improved Student Learning*
(New York: Wallace Foundation, 2010), 42, 50, http://www.wallacefoundation.org
/knowledge-center/school-leadership/key-research/Documents/Investigating-the
-Links-to-Improved-Student-Learning.pdf.
7. Lynda Tredway, Rebecca Cheung, Viet Nguyen, Daphannie Stephens, Linda Leader-Picone, and Janette Hernandez, *Leadership Connection Rubric: Supporting Equity in the
Schools We Need*, 2nd ed. (Berkeley, CA: Leadership Connection, 2015), https://gse
.berkeley.edu/sites/default/files/gse-archive-9/LCRubric%20Second%20Edition
_Web.pdf.
8. Tredway et al., *Leadership Connection Rubric*, 3.
9. University of California, Berkeley, Graduate School of Education, "Principal Leadership Institute," accessed August 13, 2019, https://bse.berkeley.edu/academics
/professional-programs/principal-leadership-institute.
10. Soheyla Taie and Rebecca Goldring, *Characteristics of Public Elementary and Secondary
School Principals in the United States: Results from the 2015–16 National Teacher and Principal Survey* (Washington, DC: US Department of Education, National Center for Education Statistics, 2017), https://nces.ed.gov/pubsearch/pubsinfo.asp?pubid=2017070.
11. Alvin Ailey American Dance Theatre, "AileyCamp," accessed December 27, 2018,
https://www.alvinailey.org/about/arts-education-community-programs/aileycamp.
12. Rebecca Cheung, *Impact Report: Diversifying the Principal Workforce* (Berkeley, CA: UC
Berkeley Principal Leadership Institute, 2017).
13. Cheung, *Impact Report*, 2.
14. Cheung, *Impact Report*.

CHAPTER 4

1. Long Beach Unified School District, "About—Long Beach Unified School District,"
accessed May 1, 2019, http://www.lbschools.net/district/; Long Beach Unified School
District, "LBUSD Facts at a Glance," accessed July 5, 2023, https://www.lbschools
.net/about/about-long-beach-unified-school-district.
2. The Linked Learning approach integrates rigorous academics with sequenced, high-quality career-technical education, work-based learning, and supports. See Linked
Learning Alliance, "About the Linked Learning Approach," accessed June 6, 2019,
http://www.linkedlearning.org/en/about/.
3. Long Beach Unified School District, "Leadership Evaluation, Domains and Dimensions," accessed May 1, 2019, https://www.lbschools.net/departments/equity
-leadership-and-talent-development/eltd-pipeline-programs/lbusd-leadership
-evaluation-domains-dimensions.
4. Long Beach Unified School District, "Leadership Evaluation, Domains and
Dimensions."

5. Joseph Grenny, Ron McMillan, Al Switzler, and Kerry Patterson, *Crucial Conversations: Tools for Talking When Stakes Are High* (New York: McGraw-Hill, 2021).
6. Michael Fullan, *The Principal: Three Keys to Maximizing Impact* (San Francisco: Jossey-Bass, 2014).
7. Dylan Wiliam, *Embedded Formative Assessment: Practical Strategies and Tools for K–12 Teachers* (Bloomington, IN: Solution Tree, 2011).
8. Long Beach Unified School District, *Principal Evaluation Handbook*; Gary Bloom and Martin L. Krovetz, *Powerful Partnerships: A Handbook for Principals Mentoring Assistant Principals* (Thousand Oaks, CA: Corwin Press, 2009).
9. Long Beach Unified School District, "Leadership Evaluation, Domains and Dimensions."
10. Desiree Carver-Thomas and Anne Podolsky, *Long Beach Unified School District: Positive Outliers Case Study* (Palo Alto, CA: Learning Policy Institute, 2019), https://learningpolicyinstitute.org/sites/default/files/product-files/Positive_Outliers_Qualitative_CS_Long_Beach_REPORT.pdf.
11. Carver-Thomas and Podolsky, *Long Beach Unified School District*.

CHAPTER 5
1. Arkansas Leadership Academy, "About Us," accessed April 16, 2019, https://www.arkansasleadershipacademy.org/313778_2.
2. State of Arkansas, 78th General Assembly, Regular Session 1991, *Act 236* (Little Rock: Arkansas State Legislature, 1991).
3. State of Arkansas, 78th General Assembly, Regular Session 1991, *Act 236*, 5–6.
4. Arkansas Leadership Academy, "About Us."
5. State of Arkansas, 84th General Assembly, Second Extraordinary Session, *SB 46* (Little Rock: Arkansas State Legislature, 2003).
6. Transparency.Arkansas.gov, "Expenditures," accessed April 16, 2019, https://www.ark.org/dfa/transparency/expenditures.php?ina_sec_csrf=e8ad70e2563022e86a00bda8ec762619&do:expenditures&tab=byagency#expenditures_5_151393_drilldown.
7. Arkansas Department of Education, *R.I.S.E Arkansas*, accessed May 22, 2023, https://dese.ade.arkansas.gov/Offices/learning-services/rise-arkansas; Arkansas Department of Education, "R.I.S.E. Arkansas Communications Kit," accessed April 16, 2019, https://dese.ade.arkansas.gov/Offices/learning-services/rise-arkansas/rise-arkansas-communications-kit.
8. Stephanie Levin and Kathryn Bradley, *Understanding and Addressing Principal Turnover: A Review of the Research* (Reston, VA: National Association of Secondary School Principals, 2019), https://learningpolicyinstitute.org/sites/default/files/product-files/NASSP_LPI_Principal_Turnover_Research_Review_REPORT.pdf.

CHAPTER 6
1. NCEE, "Research Base," accessed April 19, 2019, https://ncee.org/nisl-program/.
2. NCEE, "Results," accessed April 19, 2019, https://ncee.org/nisl-program/.
3. National Institute for School Leadership, unpublished data, December 12, 2018.
4. National Institute for School Leadership, *The NISL Wheel: A Guide for School Leaders* (Washington, DC: National Institute for School Leadership, 2016), 5.
5. National Institute for School Leadership, *NISL's Conceptual Framework for Leadership* (Washington, DC: National Institute for School Leadership, 2017).
6. National Institute for School Leadership, "Overview," accessed May 22, 2023, https://ncee.org/nisl-program/.
7. Marc Tucker, *9 Building Blocks for a World-Class Education System* (Washington, DC: National Center on Education and the Economy, 2016), https://ncee.org/wp-content/uploads/2019/10/9-blocksv100219Print.pdf.
8. National Institute for School Leadership, *NISL's Conceptual Framework*, 8.
9. National Institute for School Leadership, *NISL Wheel*, 1.

10. National Institute for School Leadership, *NISL Wheel*, 1.
11. National Institute for School Leadership, *NISL's Conceptual Framework*.
12. Leib Sutcher, Anne Podolsky, and Danny Espinoza, *Supporting Principals' Learning: Key Features of Effective Programs* (Palo Alto, CA: Learning Policy Institute, 2017), https://learningpolicyinstitute.org/product/supporting-principals-learning-key-features-effective-programs-report.
13. National Institute for School Leadership, *The NISL Executive Development Program (EDP) Content Map* (Washington, DC: National Institute for School Leadership, 2016).
14. National Institute for School Leadership, *The Executive Development Program* (Washington, DC: National Institute for School Leadership, 2016), Unit 4.1: Welcome and Overview.
15. National Institute for School Leadership, *Executive Development Program*, Unit 4.1: Welcome and Overview.
16. Stacey M. Childress, Denis P. Doyle, and David A. Thomas, *Leading for Equity: The Pursuit of Excellence in the Montgomery County Public Schools.* (Cambridge, MA: Harvard Education Press, 2009).
17. National Institute for School Leadership, *Executive Development Program*, Unit 2.0.2: Key Concepts.
18. NCEE, "Results."
19. John A. Nunnery, Cherng-Jyh Yen, and Steven M. Ross, *Effects of the National Institute for School Leadership's Executive Development Program on School Performance in Pennsylvania: 2006–2010 Pilot Cohort Results* (Norfolk, VA: Old Dominion University, Center for Educational Partnerships, 2011), http://files.eric.ed.gov/fulltext/ED531043.pdf.
20. John A. Nunnery, Steven M. Ross, Shanan Chappell, Shana Pribesh, and Elizabeth Hoag-Carhart, *The Impact of the NISL Executive Development Program on School Performance in Massachusetts: Cohort 2 Results* (Norfolk, VA: Old Dominion University, Center for Educational Partnerships, 2011), https://files.eric.ed.gov/fulltext/ED531042.pdf.
21. Roisin P. Corcoran, "Preparing Principals to Improve Student Achievement," *Child & Youth Care Forum* 46, no. 5 (2017): 769–781, https://doi.org/10.1007/s10566-017-9399-9.

CHAPTER 7

1. Gloria G. Frazier and Edward F. Iwanicki, *Leadership Performance Strands, Skills and Rubrics* (Fayetteville, AR: Arkansas Leadership Academy, 2015), 9.
2. National Institute for School Leadership, *NISL's Conceptual Framework for Leadership* (Washington, DC: National Institute for School Leadership, 2017), 3.
3. Frazier and Iwanicki, *Leadership Performance Strands, Skills and Rubrics*, 10.
4. Frazier and Iwanicki, *Leadership Performance Strands, Skills and Rubrics*, 13.

CHAPTER 8

1. University of California, Berkeley School of Education, "Leadership Support Program," 2022, https://gse.berkeley.edu/academics/professional-programs/principal-leadership-institute/lsp.

APPENDIX

1. Linda Darling-Hammond, Jeannie Oakes, Steven K. Wojcikiewicz, Maria E. Hyler, Roneeta Guha, Anne Podolsky, Tara Kini, Channa M. Cook-Harvey, Charmaine N. Jackson Mercer, and Akeelah Harrell, *Preparing Teachers for Deeper Learning* (Cambridge, MA: Harvard Education Press, 2019.)

ACKNOWLEDGMENTS

We are extremely grateful to the many people who supported this work. We first thank the school leaders—program participants and graduates—who generously shared their experiences with us. They told us about their leadership goals and strategies, their program experiences, their successes and their challenges. They welcomed us into their schools, allowed us to watch them work, and took time out of their busy days to walk us through classrooms, introduce us to teachers, and answer our questions.

We are grateful to the program faculty and staff—the directors, teaching faculty, clinical faculty, coaches, mentors, and district partners—who shared their time and experience so we could get a deep understanding of all that they were trying to do, the why and the how. They organized and hosted our visits, compiled stacks of background documents, and shared reams of data.

This book benefited from the insights and expertise of two external reviewers: Kenneth Leithwood, professor emeritus, University of Toronto, Ontario Institute for Studies in Education; and Margaret Terry Orr, professor, Fordham University. We thank them for the care and attention they gave the book. Their feedback was invaluable. We also appreciate the two anonymous reviewers whose comments and advice helped bring the book into focus.

We thank our Learning Policy Institute colleagues for their support and contributions to this research. We especially benefited from the support of Linda Darling-Hammond, whose vast expertise, thoughtful advice, and tough questions pushed our thinking and strengthened our findings. We also thank the LPI Communications Team for their invaluable support in fine-tuning the manuscript. Without their generosity of time and spirit, this work would not have been possible.

Finally, we greatly appreciate the munificence of the Carnegie Corporation of New York, which provided major funding for the study. We also are grateful to the Heising-Simons Foundation, William and Flora Hewlett Foundation, Raikes Foundation, Sandler Foundation, and MacKenzie Scott for making this work possible by providing core operating support for the Learning Policy Institute.

ABOUT THE AUTHORS

MARJORIE E. WECHSLER is the principal research manager at the Learning Policy Institute and colead of LPI's Educator Quality team. She leads mixed-methods research studies related to teacher and leader development, school- and district-level reform, and systems approaches to educational improvement. Much of her work focuses on policies and strategies to advance equity in educational opportunities and outcomes. Her books include *On the Road to High-Quality Early Learning: Changing Children's Lives*, *Disrupting Disruption: The Steady Work of Transforming Schools*, and *Developing Expert Principals: Professional Learning That Matters*. Wechsler received her PhD in education administration and policy analysis from Stanford University, an EdM in education policy from Harvard University, and a teaching credential and BA from Brandeis University in psychology.

STEVEN K. WOJCIKIEWICZ is a senior researcher and policy advisor at the Learning Policy Institute, focusing on educator preparation research, practice, and policy. He is a coauthor of the book *Preparing Teachers for Deeper Learning* and of several case studies of educator preparation programs from that project. Wojcikiewicz has two decades of experience in education as a high school teacher, experiential educator, and university teacher educator and in policy roles with a teachers' union and a nonprofit advocacy group. Wojcikiewicz has a PhD in educational psychology and educational technology from Michigan State University, an MA in teaching from the University of Portland, and a BA in history and economics from the University of Notre Dame.

JULIE ADAMS is a former research and policy associate at the Learning Policy Institute and is a current graduate student at the University of Pennsylvania's Graduate School of Education. While at LPI, she served on the Whole Child Education team and focused primarily on research related to performance-based assessments and college access. Before LPI, Adams worked at ETR, where she supported research on equity and inclusion in STEM education. She holds a BA in psychology from the University of California, Santa Cruz.

DESIREE CARVER-THOMAS is a researcher and policy analyst at the Learning Policy Institute. Her research has focused on equity with regard to educator quality issues, including teacher supply and demand, teacher diversity, and school and district leader preparation and development. She is the author of *Diversifying the Teaching Profession: How to Recruit and Retain Teachers of Color* and lead author of *Teacher Turnover: Why It Matters and What We Can Do About It*. Previously, she was an elementary special education teacher in New York City public schools. Carver-Thomas holds an MPP from the Goldman School of Public Policy at UC Berkeley, an MS in teaching from Fordham University, and a BA in comparative ethnic studies with a concentration in anthropology from Columbia University.

CHANNA M. COOK is the executive director of district and school support at the Sacramento County Office of Education, where she leads the team providing customized support to schools and districts in Sacramento County. Previously, Cook was the director of social-emotional learning at Folsom Cordova Unified School District, where she designed and led the implementation of a districtwide approach to meeting the needs of the whole child. Before joining FCUSD, Cook was a senior researcher at the Learning Policy Institute, where her research focused on social-emotional learning, whole-child approaches to schooling, deeper learning, and trauma-informed practices. She began her career as a high school English teacher and literacy coach in Los Angeles Unified School District, and she cofounded and served as principal of a charter school in Louisiana. Cook has a PhD, MA, and BA from Stanford University and an MS in educational leadership from Pepperdine University.

DANIEL ESPINOZA is a research and policy associate at the Learning Policy Institute. His research involves quantitative and qualitative methods. He is the lead author of the LPI report *Taking the Long View: State Efforts to Solve Teacher Shortages by Strengthening the Profession* and *Investing in Effective School Leadership: How States Are Taking Advantage of Opportunities Under ESSA*. He is a coauthor of *Supporting Principals' Learning: Key Features of Effective Programs, Improving Education the New Mexico Way: An Evidence-Based Approach*, and *Students Experiencing Homelessness: The Conditions and Outcomes* *of Homelessness Among California Students.* Espinoza holds a BA in both international economics and political science from the University of Notre Dame.

MADELYN GARDNER is a doctoral student at the Harvard Graduate School of Education. Her research interests lie at the intersection of human development and public policy, with a particular focus on unpacking the elements of early learning experiences that benefit children's learning and growth. Previously, Gardner worked at the Learning Policy Institute, where she conducted research on issues of access, quality, and equity in state early learning systems, as well as educator preparation and development. Gardner holds an MA in international education policy from Stanford University and a BA with honors in anthropology from Grinnell College.

MARIA E. HYLER serves as the director of the Learning Policy Institute's Washington, DC, office and is a senior researcher. Additionally, she directs the EdPrepLab in partnership with Bank Street Graduate School of Education. Before taking her position at LPI, Hyler served as an assistant professor at the University of Maryland, College Park. She began her career teaching tenth and eleventh graders in Belmont, California, where she achieved National Board Certification in Adolescent Young Adult English Language Arts. Hyler received a PhD in curriculum and instruction from Stanford University, an MEd with a teaching credential from Harvard Graduate School of Education, and a dual degree in English and Africana Studies from Wellesley College.

ANNE PODOLSKY is a doctoral student at Stanford University and a researcher at the Learning Policy Institute. Her research examines how principals and teachers can be trained, supported, and organized to best support all students. Podolsky is an Illinois State Board of Education certified teacher and a member of the State Bar of California. Podolsky holds a JD from the University of San Diego School of Law, an MA in education policy from Stanford University, and a BS in elementary education from Loyola University Chicago (summa cum laude).

INDEX